STARING

STARING
How We Look

ROSEMARIE GARLAND-THOMSON

OXFORD
UNIVERSITY PRESS

2009

OXFORD

UNIVERSITY PRESS

Oxford University Press, Inc., publishes works that further
Oxford University's objective of excellence
in research, scholarship, and education.

Oxford   New York
Auckland   Cape Town   Dar es Salaam   Hong Kong   Karachi
Kuala Lumpur   Madrid   Melbourne   Mexico City   Nairobi
New Delhi   Shanghai   Taipei   Toronto

With offices in
Argentina   Austria   Brazil   Chile   Czech Republic   France   Greece
Guatemala   Hungary   Italy   Japan   Poland   Portugal   Singapore
South Korea   Switzerland   Thailand   Turkey   Ukraine   Vietnam

Copyright © 2009 by Oxford University Press, Inc.

Published by Oxford University Press, Inc.
198 Madison Avenue, New York, New York 10016

www.oup.com

Oxford is a registered trademark of Oxford University Press

Library of Congress Cataloging-in-Publication Data
Thomson, Rosemarie Garland.
Staring : how we look / Rosemarie Garland-Thomson.
p. cm.
Includes bibliographical references and index.
ISBN 978-0-19-532679-6; 978-0-19-532680-2 (pbk.)
1. Gaze.   I. Title.
B846.T46 2009
302.5'4—dc22   2008034410

Printed in the United States of America
on acid-free paper

To Allison Hobgood and Sarah Peterson, who are exemplary future
scholars and intellectual heirs. You are a sight to behold.

ACKNOWLEDGMENTS

I am grateful for the support of many people and institutions that helped bring this book to life. The Emory University Fox Center for Humanistic Inquiry, the Emory University Research Committee, the Emory University Manuscript Development Program, the Bogliasco Foundation, the National Endowment for the Humanities, and research support from Howard University provided time to think, research, and write at various stages and incarnations of this project. Generous support from Deans Lisa Tedesco and Robert A. Paul at Emory University made possible the compelling illustrations.

I thank the many individuals who supported the project, contributed ideas and images, and served as colleagues-in-scholarship. Niko Pfund, publisher at Oxford University Press, enthusiastically encouraged me about staring from the beginning; Oxford University Press's editorial team of Shannon McLachlan and Brendan O'Neill, the production team of Gwen Colvin and copyeditor Dr. Katherine Ulrich, and the anonymous readers have all been scrupulous and professional throughout the publishing process. Marquard Smith, editor of the *Journal of Visual Culture*, and Jim Phelan, editor of *Narrative*, strengthened the book. Doug Auld, Kevin Connolly, Mark Gilbert, Riva Lehrer, and Chris Rush generously contributed their marvelous art. Theresia Degener, Harriet McBryde Johnson, Simi Linton, Cheryl Marie Wade, and David Roche kindly provided photographs of themselves.

My gratitude goes to colleagues at Emory University: the Senior Fellows and interim director Steve Everett during my residency at the Fox Center for Humanistic Inquiry; my colleagues in the Department of Women's Studies Research Seminar; Amy Benson Brown, director of the Manuscript Development Program; Martha Fineman, director of the Vulnerability Studies Project and the Feminism and Legal Theory Project. Allison Hobgood, Sarah Peterson, Melissa Anderson, and Elizabeth Simoneau were dedicated, resourceful, and perpetually cheerful research assistants without whom this book would not be.

Dear colleagues and friends from the Washington, D.C., Body Studies Group, the National Endowment for the Humanities Summer Institute on Disability, and the Society for Disability Studies, as well as the larger disability studies community, sustained my work. Many kind colleagues responded to my ideas about looking and kept an eye out for me, as it were: Rachel Adams, Brenda Brueggemann, Lisa Cartwright, Lenny Cassuto, Bill Cohen, Sumi Colligan, Michael Davidson, Lennard Davis, Anne Finger, Ann Fox, Sander Gilman, Kim Hall, Diane Price Herndl, Martha Stoddard Holmes, Lynne Huffer, Mark Jeffries, Joy and John Kasson, Georgina Kleege, Chris Krentz, Catherine Kudlick, Petra Kuppers, Cindy LaCom, Gary Laderman, Simi and David Linton, Paul Longmore, Dee McGraw, Ben Reiss, Robert McRuer, David Mitchell, Carrie Sandahl, Susan Schweik, Pamela Scully, Tobin Siebers, Sharon Snyder, Nikki Sullivan, and Gail Weiss. Most every colleague I encountered during this project had something perceptive to say about staring; I am grateful for all that collective wisdom and interest.

In particular, this book honors the many starees who generously shared their experiences with staring and those who graciously offered images of themselves.

Portions of this book appeared in earlier forms in Paul Longmore and Laurie Umansky's *The New Disability History* (New York University Press, 2000), Phillip Auslander and Carrie Sandahl's *Bodies in Commotion: Disability and Performance* (University of Michigan Press, 2004), the *Journal of Visual Culture* (summer 2006), and *Narrative* (January 2007).

CONTENTS

week 2

week 3

- week 12

PART I

ABOUT STARING

— introduces staring as a complex +
compelling social exchange in which
we all participate

1

Why Do We Stare?

[handwritten note: put page #s for reference in notes]

LOOKING INTO STARING

Staring raises questions. Who stares? Why do we stare? When do we stare? What do we stare at? Why can't we stop staring? What do we do when we are stared at? Should we stare?

We stare because we are curious, and we are curious about staring. *Staring: How We Look* aims to scratch that inquisitive itch by thinking carefully about the stare. It explores staring's possibilities and shows that staring is more than meets the eye.

Everybody stares.[1] Staring is an ocular response to what we don't expect to see. Novelty arouses our eyes.[2] More than just looking, staring is an urgent eye jerk of intense interest.[3] Mike Ervin calls it "the car wreck phenomenon" (2005 interview).[4] We stare when ordinary seeing fails, when we want to know more. So staring is an interrogative gesture that asks what's going on and demands the story. The eyes hang on, working to recognize what seems illegible, order what seems unruly, know what seems strange. Staring begins as an impulse that curiosity can carry forward into engagement (figure 1.1).

[handwritten note in right margin: involuntary]

Spectacles elicit wonderment, but when we stare at one another something more complicated happens. We don't usually stare at people we know, but instead when unfamiliar people take us by surprise. This kind of staring between strangers, this book suggests, offers the most revealing instance of the stare: how it works and what it can do. An encounter between a starer and a staree sets in motion an interpersonal relationship, however momentary, that has consequences. This intense visual engagement creates a circuit of communication and meaning-making. Staring bespeaks involvement, and being stared at demands a response. A staring encounter is a dynamic struggle—starers inquire, starees lock eyes or flee, and starers advance or

Figure 1.1. Appleton's Tianga Jungle Girl Show, 1956, Rugby, England. Jack Leeson Collection, National Fairground Archive, University of Sheffield.

retreat; one moves forward and the other moves back. A staring interchange can tickle or alienate, persist or evolve. Staring's brief bond can also be intimate, generating a sense of obligation between persons, what Joshua Meile calls "an unavoidable consequence of empathy" (2005 interview).[5] Staring, then, shows us something about how we look *at* each other and how we look *to* each other. "Appearances," according to sociologist Tanya Titchkowsky, "are enactments" (2007, 17). In other words, things happen when people stare.

The lively scene on this book's cover and also on the next page suggests staring's potentially productive interactions. In bold planes and vivid colors, American artist Jacob Lawrence's 1938 painting *Blind Beggars* (figure 1.2) depicts a crowded urban streetscape, probably in Harlem. A pick-up parade of children marches chaotically down the sidewalk, whooping, gesturing wildly, twirling flags, banging drums, and waving sticks. From a window above the street, a woman leans out gawking at the action. The wide-eyed and big-grinned children form an entourage surrounding a dignified, dapper gentleman in a suit and tie and a well-dressed, demure lady walking arm in arm. The couple is the clear center of interest. Everyone is staring at them. Both wear dark glasses and each sweeps the street ahead with a guide cane blind people use. The man carries a tin cup in his other hand. The beggars do not grovel, seek pity, or appear downtrodden. No one turns uneasy eyes away from them. Everyone's getting something out of this. The children are delighted. The woman in the window is fascinated. The starees are the king and queen of the street, blind Pied Pipers running the show. The raucous

Voyeurism- the practice of gaining sexual pleasure from watching others when they are naked or engaged in sexual activity → porn

Figure 1.2. Jacob Lawrence, *Blind Beggars* (1938).

scene of *Blind Beggars* shows how staring can be a mutually vivifying visual dance in which starers and starees engage one another.

Even though we like to stare, everybody knows we are not supposed to do it. Mothers scold gawking children. Etiquette manuals caution against untoward eyeing. The timid wither under riveting stares. Indiscreet looking invades another's space. People just simply don't like to be stared at.[6] As with other bodily impulses such as eating and sex, staring elicits strict social regulation. So staring is often a furtive, guilty pleasure. Never far from voyeurism, it can be an inappropriate and mutually embarrassing act. Starers must defend against accusations of vulgar overinvolvement, and starees must defend against intrusive overexposure. Consequentially, staring can roil up common unease on both sides of those ogling eyes.

This contradiction between the desire to stare and the social prohibitions against it fills staring encounters with angst that can be productive, leading starers to new insights. Triggered by the sight of someone who seems unlike us, staring can begin an exploratory expedition into ourselves and outward into new worlds. Because we come to expect one another to have certain kinds of bodies and behaviors, stares flare up when we glimpse people who look or act in ways that contradict our expectations. Seeing startlingly stareable people challenges our assumptions by interrupting complacent visual business-as-usual. Staring offers an occasion to rethink the status quo. Who we are can shift into focus by staring at who we think we are not.

facial cancer

Figure 1.3. Mark Gilbert, *Henry De. L.* (1999). Oil on canvas, 72 in. × 42 in.

We can see how a productive staring exchange might work by looking at a portrait of Henry de Lotbiniere (figure 1.3) that was part of the Saving Face exhibition by painter Mark Gilbert shown at the British National Portrait Gallery in 2002. De Lotbiniere, a London barrister who underwent fifteen operations for facial cancer over thirteen years, presents himself to the public eye through Gilbert's portrait. The effect of the painting is to stage a staring encounter between viewers and de Lotbiniere that makes him seem simultaneously strange and familiar, very like his starers and very unlike them. The painting itself instructs viewers how to look at de Lotbiniere. To use W. J. T. Mitchell's (2005) formulation, this picture wants you to stare. It does so by nestling the barrister's quite stareable face in the context of a particular yet ordinary person. His unusual face is one of many distinguishing features; he has long legs, large feet, expressive hands, a strong jaw, and, of course, a barrister's wig and robes. De Lotbiniere's single eye steadily meets and measures the eyes of his viewers, drawing them toward his astonishing face, which is deep in the background yet acts as the commanding focus of the portrait. De Lotbiniere's seated body juts out from his face into the foreground of the painting, drawing the viewer caught by the barrister's unsettling eye-to-eye contact on a visual tour of the robed, dignified man that culminates in his comfortably crossed knees and two typically shod feet. The effect of the portrait is to manipulate our eyes by both calling up and calling off our stares. It offers for contemplation the surprising sight of de Lotbiniere's unorthodox face at the same time that it situates that face in the reassuringly familiar body of an ordinary barrister. De Lotbiniere's presentation enlists staring to tell a story about him. It invites starers to wonder about his unusual face, to find coherence in a sight that at first seems incomprehensible, to reconcile the Cyclops with the lawyer. If starers stay the course, their eyes will work toward reducing the strangeness of de Lotbiniere's face by giving it a story. Whatever that story may be, it will not be the same one that started them staring.

Any of us can be a starer or a staree. To be a staree is to show a starer something new, to catch a starer off-guard with an unfamiliar sight. What counts as a new sight in the shared visual landscape constantly shifts depending on a starer's expectations, surroundings, mood, level of engagement, individual history, and acculturation. Once triggered, a stare can yield its bearer myriad responses, from curiosity to confusion, attraction, discomfort, even repulsion. Starees, of course, are sometimes reluctant participants in their starers' visual search for something new; they have their own lives to live. Moreover, people become more or less stareable depending on the context. Gilbert's barrister, for example, might not be particularly stareable in an oncology waiting room or amongst friends and family. Staring encounters nonetheless draft starees into a story of the starer's making, whatever that story might be, whether they like it or not. Because lived staring encounters are spontaneous and dynamic—in the way that Gilbert's staged staring encounter with the barrister is not—they can be pliable under the guidance of an experienced staree. Indeed, accomplished starees often develop a repertoire of strategies they use to choreograph staring encounters.[7]

A snapshot of two practiced starees hints at the skillset starees can wield when they enter the public eye. Theresia Degener, a lawyer, professor, and disability rights activist, and Gisela Hermes, a professor of disability studies in Germany, linger by a riverbank on a summer afternoon in this casual

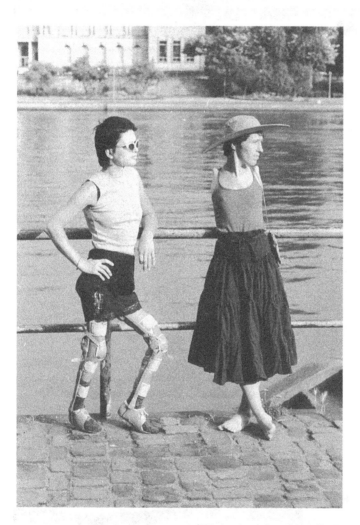

Figure 1.4. Martin Glueck, photo of Dr. Theresia Degener and Gisela Hermes.

photo (figure 1.4), perhaps on vacation, perhaps with another companion who snaps the picture. The friends costume and pose themselves as we would expect in such a setting. Degener sports a sun hat, flowing skirt, and bare feet. Hermes wears shorts and chic sunglasses and stands nonchalantly with arms akimbo. Both women gaze with interest at some sight further on down the river. This altogether unremarkable scene is interrupted, however, by a single arrestingly conspicuous feature of each woman's body that is juxtaposed with her ordinariness. Degener is armless and Hermes' delicate legs are laddered from hip to heel by elaborate supportive braces. This scene is both visually quiescent and eye-catching, familiar and strange at the same time. The exposure of armless shoulders and anomalous legs is rare outside medical venues or sideshows. Most striking perhaps is the apparent comfort with their unusual bodies that these women's comportment and clothing suggest. In fact, the women seem simply to be going about their day, unapologetically taking up what conversation analyst Harvey Sacks (1984) calls "doing being ordinary." They make, in short, an extraordinary sight ordinary. When people with stareable bodies such as Degener and Hermes enter into the public eye, when they no longer hide themselves or allow themselves to be hidden, the visual landscape enlarges. Their public presence can expand the range of the bodies we expect to see and broaden the terrain where we expect to see such bodies. This new public landscape is in part a product of the laws, social practices, and changed attitudes wrought by the larger civil rights movement—including the disability rights movement.[8] These encounters work to broaden collective expectations of who can and should be seen in the public sphere and help create a richer and more diverse human community. This is what starees can show us all.

AN ANATOMY OF STARING

Staring: How We Look is an anatomy of staring.[9] It dissects staring encounters to expose their hidden vitality. *Staring* is a vivisection that reveals what hides in a seemingly obvious visual gesture. Staring, it proposes, is an intense visual exchange that makes meaning.[10] Staring here is more than just looking. The stare is distinct from the gaze, which has been extensively defined as an oppressive act of disciplinary looking that subordinates its victim.[11] As we will see in the chapters that follow, starers engage in several variations of intense looking: among them are the blank stare, the baroque stare, the separated stare, the engaged stare, the stimulus-driven stare, the goal-driven stare, and the dominating stare. At the heart of this anatomy is the matter of appearance, of the ways we see each other and the ways we are seen. It unsettles common understandings that staring is rudeness, voyeurism, or surveillance or that starers are perpetrators and starees victims. Instead, this vivisection lays bare staring's generative potential.

The "we" of this book is a rhetorical convention to draw readers into an identification with the book's point of view, with its contention that staring is a universal impulse. The "we" does not imply any exclusive group, but rather it recruits an ideal reader: the general, educated reader or academic who is curious about why we stare. William Ian Miller calls this convention the "invitational we," which is "the voice of attempted sympathy and imagination."[12] This rhetorical strategy is an effort to avoid the flattening pronominal dichotomy of "we" and "they" that divides starers from starees.

The use of "we" yokes starers and starees in a mutually defining process that helps reveal how social relations create identities. By framing staring as a psychologically fraught and socially charged encounter, the book addresses how identity emerges through interactive processes. In this way, *Staring* expands the broad critical discussion about visuality in modernity through its focus on disability identity formation. In other words, it shows how staring works, what it does, and how it makes us who we are. This anatomy strives to reveal connections among our own staring practices, interpersonal relations, and the meanings we give to human variations.

To dissect staring, the book approaches staring from a distinctly social model, using several analytical instruments: the social sciences of visual communication, interactionism, cognitive and social psychology; the history of visuality and curiosity; and most of all, the humanistic disciplines of philosophy, disability and feminist theories, ritual and performance studies, and literary criticism. It uses these tools on an eclectic collection of "scenes of staring" that serve as case studies. These scenes take the form of narrative accounts, artistic representations, photographs, films, and performances. In all, *Staring: How We Look* is stalwartly humanistic in its approach. Its perspective is more that of the literary critic and philosopher than the historian or social scientist. To bring forward the generative rather than the oppressive aspects of staring, it leans more toward Erving Goffman than Michel Foucault, more toward Charles Taylor and Martin Buber than Jean-Paul Sartre, more toward D. W. Winnicott than Jacques Lacan.

Because most studies and analyses of staring focus on starers, bringing forward the roles of starees is crucial to presenting a full account of staring. Human starees, rather than car wrecks or sublime spectacles, epitomize the staring encounter and are the center of this book. To get at what starees do and how they understand these intense interpersonal visual exchanges, this anatomy of staring draws from self presentations, visual representations, and published accounts by and of starees as well as interviews with people who have stareable traits, all of whom have spent years—sometimes lifetimes—managing staring encounters. Developing a balanced account of starer/staree interactions changes the usual understanding of staring as a one-way act. Doing so highlights the dynamic nature of staring encounters, recasts starees as subjects not objects, and reveals new perspectives.

The book consists of six parts, each of which addresses an aspect of the staring relationship. "About Staring" introduces staring as a complex and compelling social exchange in which we all participate. "What Is Staring?" focuses on the roles and perspectives of starers, laying out the four interrelated aspects of staring: physical response, cultural phenomenon, social relationship, and knowledge gathering endeavor. "Don't Stare" explores the history, social regulation, and cultural contradictions of staring. "Starers and Starees" serves as a transition from the focus on starers to one on starees. "Scenes of Staring" develops an extended analysis of the four parts of human anatomy most likely to draw the stare: faces, hands, breasts, and bodies. Finally, "A Last Look" explores the ethics of looking and offers a model of staring as an opportunity for mutual recognition.

major ideas

- Why do we stare?
- definitions
  → from all week 2 reading
  → top of notes page
- consequences of staring

— focuses on the roles and perspectives of starers, laying out the four interrelated aspects of staring

1. physical response
2. cultural phenomenon
3. social relationship
4. knowledge gathering endeavor

PART II

WHAT IS STARING?

> . . . staring, in its pure and simple essence, is the time required by the brain to make sense of the unexpected.
> —Jeanne McDermott, mother of Nathaniel, who was born with Apert's syndrome

> A stare has, essentially, the character of a compulsion; it is steady, unmodulated, "fixed."
> —Susan Sontag, "The Aesthetics of Silence" (1969)

Staring is both simple and complex, both natural and cultural. It has four elemental qualities. First, as the quotes above suggest, staring is a physiological response. Disturbances in the visual status quo literally catch our eye, drawing us into a staring relationship with a startling sight. Staring is a more forceful form of looking than glancing, glimpsing, scanning, and other forms of casual looking. Staring is profligate interest, stunned wonder, obsessive ocularity. The daily traffic reports capture staring's disruptive potential with the term "rubbernecking," a canny summation of our reflexive compulsion to look. In line at the supermarket, a freak on the tabloid cover or the sensational photo of a murder victim lures our hapless eyes, trumpeting harsh evidence of the randomness of human embodiment and our own mortality. We may gaze at what we desire, but we stare at what astonishes us (figure 2.1).

Second, like all physical impulses, staring has a history sedimented over time and across space that is specific to each culture, which in turn shapes its meaning and practice. The intensity of our physical urge to stare has been strictly monitored by social rules ranging from ancient ritual protections against the "evil eye" to modern-day mothers' wary pronouncement of "Don't stare!" In modern, urban culture where so many of our daily visual interactions are anonymous, staring becomes an uneasy fusion of curiosity and voyeurism.

Third, staring establishes a social relationship between starer and staree. It is an interpersonal action through which we act out who we imagine ourselves and others to be. The impulse to look at each other is a natural human social response. Dogs sniff each other; we look at each other. Peek-a-boo is one of the earliest human routines. Freud told us that fort-da—the formative exercise of seeing objects being there and not there, of appearing and disappearing—establishes the borders of the self. The rawest and most

A GAWP OF TOURISTS

Figure 2.1. Simon Bond, "A Gawp of Tourists," December 14, 2007.
Courtesy of www.cartoonstock.com.

fundamental form of staring is a face-to-face encounter: a visual confronta-tion involving engagement, avoidance, mutuality, or some combination that creates an often uneasy bond between two people. Moving along the city street or on a crowded subway train, the peculiar appearance of an ampu-tated leg or a madman in his fantasy rant arrests our eye and we gawk in spite of ourselves, awkwardly fracturing the visual anonymity that politeness demands. Our language catalogs staring's interpersonal charge, its capacity to ambush starer and staree alike, taking on a life of its own that can extend beyond the intentions of its bearer or its target. Both "stolen glances" and "fixed stares" are inappropriate behavior. To "fasten one's eyes" on an object suggests a vulnerable enthrallment or an overriding compulsion. We speak of "staring daggers," "penetrating looks," "piercing eyes," "riveting glances," and "looking somebody up and down." Such phrases reflect the intensity of being on either side of a staring encounter.

Fourth, staring is a conduit to knowledge. Stares are urgent efforts to make the unknown known, to render legible something that seems at first glance incomprehensible. In this way, staring becomes a starer's quest to know and a staree's opportunity to be known. Whatever or whomever embodies the unpredictable, strange, or disordered prompts stares and demands putting order to apparent disarray, taming the world with our eyes. Because we are all starers, knowledge gathering is the most productive aspect of staring in that it can offer an opportunity to recognize one another in new ways.

major ideas
- types of stares → also on pg. 9
- 4 qualities of a stare

2

A Physical Response

... the human mind always burns to hear and take in novelties.
—Gervase of Tillbury, *Otia imperialia*, circa 1210

Staring is a universal part of our cognitive architecture that natural selection has bequeathed us. The evolutionary origin of staring is a startle response. When staring is intentional—as in the long loving look or the hostile glare— we are masters of our eyes. When an unexpected sight grabs our attention, however, staring is spontaneous and volatile. As the epigraph to the previous section says, "staring, in its pure and simple essence, is the time required by the brain to make sense of the unexpected."[1] We cannot, even when we try, ignore compelling visual stimuli; we can only withdraw the stare once it is in play (Yantis 1998, 239). Intense, persistent looking and the ability to interpret such stares are fundamental to our survival as social beings as well. Human infants and mothers stare long and emphatically at each other to cement their relationship (Baron-Cohen 1985, 39). We enact social hierarchies through visual dominance displays (Ellyson and Dovido 1995). Even very young infants show surprise by staring for longer periods at scenes that violate the laws of physics or seem physically implausible than they look at a predictable or expected event.[2] Staring not only signals alertness in the starer, it alerts the staree. Another's stare actually excites electrical activity in the brain (Baron-Cohen 1995, 98). The staring encounter arouses us as well. Our heart rate increases when we are stared at; being subjected to a stare even registers on a cortical EEG. So viscerally potent is the staring encounter that we can even feel stares directed at us. In fact, humans from infancy can detect unseen stares. We not only believe that we can tell when we are being stared at, but repeated experiments dating as early as the late nineteenth century suggest that in fact we do (Colwell et al. 2000). Staring, then, has vivid physiological effects for both starer and staree that emanate from the neural automata and spread through the entire body.

VISUAL THRILLS

The question of what we stare at has a simple answer: we stare at what interests us. Things interest us, of course, for differing reasons and elicit stares with correspondingly varied goals. The schoolteacher tries to intimidate the unruly boy; the lover and the pilgrim seek to adore; the bored look for excitement; the scientist searches for truth. What interests us most, however, is novelty. For centuries people have known that the "mind always burns to hear and take in novelties."[3] In his book on the science of satisfaction, the physician Gregory Berns (2005) explains that brain imaging experiments show the neurotransmitter dopamine flowing most fully when we experience novel events. Dopamine is the chemical that the brain releases in response to pleasure. The pleasure of novelty, the dopamine rush, comes from the "surprise" that stimulates the brain. Berns concludes that novelty is "the one thing we all want" (14). "You may not always like novelty," Berns says, "but your brain does" (xiii). Searching for the pleasure novelty brings, we do not seek a thing for itself but rather for the thrill of surprise it brings. So the snagging of our eyes by something unusual pumps out the dopamine, providing us pleasure.

What is unusual, of course, depends upon what we expect to see. A common sight in one place can be uncommon in another; as noted in the previous chapter, de Lotbiniere might not be stareable in a cancer ward. Social expectations shape our ocular sorting processes, making certain appearances and actions unusual and cataloging people as alien or native, extraordinary or ordinary. Zora Neale Hurston wrote, for instance, that she became "colored" only when she was surrounded by white people (1928). Gender expectations make the bald head of a woman indicate chemotherapy treatment whereas viewers might read the same smooth pate on a man as the stylish marking of a hip athlete. Similarly, a woman with enough facial hair to suggest a beard merits a stare while a man with a bushy beard is unremarkable.

But the jolt of the unusual is fleeting. A dopamine rush inevitably ebbs as novelty diminishes. Novelty is fragile and staring volatile because the longer we look, the more accustomed a once surprising sight becomes. Staring researcher and social psychologist Ellen J. Langer found that people stare at "novel stimuli" as a form of "exploratory behavior" (Langer et al. 1976, 461). The surprise that motivates staring produces, in other words, an expedition in search of information. Drawn by the inexplicable, we try to integrate new information into what we already know to reduce our uncertainty about the world. Both Berns and Langer assert that what humans really want is predictability in what we grudgingly know to be an unpredictable world.[4] Ironically, at the root of our craving for novelty is an anxious drive to be rid of it so that we can sink into a calmer world where nothing startles or demands our visual attention.

Here is the contradiction at the heart of staring, then: the extraordinary excites but alarms us; the ordinary assures but bores us. We want surprise, but perhaps even more we want to tame that pleasurable astonishment, to domesticate the strange sight into something so common as to be unnoticeable. These clashing impulses make staring self-cancelling, abating once we reassert the equilibrium of familiarity. Langer says that we judiciously court the novel, trying to control our visual explorations. In other words, we prefer to stare for our own reasons and on our own terms rather than be forced into a stare by something or someone stareable. For example, the middle-class value of traveling, seeking a diverse environment, or even favoring ethnic food can be seen as forms of deliberate, and therefore controlled, stimulation through novelty, positioned within a model of consumption that indicates upper-class status. Such intentional novelty seeking differs from a reactive stare driven by the novel object. The rawest, most basic form of staring is the physiological expression of being caught off guard, captured by the unexpected. Staring is at once a pleasurable encounter with novel stimuli and a disconcerting hijacking of our visual agency by the impulse to stare. We at once want and do not want to gawk at such compelling sights.

Because we both crave and dread unpredictable sights, staring encounters are fraught with anxious contradiction. The functional and formal conditions of our bodies that are termed disabilities are one of the most unpredictable aspects of life. Like death itself, disabilities come to us unbidden as we move through a world that wears us down even while it sustains us. Seeing disability reminds us of what Bryan S. Turner (2006) calls "ontological contingency," the truth of our body's vulnerability to the randomness of fate. Each one of us ineluctably acquires one or more disabilities—naming them variably as illness, disease, injury, old age, failure, dysfunction, or dependence. This inconvenient truth nudges most of us who think of ourselves as able-bodied toward imagining disability as an uncommon visitation that mostly happens to someone else, as a fate somehow elective rather than inevitable. In response, we have refused to see disability. Avowing disability as tragic or shameful, we have hidden away disabled people in asylums, segregated schools, hospitals, and nursing homes.[5] When we ourselves develop disabilities, we often hide them as well, sometimes through semantic slights-of-hand, sometimes through normalizing medical procedures that erase disability, and sometimes through closeting our conditions. This hiding of disability has made it seem unusual or foreign rather than fundamental to our human embodiedness. Rather than accepting disability and accommodating it as an expected part of every life course, we are stunned and alienated when it appears to us in others or ourselves.[6] When we do see the usually concealed sight of disability writ boldly on others, we stare in fascinated disbelief and uneasy identification. Why, we ask with our eyes, does that person with dwarfism, that amputee, that drooler, look so much like and yet so different from me? Such confusing sights both affirm our shared humanity and challenge our complacent understandings. The visibly disabled body intrudes on our routine visual landscape and compels our attention, often obscuring the personhood of its bearer. Sometimes our startled eyes can stay with such a sight, and sometimes they flee in strained distress. The appearance of disability in the public sphere makes, then, for a stareable sight. As such, the way we imagine human disability provides us with one of the best opportunities to understand how we stare.

LOOKING RIGHT AND LOOKING WRONG

We harness the physiological impulse to stare to the pragmatic project of connecting with the world and making it coherent to us by using staring to gather information. This goal-driven form of exploratory visual behavior can be called paying attention, which is a form of social capital, part of the required skill set for living.[7] The problem of paying attention is how to keep the interest that triggers staring alive when novelty abates. This type of staring as information collection requires concentrated, focused, and prolonged looking. To pay attention is to make staring productive and controlled, to continue the visual engagement when surprise no longer drives scrutiny, to resist ocular boredom and the lure of distracting newly novel sights. The wide-eyed gawking that Langer calls stimulus-driven exploratory behavior is promiscuous looking; it is always at risk of being seduced away by a fresher, newly stimulating sight. Paying attention, in contrast, is visual monogamy, a deferral of dopamine's quickie gratification.

Paying attention involves multisensory perception, vision being the primary vehicle for focused concentration. Jonathan Crary defines attention as "an imprecise way of designating the relative capacity of a subject to selectively isolate certain contents of a sensory field at the expense of others in the interests of maintaining an orderly and productive world" (1999, 17). Proper attention is goal-driven, deliberately controlled by our intentions and strategies (Yantis 1998). As early as 1890, William James, the father of modern psychology, distinguished this kind of "active" mode of looking from "passive" attention.[8] Shifts in attention must be closely monitored to ensure sustained concentration and focus amid a riot of visual stimuli. To pay attention demands that we tame reckless eyeballing, that we domesticate the rush of the new into sensible observation.

Rather than reactive staring, attention expects us to sort through what we see to create and maintain coherence. This visual organizing determines foreground and background and arranges relations among the elements perceived. Psychologists call this process of visual recognition "orientation" (Pashler 1998, 194).[9] Orientation is the attempt to impose a frame of reference on the chaos of a visual field by integrating what is unknown into what is already known. The many common visual orientation exercises, such as seeking meaning in inkblots, clouds, or the well-known image that moves from a vase to two facial profiles, require scrutiny to impose a logical narrative on what at first glance seems to be random visual stimuli. When items with visual salience, like the flashing lights of an ambulance, the red stoplight, the bold font on a page, capture our attention, such visual clues help us with the work of establishing background and foreground and summoning familiar narratives. But the kind of preparation that converts a stare into information collection is difficult for us. Experiments suggest that even a voluntary act of will to prepare a frame of reference in advance of a visual stimulus does not allow us to recognize what we see (Pashler 1998, 194). In other words, attention is fragile because we cannot help but stare when we are surprised by new sights.

ex of orientation

Stareable sights seduce us into an attention crisis in which random visual intrusions, not a disciplined will, assert control. The visual excitation of what William James called "strange things" grabs our attention automatically (1890, 416–17). They captivate our focus even if we deliberately attempt to ignore them (Yantis 1998). Despite our vigilance, strange sights jerk us away from the restrained enterprise of sorting, sifting, selecting the visual raw material that the vast spectacle of life proffers, and making solid sense of it.[10] Staring is like visual vertigo, a normal physical reaction to confounding stimuli.

Most often the attentive spectator is a passive scanner of images and stimuli that must be organized efficiently with the minimum response, a human computer digesting, discarding, and directing information in order to guide attention and action. The task of the modern individual is to move appropriately and effectively from disengaged spectator to attentive perceiver in order to slide easily into the social order. The starer, in contrast, is an undisciplined spectator arrested in an earlier developmental stage or one resistant to the attentiveness of the modern networker. The starer is a properly attentive spectator befuddled, halted in mid-glance, mobility throttled, processing checked, network run amuck. The starer is indeed the opposite of the attentive spectator who cruises through the mundane landscape, deftly shifting and sifting through the visual field, conferring narrative mastery on all that he surveys.

So the challenge of proper looking is converting the impulse to stare into attention, which is socially acceptable. To grasp our world and get things done right, we need to manage our orientation quite rigorously. The neurological process of sorting visual stimuli is demanding work, but like breathing, a largely unconscious and habitual one. When orientation functions to keep us on target, we are paying attention and are competent beings in the social world.[11] When a stimulus involuntarily nabs our attention, we risk being jerked from attention to staring. Attention-deficit disorder is the clinical diagnosis with which medicine categorizes someone who is overly susceptible to such involuntary shifts in attention. The display of shattered attention, of a poorly controlled urge to stare, when embedded in an environment of the properly attentive, such as a well-ordered classroom, creates a classifiable problem. The current rampant diagnosis of attention-deficit disorder among perceptually scattered children can be understood as an attempt to correct their mismanaged staring. Attention-deficit disorder, understood now as a disabling condition, is doubly stigmatizing. The attention-deficit student disrupts the homogeneity with which the "normal" children look at the chalkboard, and thus "looks wrong" precisely because he or she has not mastered the social conventions controlling our stares. Thus, this form of improper looking turns the attention-deficit starer into a spectacle of undisciplined visuality, of both wrong looking and looking wrong. To look right is to appear attentive; to look wrong is to appear to stare improperly.

In addition to deficient attention, another form of improper looking is the blank stare. The blank stare is a variation on unfocused looking that indicates distraction, looking without processing the information we see. To look intensely for too long dissolves perception and resolves into a blank stare. Extended looking threatens to reverse attentiveness. A blank stare is the inability to turn surprise into knowledge. It is being stuck in between the waning dopamine rush that the staring urge yields and the ultimate satisfaction of reducing unpredictability by incorporating a compelling sight into our scheme of understanding. This refusal of attentiveness signals alienation. The blank stare, according to David Michael Levin, marks society's outcasts (1988; 1993). The inequities of our economic and social order, Levin asserts, are "reflected back to us from the eyes of its victims, the subjects it has destroyed—if only we dare to look, with the simple presence of honesty, into the vacant stares of our prisoners, into the glassy stares of workers after their shift on the assembly line, and into the dead stares of the elderly, abandoned by the institutions of our 'humanity' and waiting for the call of death" (1988, 127). The visual comportment of people with significant disabilities—often those with cognitive, developmental, or perceptual impairments—catalog them as blank starers. The supposed dumb look, blind eye, and idiotic expression are highly stigmatized ways of appearing that draw interrogative stares from those who are properly focused. This type of purportedly empty stare demands no response, initiates no interchange, and produces no knowledge. Blank stares function, then, as visual impotence.

The distracted stares of attention-deficit disorder or blank stares of inattention point to a failure to adroitly separate the ocular wheat from the chaff. Such lookers visually manifest a failure of knowing.[12] Their stares signify an inability to make sense of what is seen, exemplifying what psychologists call disorientation as opposed to effective orientation. As with eye contact in general, attentiveness is brittle.[13] Like trying to start a car engine with a low battery, attention repeatedly sparks toward coherence until its iterations sputter into a nothingness born of futility. The demeanors of deficient attention and blank stares unsettle their witnesses and stigmatize their bearers. The world, not the individual, is in control. Thus staring is the opposite of paying attention because the starer is not master of the encounter.

With these habitual starers, staring betrays a basic confusion, a thwarting of coherence, a betrayal of perceptual synthesis. These stares are potential mastery transformed into lingering moments of chagrin. Instead, our eye behavior must be carefully controlled if we are to display a positive image of ourselves to others. Proper looking should not edge into blank or unfocused stares in what Erving Goffman (1959) calls our "presentation of self in everyday life."[14] We must look like we are paying attention, but never like we are staring.

major ideas :
- *staring vs. paying attention*
- *definitions*
- *gender*

3

A Cultural History

> Because the eye loves novelty and can get used to almost any
> scene, even one of horror, much of life can drift into the vague
> background of our attention.
> —Diane Ackerman, *A Natural History of the Senses,* 235

Culture regulates all human behavior, including physiological processes: sex, eating, elimination, comportment, eye behavior—indeed, everything our bodies do. How we look at each other begins as instinct but quickly takes its place alongside other natural bodily functions as a carrier of social meaning. In this sense, all visual behavior, especially the intense urge to stare, has a cultural history.

THE UNEASY PRIMACY OF VISION

The modern world, in particular our era, is ocularcentric[1]; it depends on sight as the primary sensory conduit to the world.[2] We relish looking, produce endless images, and root our understanding of the world in observation. Indeed, most information comes to us through sight in this intensely technological world saturated with advertising and crowded with computer, television, and video screens. Yet our reliance on seeing as believing has bred a spirited skepticism. From the Protestant distrust of graven images to our secular fascination with magic, sleight-of-hand, or ghosts, we avidly question the truth of what we see.[3] Vision is celebrated and scorned, pronounced to be manipulative, liberating, rapacious, pornographic, gendered, or dominating. Nearly everyone seems to agree that vision shapes the modern citizenry.[4]

We build the world to accommodate the demands of seeing. Because technologies of printing supplanted spoken voices as a way to communicate, we are awash in printed words. Forests worldwide have disappeared in the service of pulp mills. New magazines are born by the hour, and books are everywhere. We have become sedentary in part because technologies of vision now bring the world to our living rooms. With the Internet and text messaging, we connect to one another and roam a universe of information.

The built environment also enforces a hierarchy of the senses. Automobile-dependent cities or suburbs, for example, restrict the mobility of blind people.[5] We seldom even consider the advantages of blindness, such as being able to navigate without artificial light or engaging fully with other senses such as touch and smell. Those without a sense of smell—we do not even have a common word for this deprivation—seem only mildly compromised in contrast to the blind. In fact, smell-lessness might even seem an advantage for some modern ascetic demands such as female slimness.

The modern imagination, moreover, has long seized upon the dynamics of looking as a source of narrative boldness and a vehicle for making meaning. Our preference for sight dates back to at least the classical Greco-Roman burgeoning of architectural and artistic iconography that celebrates looking as a source of knowledge. The ideal appeared in a perfectly proportioned statue or temple. But even the Greeks, with their paradoxical faith in both vision and abstraction, mistrusted the power of sight at the same time they celebrated it. Whereas Aristotle respected the senses, Plato worried about the power of images to obscure fundamental truths. The classical myths of Narcissus, who was seduced and drowned by his own reflection; of Orpheus, who lost his lovely Eurydice forever by turning back to look; and of Medusa, who turned men to stone with her stare, each testify to what Martin Jay calls "vision's malevolent power" (1993, 28). A founding image of our culture, Medusa's fierce look, surrounded by threatening serpentine locks, is widespread in both ancient Greek myth and the archeological record that survives today. Medusa's vivid story demonstrates the uneasy power of the stare. After the clever hero, Perseus, severed her head by using a mirror to avoid her petrifying gaze, he appropriated her power to vanquish his enemies and rivals.

A persistent fascination with staring endures in the traditional curse of the evil eye (Siebers 1983). Like the Medusa myth, the evil eye superstition is about the primacy, and power, of vision. This belief in ocular potency for enacting evil in the world is apparently universal. From the ancient Roman *oculus fascinus*, the Italian *mal occhio*, the Dutch *booze blik*, to the Ethiopian *ayenat*, almost all cultures have a word for the evil eye (Gifford 1958, 6). Like Perseus brandishing Medusa's head, people across cultures ward off enemies and other hexes with a symbol of the eye. Amulets, the precursors to modern jewelry, served a symbolic function similar to Medusa's head by turning like against like in homeopathic fashion. Amulets work as remnants, much like relics, containing concentrated and residual power. Plutarch says amulets "engage the forces of attraction; they defeat fascination with fascination" (Siebers 1983, 7). With the banishment of superstition and enchantment, modern English has redefined words such as "fascinating" and "charming." But the linguistic remainder of the evil eye persists in the root word "fascinate," which comes from the Latin word *fascinatus,* meaning evil spell. We have shifted our obsessions with staring from superstition to science, but the force of the stare remains.

Vision was important to the medieval Church, delivering the Christian story in visual form to illiterate masses. Religious practices such as the veneration of images, the spectacle of mystery plays, the flood of stained-glass-colored light in Gothic cathedrals, the cult of relics, and the illumination of manuscripts depend on seeing for their didactic effect. A powerful force, vision was also the vehicle of temptation, and this link between vision and temptation developed during the Protestant Reformation into a widespread iconophobia even while the Eastern Orthodox churches remained iconophile. For Protestants, the observable world was evanescent and profane, and it obscured the spiritual realm. The Reformation was deeply distrustful of the extravagantly visual, elevating the spare word of God above the image and emptying the Cross of the scene of the wounded Christ. In contrast, the Counter-Reformation used the opulence and "aggrandizement of the eye" of the Baroque in attempts to return the Catholic Church to dominance (Jay 1993, 46). Though Protestantism replaced the image with the word, it still relied on sight to spread its religion. The inscribed and later printed Word of God was made available to individual followers in the form of Protestant Bibles, and Christian martyrdom as a form of witnessing and visions of a resurrected Jesus restored to wholeness persisted.

As the seventeenth century took hold, seeing developed new forms in a secularizing, democratizing world. Observation replaced witnessing with the rise of rationalism and scientific inquiry. Literacy and the printed word flourished. The modernizing world celebrated earthly rather than heavenly sights in art and technology. The early modern period gave us perspective—the artistic convention invented in Renaissance Italy that replicated human vision in artistic representation and created the illusion of reality. The visual technique of perspective both reflected and contributed to the development of individualism by validating the single spectator whose point of view controls the scene (Berger 1972). Thus perspective helps to transform the individual viewer into a gatekeeper of knowledge regarding the scene depicted, shutting down the possibility of competing knowledges that might emerge

how sight was used

from the multiple points of view suggested by medieval painting or, later, Cubist art. The way of seeing captured by perspective and later by scientific inquiry leads to a comprehensive scrutiny that allows an observer to avoid direct involvement with the object of observation. This shift gives rise to the notion of objectivity as disengaged looking (Jonas 1979). Renaissance humanistic perspective thus laid the groundwork for the idea of intense looking at the heart of scientific observation.

Such secular vision became even more central to later modernity. Science rose to prominence as an explanatory system in the eighteenth century. Increasingly, science eclipsed the authority of the Church, which was becoming privatized and domesticated under an egalitarianism based on freedoms posited as secular rights and firmly grounded in the material world rather than the hereafter. The conviction that visual observation is the source of truth supports the entire enterprise of science. Scientific observation and its twin, medical diagnosis, require sustained, intense looking that is imagined as untainted by the viewer's subjectivity. The stethoscope and the microscope came between the observer and observed and increased the objective character of scientific and medical vision. Later, technology such as X-rays, sonography, and genetic testing augmented the inquisitive eye, expanding the limits of vision from the exterior to the interior of the body and further depersonalizing encounters between experts and the objects of their expertise (Cartwright 1995).

The new empirical knowledge of medical science clarified and improved human life. A microscopic world emerged that made vaccines, antisepsis, and antibiotics available (Pernick 1985). Anesthesia ameliorated pain. But science also used vision and visual images to categorize and rank people. Evidence gathered from observing the exterior of bodies was thought to reveal people's character and index their value as humans. Older ways of visually ranking people, such as sumptuary laws regulating ostentatious dress, gave way to newer scientific practices, such as phrenology and physiognomy, that studied the surface and shape of the body for clues to psychological and moral states. Anthropometry used images of people to measure bodies and arrange body types on a scale of values (Terry and Urla 1995). Medical-scientific experts have viewed, measured, and evaluated women, people of color, and the poor. Almost always they were found wanting.[6]

So while the growing dominance of medical science in modernity eased disease, pain, and death, it also extended its notion of human pathology into the social world in discriminatory ways (Canguilhem 1989). Medical diagnosis, or what Michel Foucault (1979) calls the "clinical gaze," is one form of person-to-person staring that is highly impersonal, scripted, and asymmetrical. This modern form of religious confession, Foucault argues, exposes the body before the judgment and interpretation of authority. The invasive stare of the medical expert probes the patient's body and pronounces its fate. Although the clinician may aim the diagnostic stare at many parts of the body, this kind of visual scrutiny seldom encompasses the whole person but rather focuses on the aspects that are suspected of revealing pathology. Like the pre-Reformation church, scientific knowledge is practiced by elites, and the word of science is disseminated by experts. A form of institutional vision, medical scientific looking can be wielded only by those with the appropriate authority and credentials. As such, it differs from the more egalitarian seeing directed at one another to which we have access in daily life.

In late capitalism, the predominant form of looking, the mass exercise of ocularcentricity, is what we might call consumer vision. The rapid changes of industrial capitalism made us into consumers, a new kind of person who emerges in the nineteenth century to eclipse the producer. In a mobile urbanized environment where face-to-face encounters are usually anonymous, the modern individual circulates in space, status, and interpersonal relations (Crary 1999). We are ever on the move, restlessly driven by modernity's mandate to consume, perpetually distracted by an avalanche of information and stimulation, and shaped into conformity by a network of intricately structured institutions. This consumer vision then becomes the primary means of apprehending the world the modern individual must negotiate.

If as Lizabeth Cohen (2003) suggests, one central task of citizenship in our era is consuming, looking is at the heart of this demanding and exhilarating job.[7] The cultural call to be consumers primarily requires looking at commodities, not people. Consumer vision often entails not the intense, focused scrutiny of staring but rather the casual visual cruising of window-shopping or Web surfing. The flaneur, the bourgeois spectator Baudelaire celebrated as the representative modern man, visually wanders through the urban landscape exercising his privilege of disengaged, amused looking.[8] The flaneur is entertained, but never captivated; delighted but never enthralled.[9]

The consumer is a contemporary version of the flaneur, roaming the mall as a destination, not so much to actually buy but rather to take in the spectacle and to look for possible action. Buying and socializing merge at the mall, complicating looking. Even though the mall reaches for desire and novelty, we become inured to the predictable visual field of the stale consumer spectacle it offers. At the same time, the mall also extends the possibility of the novel scene. The modern consumer must visually scan the shopping landscape, sorting among competing images in search of the stimulation that occasions attention and exchange.[10]

This tension between ennui and enthrallment defines modern looking, reinforcing the physiology of novelty's fragile hold on our eyes. In consumer culture, endlessly repeated images leap toward us, each more aggressive and sensational than the next. Modern visual culture is defined by mass spectacles that are accumulations of identical items that at once deaden and draw our visual attention. Like beauty pageants or entertainment extravaganzas such as the Rockettes, the lavish accretion of sameness produces what Siegfried Kracauer (1995) calls the "mass ornament," which attracts not by novelty but by stunning repetition.[11] We defend against the visual overstimulation of modern life with the uninvolved looking of the window shopper, glancing and scanning in search of a truly arresting sight. As social scientists such as Berns and Langer suggest, the human act of staring is a longing for vivid particularity to enliven the insensate flatness of repetitive sights. Staring indicates our encounter with novelty, with coming across compelling visual stimuli amid the bloated stasis of mass visual culture. The novel item attracts, but the novel person seizes our eye more intimately.

NOVELTY AND NORMALITY

Novel is a relative term. What the sociologist Max Weber (1968) called rationalization shapes the way we see others and ourselves. Rationalization developed as a way for modern societies to control the rapidly growing amount of information, products, processes, and movement that industrialization created.[12] Rationalization abstracts and simplifies us through bureaucratic structures. Things and people must fit into preexisting patterns and templates for modern information systems to process them. Rationalization appears in our everyday lives as ready-to-wear clothing, interchangeable parts, check boxes on forms, and social security numbers.

Rationalization does not actually reduce human variation; rather it erases our particularities from the record of who we are and how we live. This pervasive smoothing out of human complexity and variation molds how we understand ourselves and others. The statistical figure of the "average man" becomes the common denominator against which we are measured (Quetelet 1842). Invented by Belgian statistician Adolphe Quetelet in 1842, *average man* is a statistical phantom who stands in for us all. In fact, the hypothetical figures we think of as average coincide with no actual persons, but are abstracted from data to yield descriptive models.

The description of average has led, largely under the pressure of medicalization, to a prescription for normality. The standard model of human form and function that has come to be called *normal* shapes our actual bodies and the way we imagine them. The measure of the good, true, and healthy, normal also determines the status and value of people in the modern world. Normal both describes and prescribes, according to the philosopher Ian Hacking: "The normal stands indifferently for what is typical, the unenthusiastic objective average, but it also stands for what has been, good health, and what shall be, our chosen destiny. That is why the . . . word 'normal' has become one of the most powerful ideological tools of the twentieth century" (Hacking 1990, 169).[13] And normality, as Lennard Davis (1995) tells us, is enforced. It is the destination to which we all hasten and the stick used to drive us there. We are obliged to act, feel, look, and be normal—at almost any cost. The exacting requirement to achieve the norm—from clothes and cars to faces and bodies—creates enormous commercial markets that fuel consumer capitalism. Abnormal costs as well. One goal of medical science is to cordon off the pathological from the normal.[14] The pathological shores up the normal, which is "the centre from which deviation departs," according to Hacking (1990, 164). People who deviate from formal, functional, or behavioral norms lose the advantages of being normal. In this way, the label *abnormal* reduces people's economic and social status and relegates them to the outer edges of the human community (figure 3.1).

Figure 3.1. Satire of the Hottentot Venus (Saartjie Baartman). Aaron Martinet (1762–1841) and Louis François Charon (1783–1831). September 1815.
© The Trustees of the British Museum.

In everyday life, we tend to experience what medical science terms *normal* and *abnormal* as the usual and unusual. As we saw in chapter 2, we are drawn toward what is visually unusual, toward novelty as a form of psychological stimulation and an antidote to visual boredom. Even more, the new has value in our contemporary, forward-looking society, partly because consumer culture requires us to be hungry for the newness that constant consumption demands. But what is novel can be quickly glossed by "ideological tools" such as rationalization and normality. So while contemporary landscapes provide us with novelty, that novelty is at the same time policed by the conflicting requirement for sameness that rationalization dictates. Medical science's influential preference for normality and prejudice against abnormality can render novelty in human form repugnant to us. Modern culture strictly prescribes our behavior, appearance, and our relations with one another, even while we celebrate freedom and choice. Stareable sights break the rules we live by, which is what makes them unusual. We may want to see the unusual but perhaps not be the unusual. Novelty, in this context, is both what we seek and avoid.

major ideas:
culture
vision
vision in religion vs. science
normality
definitions

4

A Social Relationship

> One is not to be the cause of alarm or undue concern, . . . one is
> to behave as to be safely disattendable.
> —William Ian Miller, *The Anatomy of Disgust* (1997, 199)

An eye-snagging stare of intense attention opens a social relationship between two people. The kind of visual scrutiny leveled by a stare is both impersonal and intimate. On the one hand, staring is a social activity governed by rules of engagement, an etiquette of looking that people generally know and observe. On the other hand, staring affords a spontaneous moment of interpersonal connection, however brief, during which two people have the opportunity to regard and be known to one another. So while social rules script staring, individual improvisation can take the staring encounter in fruitful directions.

Staring, in other words, makes things happen between people.

THE ORDINARY AND EXPECTED

How we live together influences how we look at one another and what we expect to see. In our modern urban public landscape, most of the people we encounter face to face are personally unknown to us. Such anonymity is a recent form of human relating. The vast majority of all humans have lived in bands, tribes, or villages where they knew everyone they saw. Since almost all of us in urban or semiurban communities are surrounded by too many people for us to know personally, we navigate daily what Lynn H. Lofland (1973) calls a "world of strangers" where people are unfamiliar yet seen by one another.[1]

To behave toward unknown others effectively and ethically, we need to gather information about them. We use their appearance as clues to who they are and how to relate to them. What you look like, rather than who you are, often determines how people respond to you. Social interactions among strangers are generally highly scripted, delicately choreographed situations in which persons read one another and assemble on the spot a behavioral repertoire to draw from in relating to one another. Sorting through the web of perceptual indicators allows us to categorize the unknown others that surround us so we can respond to them. We need to determine whether the strangers we encounter are going to help us, mug us, bother us, see us again, or just leave us alone. Intricate visual codes such as costuming, insignia, behavior, expression, and comportment—not to mention race, gender, age, size, and visible disabilities—converge to create conclusions about strangers.[2]

Modernity and its attendant rationalization have made our fellow citizens less distinct from one another, less legible to us. In preindustrial life, law and custom differentiated people rigidly according to status, gender, rank, and occupation and marked those distinctions clearly, usually through costuming or symbolic decoration. Roman citizens wore only white togas; medieval royalty wore crowns and robes; feudal guild members had elaborately distinct uniforms; European women wore only skirts; English barristers donned wigs and ribbons; criminals and beggars were branded or mutilated; monks wore cassocks; only Frankish elites were allowed to have long hair; adulteresses' breasts displayed the letter A; Jews wore yellow stars (Lofland 1973, 44–48).[3]

Now The Gap, Brooks Brothers, Aveda, and aesthetic surgery clinics produce a common appearance, even as they promise distinction. Industrialization has standardized our appearance with ready-made clothes and a mass-produced material environment; consumer culture urges brands, styles, body shapes, and even skin colors upon us. The promise of democratic social mobility gets expressed through achieving the right look. Even panhandlers often wear Nikes, albeit scruffy and often imitation. This standardization of our appearance herds us toward an undifferentiated self-presentation that signals a quasi-middle-class status. While subtle distinctions register economic differences—Wal-Mart garb can be distinguished from Armani adornment—our advice for success is usually to look discreet. World leaders, women, and janitors now can show up at important occasions in similar dark, tailored suits. Teeth whiteners and orthodontics, diets and fitness regimes, as well as unisex hair salons try to regularize our actual bodies, crowding us toward the center of the bell curve of human variation.[4] Visual extravagance is often a bold grab for attention, understood usually as a counterculture move or a risky affront to good taste. So while the consumerist rhetoric of choice, individualism, nonconformity, and diversity prattles about being yourself,

[handwritten margin note: don't have something like this anymore]

[handwritten note at bottom: don't stand out / fit in]

the swift current of late modernity sweeps us all toward sameness. As we saw in chapter 3, we are urged to become incarnations of the "average man".

To recognize, in anything but the most superficial manner, individuals amid the flood of mass-produced strangers we encounter would overwhelm us. The solution is simply not to engage with them, to notice them as little as possible unless necessary, and to surround ourselves with shields of privacy. The visual dynamic of this demurral is both a reluctance to look at one another and a refuge in being invisible to each other, being what William Ian Miller in this chapter's epigraph calls "disattendable." Visual interchange in public spaces flattens us to our surfaces, glosses over our complexities. Since we cannot recognize each other fully and deeply as we could with our familiars, we both expect and accord each other what the sociologist Erving Goffman calls "civil inattention" (1980, 83–88). Getting through our day amid this tangle of others depends on such ocular complacency. Staring at one another interrupts this tacit arrangement by exposing us to what might be called uncivil attention (figure 4.1).

Achieving a delicate balance between avoiding attention and achieving recognition requires vigilant management. In face-to-face interactions with both strangers and those we know, we strive to manage the impressions we convey. As Goffman (1959) suggests, we embellish and obscure aspects of ourselves in order to stage a credible and creditable act. "Performed with ease or clumsiness, awareness or not, guile or good faith," Goffman asserts that this self-presentation "is none the less something that must be enacted or portrayed, something that must be realized" (1959, 75). To project positive impressions, our performances tend to exemplify the prescribed values of the society we live in, usually more so than do our actual behaviors or private facts about ourselves. Our bodies are the props that deliver this performance. As long as they are compliant they remain largely invisible, even to us.

We stare at what visually leaps toward us, then, while trying not to be too eye-catching ourselves. To avoid uncivil attention, we must be ordinary to keep within the center of the bell curve and avoid social sanction. Conversation analyst Harvey Sacks (1984) has pointed to the work involved as "doing being ordinary."[5] To be ordinary is to be normal, properly presentable. Indeed, one of the major liberties accorded to the ordinary is civil inattention—that is, the freedom to be inconspicuous, not to be a staree.

Not everyone can or wants to cultivate such civil inattention, however. The cultural revolts of the 1960s—hippiedom, the women's movement, and Black nationalism—repudiated the social ethic of disattendability by adopting extravagantly differentiating costuming and behavior for political purposes. Hippies flouted all conventions, producing long-haired

Wanted to be noticed

Figure 4.1. Mike Baldwin, "Stares/Stairs," December 14, 2005. Courtesy of
www.cartoonstock.com.

males with love beads, outrageous styles, and drug-induced impropriety.
Feminists wore pants and abandoned bras. Blacks claimed Afrocentric
beauty, wrapped themselves in Kente cloth, and cultivated Afros. People who refuse to be visually inconspicuous—such as Hell's Angels, the
pierced and tattooed, or drag queens—ironically often become simply
another instance of visual conformity because we have come to expect
resistance to convention to be expressed in certain ways. Too soon, then,
the flamboyant becomes a version of "doing being ordinary" to the inured eye.

THE UNEXPECTED AND EXTRAORDINARY

Expectations about the ways bodies should look and work affect how we see each other as well. "The ordinary—and the interruption to the expected experience," according to Geoffrey C. Bowker and Susan Leigh Star, "are delicate constructions made and remade every day" (1990, 296). Take for example the seemingly straightforward state of "attractiveness." Physical attractiveness is a form of social capital. The more attractive one's self-presentation, the more competent and esteemed one is thought to be, which translates into economic and social advantage. What social scientists term "expectation states theory" analyzes group interaction to reveal how a complex web of status cues—some categorical, like race, gender, and ability and some traits, like articulateness or confidence—works to determine "the status hierarchy where members with high expectations will participate more and will be more influential than members with low expectations" (Eiseland and Johnson 1996, 72). In other words, people who cannot convincingly present high status cues are devalued. Expectation states theory suggests then that attractiveness is not so much a collection of positive bodily attributes, but rather it is the successful presentation of a normative standard. Simply put, expectation states theory lays out how beauty really is in the eye of the beholder.

Within the ever-shifting circumstances that determine what we expect when we confront each other, some people are less successful in achieving the ordinary and are thus accorded uncivil attention. Indeed, some of us cannot be visually unremarkable, regardless of how we structure our performances of self in everyday life. When bodies begin to malfunction or look unexpected, we become aware of them. They expose themselves by becoming bodies rather than tools of our intentionality. Sick, disabled, or pained bodies both experience and invoke what Drew Leder (1990) calls "dysappearance," meaning that their differences from acquiescent bodies make them appear to us and others.[6] Extraordinary-looking bodies demand attention. The sight of an unexpected body—that is to say, a body that does not conform to our expectations for an ordinary body—is compelling because it disorders expectations. Such disorder is at once novel and disturbing. This interruption of expectations, of the visual status quo, attracts interest but can also lead to disgust, according to William Ian Miller (1997). Unusual bodies are "unsettling because they are disordering; they undo the complacency that comes with disattendability; they force us to look and notice, or to suffer self-consciousness about looking or not looking. They introduce alarm and anxiety by virtue of their power to horrify and disgust." Such bodies fascinate; they demand that we "sneak a second look" (Miller 1997, x).

Furthermore, social scientists agree that disability is a visual cue for lower expectations and discomfort for those who identify as nondisabled. Discomfort comes in part from the social illegibility of the disabled body. The social rituals in which we accord one another recognition depend on accurate reading of bodily and gestural cues. Unpredictable or indecipherable cues create anxiety. It is not that disability itself creates unease, but rather people's inability to read such cues disrupts the expected, routine nature of social relations.

We are exquisitely sensitive to the nuances of meaning encoded in appearance variations and to the rituals of social encounter that tell us who we are in relation to others. Think of the hint implied in a wink, the moral equation of good posture and upstanding citizenship, the gendered connotations of sitting with one's legs spread apart.[7] All these meanings rely on a certain bodily stability, on a relatively narrow range of variations that we learn to read with precision. Someone permanently seated in a wheelchair, however, confounds the usual interpretive web of social significances clustering around what we might call the postural arrangement of bodies. In another example, height relations express a literal hierarchy. The dais and the pulpit ceremonially raise kings and clergy above lesser beings; the arrangement of gender pairings almost always yields a man made tall by a shorter woman. The uprights among us usually do not know how to read or what to make of a wheelchair user or the person of small stature who is waist-high in the world.[8]

Moreover, moving and seeing in expected and ordinary ways are central to our sense of who we are in the modern world. In all of human history until the first third of the nineteenth century, we moved ourselves and our products by foot, boat, or draft animal. Within just one hundred years, trains, cars, and airplanes along with the material public world of streets, stairs, and runways they created expanded exponentially our capacity to move across space and time. Similarly machines such as the printing press, the camera, the x-ray machine, the microscope, the telescope, and the computer extended our eye from the immediate surroundings to the previously hidden interior of the body, the edge of the universe, the bottoms of the sea, or any place on earth. These two actions merge in what Anne Friedberg (1993) calls the "mobilized gaze," a skill required by modern life and its built environment. The ability to deftly use machines of mobility and vision furnishes access to resources and public spaces. Such skills are forms of cultural capital often unavailable to people with certain kinds of disabilities. All too often, social and economic resources and the built environment are inaccessible to many disabled people, excluding them from the privileges of being ordinary.

If staring attempts to make sense of the unexpected, the disabled body might be the exemplary form of the unforeseen. We gawk when presented with the prosthetic hook, empty sleeve, immobile limb, scarred flesh, unfocused eye, quieted body, irregular shape, or twitching extremity. These are bodies that we expect neither to see, to know, nor to have. Such stareable sights capture our eyes and demand a narrative that puts our just-disrupted world back in order.

STARING AS COMMUNICATION

We say something to one another when we stare. Staring is part of our enormous communal vocabulary of the eyes that we use to put a sharp point on what we mean, think, or want. While staring is always an interrogative gesture of interest, this emphatic way of expressing our response to others nonetheless ranges widely in meaning—from domination, adoration, curiosity, surprise, allegiance, disgust, wonder, befuddlement, openness, hostility, to reverence. Since the 1960s, investigators in the field of visual communications have conducted elaborate experiments to uncover our patterns of seeing one another in face-to-face encounters. They distinguish among several kinds of what are considered normal visual interchanges: looking is gazing at the region of eyes; eye contact is mutual looking; seeing is visual access to the whole person. A complex psychology controls human looking; we pursue the exciting and discard the dull sights. We glance at the eyes of the other randomly or intentionally, sometimes mutually locking into eye contact. Our eyes follow interesting objects, but avoid stimuli that are too arousing. Both looking and eye contact determine conversation, establish intimacy, and convey emotion (Rutter 1984; Argyle and Cook 1976).

As chapter 2 discusses, visual interaction stirs us up, makes us receptive. The stare can convey hostility, create tension, elicit avoidance, and propel escape. What is striking in these studies is the way staring at once provokes and paralyzes its object, eliciting both anger and anxiety. Whereas initial studies suggested that the intention and reception of staring is primarily negative, a more complex understanding of staring that expands this predatory model subsequently emerged. Later studies affirmed staring's ability to evoke emotion, increase involvement, and stimulate reaction, but they also recognized that the meaning staring enacted varied widely depending on the context of the encounter (Ellsworth and Langer 1976).[9] In other words, psychologists demonstrated that staring is a profoundly social act unmoored from specific meaning. So while staring's form is scripted, its capacity to create meaning is unstable and open-ended.

The duration and effect of eye contact also varies greatly from encounter to encounter, from person to person and culture to culture. If you look more often or more intently than social mores prescribe, other people judge you as a norm breaker or impolite (Argyle and Cook 1976, 96). Furthermore, because staring is an abnormal gaze pattern, it communicates more than routine, random looking.

Sometimes people try to escape a stare, sometimes they try to engage it. Overweight students flee the stare when eating, for example, but resist it when not consuming food (Lee and Goldman 1979). Inexplicable stares create a more negative response from the staree, whereas staring as a call for help tends to be heeded (Ellsworth and Langer 1976). Some people look longer and more often than others, inviting the other person in the visual dyad to look longer too. Women tend to look more than men, and people of both genders tend to look more at female partners than male ones. A continuous, direct gaze promotes intimacy and personal revelations among women, but it prompts reticence among men. Socially withdrawn people, such as schizophrenics and depressives, tend to avert their gaze in personal conversations. Not surprisingly, people look more at their visual partner when listening than when speaking. High status people are looked at more than low status people. Mutual looking is much more freighted with potential social significance. Mutual looking often transforms into staring that can range from the lovers' lingering erotic visual embrace, to the hostile ocular wrestling of an argument, or rapt astonishment at the unforeseen—or it can be broken off almost as soon as it is made by one member of the pair, such as in the snapping away of the eyes in a chance meeting on the subway. In short, unpredictable things happen when people stare at other people (Rutter 1984).

STARING AS DOMINANCE

Staring is a form of nonverbal behavior that can be used to enforce social hierarchies and regulate access to resources. Nonhuman primates engage in the dynamic of direct stare and gaze aversion, for example, to establish dominance and elicit submission.[10] In humans, a stare can also communicate social status, conferring subordination on a staree and ascendancy on a starer. Think, as a crude but telling example, of the toughness youngsters convey by defeating their peers in staring contests (Ellyson and Dovidio 1985, 115). Such staring is aggressive, often hostile, in scripted staring situations such as military boot camp where drill sergeants stare down inductees to enforce a power hierarchy.[11] The lowered brows, stiff jaw, and slash of a mouth that an angry boss directs toward a timid underling with eyes aslant is the prototype of dominance staring, the visual equivalent of a gorilla's chest pounding.

But human dominance staring is usually more complex than chest pounding. Often staring as a manifestation of dominance veils aggression with a restraint enabled by the hierarchy the staring enacts. In other words, a harsh stare can do the work of a foot on the neck because the subordinate accedes to the system of domination that is in place. Take, for example, the much analyzed concept of the male gaze, which feminism has fruitfully elaborated.[12] The male gaze is a position of privilege in social relations which entitles men to look at women and positions women as objects of that look. As John Berger succinctly puts it: "men act, women appear" (1972, 47). In other words, the male gaze is men doing something to women. This ocular gesture of dominance acts out the gendered asymmetries of patriarchy as it proliferates in institutionalized cultural forms such as films, beauty contests, advertising, striptease routines, and fashion shows. Laden with sexual desire, predation, voyeurism, intimidation, and entitlement, the male gaze often achieves the prolonged intensity of staring. Nonetheless, cultural narratives about romantic love, feminine beauty, and heterosexual or homosexual desire can obscure the male gaze's endorsement of gender dominance. Both individual intention and reception of the male gaze can thus depart from gender scripts, as for example when women relish the arousing aspects of being the object of the male stare or men intend their stares as affirming feminine attractiveness. Simply flipping through any women's fashion magazine confirms the way that erotic narratives mask power relations implicated in heterosexual relations of intense looking.

This theory of a regulating visual dynamic describes masculine and feminine positions, not necessarily actual people. Not all men can or do exercise the male gaze, and women are often posed to cast a surveying look on themselves—as before the mirror, for example—or to identify with the male position, as in watching another woman in a movie. So the male gaze not only occurs in lived gendered relations such as a man leering at strippers, but also when women look at one another from both heterosexual and lesbian positions. Regardless of which sex the partners in the exchange identify with, looking masculinizes, then, and being looked at feminizes. Moreover, this gendered dynamic is part of the set of social practices that call us into being as men or women (Sturken and Cartwright 2001, 70; Butler, 1990).[13] We internalize and identify with the gender system's requirements in the same way that the modern subject described by Michel Foucault (1979) agrees to self-monitoring. In other words, the male gaze as a form of dominance staring makes us into men and women.

The opposite of staring as a dominance display is smiling. Studies suggest that smiling not only mitigates hostility perceived by a staree but also signals a response of submission in a starer (Ellyson and Dovido 1985, 143; Rutter 1984). Smiling, like staring, is a way to manage the uneven distribution of status in social environments. Facial interactions are gendered: women smile more than men in social situations. More power is attributed to people who smile less often. Feelings of competence decrease smiling whereas feelings of incompetence increase smiling (Ellyson and Dovido 1985, 143). Visual acts such as staring and smiling help to create, enforce, and register our social positions.

Cultural othering in all its forms—the male gaze being just one instance—depends upon looking as an act of domination. The ethnographic or the colonizing look operates similarly to the gendered look, subordinating its object by enacting a power dynamic. When persons in a position that grants them authority to stare take up that power, staring functions as a form of domination, marking the staree as the exotic, outlaw, alien, or other. The colonizing look marks its bearer as legitimate and its object as outsider.[14] Like gendered looking, the colonizing gaze occurs at myriad collective social staring rituals such as World Fairs and Expositions, museums, freak shows, drag shows, and the pages of National Geographic.[15] The critic Edward Said (1979) terms this cultural scripting of the unfamiliar into the exotic Orientalism. The Orient is any place situated to the east of a recognized point of reference. This definition calls attention to the relational quality of the colonizing gaze, suggesting that the dynamic works to establish the standpoint of the colonizer at the center of things and to relegate the colonized to some faraway edge of the world.

One strategy the colonized have used to avoid being the object of domination stares is gender and racial passing. To pass as a member of the dominant group, people in the subordinate group whose physical traits or self-presentation in dress or comportment permit can appear to belong to the ascendant group. In other words, passing is an intentional quest for civil inattention in a racist or sexist environment.

Racism uses staring as a tool of domination. Franz Fanon's trenchant study of racism, *Black Skin, White Masks*, identifies its visual manifestation: "the glances of the Other fixed me there" (1991, 109). Fanon suggests here that the racist stare seals his identity as Black. In his antiracist effort to neutralize Blackness, Fanon recruits disability as the true mark of physical inadequacy from which he wishes to differentiate racial marking. A "crippled veteran" tells Fanon's brother to "resign" himself to his color, just as the veteran himself "got used to [his] stump" (140). This comparison outrages Fanon, who claims that racial difference does not make one inferior, but disability does. Fanon defends against the comparison with disability by asserting that his "chest has the power to expand without limit" (140). "I am," Fanon claims proudly, "a master and I am advised to adopt the humility of the cripple" (140). So while Fanon avows "the Negro is not" deserving of subordination, he suggests that "the cripple" is (231, 140).[16]

The kind of staring that "fixes" a person in gender, race, disability, class, or sexuality systems is an attempt to control the other. The study of the political nature of visual relations began in some sense with Simone de Beauvoir's analysis in 1949 that Woman is the essential Other. Man subordinates Woman by setting himself up as the Self, according to De Beauvoir. This mandate for men to be Man and women to be Woman pressures gender relations toward inequality. In other words, men need to assume the position of dominators and women of subordinates to uphold social order and find their place in it. In a skeptical turn, contemporary theorists in philosophy and cultural studies have understood looking itself as a form of domination and produced abundant critiques of vision.[17] For example, Fredric Jameson sneers that the "visual is essentially pornographic," its purpose being "rapt and mindless fascination" and its aim to seduce us "to stare at the world as if it were a naked body" (1990, 1). Staring here is more corrupt than gazing, an emblem of distorted vision.

This view of vision as surveillance advanced with Michel Foucault's (1979) parable of the Panopticon. The Panopticon was Jeremy Bentham's utopian and utilitarian architectural model of supervision in which a tower allowed observers to visually monitor inmates so as to discipline them.[18] Foucault recruits this architectural proposal as a metaphor for the self-regulation characteristic of modern individuals. The Panopticon enforces docility and self-control on those within visual reach through its potential for concealed domination staring. According to this revision of Freud's superego function, we have internalized the threat of visual dominance, of being regulated by the stare. This form of institutionalized spying by those with authority on those without agency is for Foucault a fundamental social act of modernity. The Panopticon might be seen as a nascent high-tech form of Medusa's evil eye. By institutionalizing the dominating stare, the idea of the Panopticon tames Medusa, stripping away her petrifying stare and replacing it with the banal surveillance camera we've all come to accept at the bank or the convenience store. Surveillance differs, however, from interpersonal face-to-face staring in that it is controlling, static, and exercised by the few on the many.

In contrast, the philosopher Jean Paul Sartre offers a parable of interpersonal shaming through domination staring. The significance of the primal scene for Sartre is not simply seeing the sex act but rather imagining being caught staring at the primal sexual act through a keyhole. Driven by "jealousy, curiosity, or vice," a starer is vulnerable for indulging in such profligate and inappropriate looking (Sartre 1956, 235–36). This scene asserts the perversity of staring and the anxiety of being a staree. For Sartre, the Other is not the object of the dominating stare but instead the Other threatens witnessing the self as staree. "The Other *looks* at me," Sartre claims, "and as such he holds the secret of my being, he knows what I *am*. . . . The Other has the advantage over me" (473). Whereas Fanon sees this dynamic as forming racial identity, here Sartre offers a triangulation complicating a simple formula of visual domination and subjection. Sartre is stared at while himself staring. The risk, then, in visually objectifying another is being caught doing it. Such fascinated looking is simultaneous domination and subjection. The lesson of this parable is that the excessive, indecorous enthrallment of staring subjugates the starer by begetting shame.

Sartre's keyhole metaphor is a limited model of staring however. His keyhole captures the furtive and unseemly nature of a stare. This vantage point, like Foucault's Panopticon, provides a "cone of vision" that opens out from the eye of a viewer (Melville 1996, 104). But staring without the restriction of a keyhole reverses the shape of this visual cone. In fact, staring in modern urban life is most often a form of involuntary telescoping in which our roving, casual visual scanning focuses in on an unexpected sight.

Understanding the kind of staring that enacts dominance is useful for illuminating inequities in power relations. The limitation, however, of focusing on this narrow but currently popular interpretation of visual social relations is that it can foreclose on the complexities of how we look at one another. Sartre goes a way in questioning the idea of the crushing force of a starer's eye by showing his keyhole peeper to be simultaneously a starer and staree. Nonetheless, Sartre's model of staring shuts down rather than opens up the encounter. Sartre's starer/staree is "known" by his starer, but that knowledge results in an "advantage over" that is ultimately a domination that threatens the staree. The knowledge that the staring other gets from the encounter crushes the staree with shame for his own eager but furtive looking.

STARING AS STIGMA ASSIGNMENT

Domination staring gives a starer power over a staree. Staring can also be a social act that stigmatizes by designating people whose bodies or behaviors cannot be readily absorbed into the visual status quo. Stigmatizing, according to sociologist Erving Goffman (1986), is social discrediting of those we perceive as different, as lesser than we are. Stigmatizing pushes others away rather than dominating them. Stigma, Goffman suggests, is not in the bodies of people considered disreputable but in social relations that deem some superior and others inferior. In other words, social interactions—such as staring—assign stigma to certain perceived traits. Goffman describes a hierarchy of stigma designations that begins with disability—or what he rather harshly terms "abominations of the body" (1986, 4). Next are character aspersions such as dishonesty, weak will, or unnatural passions, which people associate with conditions such as alcoholism, homosexuality, mental disability, criminality, and unemployment. Finally are what he calls the "tribal affiliations" of race, ethnicity, nationality, and religion. The people remaining without supposed besmirchments are the "normals" (5). Everyone with potentially discreditable traits must navigate a web of shifting social expectations and sources of status. Stigma, in short, is prejudicial judgment against appearing different from the "normals."

When the social sorting process of stigmatization shaves off everyone from the mildly discredited to the "abominations," the lingering untainted "normals" are an elite minority. Goffman (1986) sums up this archetypal "normal" as the "only one complete unblushing male in America: a young, married, white, urban, northern, heterosexual, Protestant father of college education, fully employed, of good complexion, weight and height, and a recent record in sports" (128). The ironic point in this description is that the prototypical figure of normalcy is not what we actually see everywhere but rather is what we expect to see. The illusion of the normal is often what people reach for in creating self-presentations, particularly those in the public eye such as politicians, executives, or news anchors, for example. This phantom figure of the "normate" is "the veiled subject position of the cultural self, the figure outlined by the array of deviant others whose marked bodies shore up the normate's boundaries" (Garland Thomson 1996, 8).[19] Actual normates are as scarce as hen's teeth, whereas imagined normates preside over the public landscape. So while the "abominations" that life makes of so many of us are always among us, their presence is a perpetual surprise. We become inured to our own "abominations" for the most part, so when the uncivil attention of the stigmatizing process comes our way, it seems an indignity, as we saw with Fanon's experience of racism.

Stigmatizing is a social process that hurdles a body from the safe shadows of ordinariness into the bull's-eye of judgment. As appearance became standardized in the modern world, particularity came to be understood as aberration rather than simple variation or distinctiveness. The seen body is our primary mode of perceiving and understanding scale, symmetry, balance, which are the coordinates of ordinariness. Comparisons to what we expect determine our understanding of "abominations," of the disproportionate, grotesque, deformed, miniature, gigantic, or unusual (Stewart 1984). A proto-ordinary body becomes an authentic body, the one we think of as normal or call able-bodied.

The stigmatizing process is uncomfortable for everybody involved. Stigma comes to people not only from violating ordinariness but also from disrupting the effortless mutual granting of civil inattention that gets us through our day. Social co-presence requires that we do not spark one another's fears, anxiety, embarrassment, or disgust. "The stigmatized," as William Ian Miller notes, "disrupt the smooth-running social order that normals righteously demand" (1997, 200). The ocular intrusion of people who cannot achieve inconspicuousness is itself an occasion for discrimination. The visually indiscreet ignite the uncomfortable partnership of staring. To be a stareable sight is unseemly, then, in part because it outs the starer for inappropriate looking. To use Sartre's shame model of looking, staring as stigma assignment doubly shames starees—both for their supposed flaws and for exposing their starers. Staring, then, can be a matter of looking wrong and wrong looking for everyone in the encounter.

We make the unexpected out of what we have learned to expect, out of understandings of the world that come to us and that we remake. For instance, the concept of "tribal affiliations" illustrates how received culture structures expectations. The more commonalities we share, the more salient minor differences seem. This patterning of allegiances and exclusions is the root of nationalism and ethnicity, according to Michael Ignatieff (1997). Developing Freud's notion of "the narcissism of minor differences," Ignatieff asserts that we sort variations in behaviors, values, and corporeal traits into essential cultural difference we call ethnicity (48). Nationalism is the narcissistic overvaluing of differences rather than commonalities, a distortion that defines those different from us as outsiders, and an occasion for conflict. In another example, what we take to be gender, sexual, racial, and ability differences are largely minor but receive great social significance. Human variation matters when some characteristics merit privilege and others are sources of stigma.[20]

Human variation, in other words, is seldom neutral. "Abominations of the body" are in the eye of the well-acculturated beholder. Modern culture's erasure of mortality and its harbinger, bodily vulnerability, make disabled bodies seem extraordinary rather than ordinary, abnormal instead of mundane—even though in fact the changes in our function and form that we think of as disabilities are the common effects of living and are fundamental to the human condition. What Goffman describes as "abominations" come to most ordinary lives eventually. If we live long enough, we will all become disabled.[21]

main ideas

appearance
attractiveness
communication
smiling
dominance
stigma

disability
↓
dishonesty, weak will
unnatural passions
↓
race, ethnicity,
nationality, religion
↓
normals

5

Knowledge Gathering

> An observer sees within a prescribed set of possibilities.
> —Jonathan Crary, *Techniques of the Observer* (1990, 6)

CURIOUS STARING

We have inherited an uneasy tension between seeing and knowing. Philosophy is in part a conversation about the relations between appearances and reality. Plato, for example, warned that truth lies not in the visible, that appearances in fact obfuscate truth. Our insistence that we see things with our own eyes has alternately been punished and rewarded. This chapter addresses the rewards of curiosity, while the next examines its dangers. Curiosity is the itch to know; it shifts desire of the eye to desire of the mind. Like staring, curiosity seeks. Both are acquisitive, grasping, appetitive. Staring is an ocular inquiry; curiosity is an intellectual inquiry. The eye leads; the mind follows.

Human curiosity animates our modern world, revealing the tacit, taming the novel, and undertaking the unknown.[1] Despite traditional misgivings, the pursuit of curiosity—even more than the Jeffersonian pursuit of happiness—characterizes modern individuals. Curiosity is interest headed toward possession. Vision may ignite curiosity, but mobility and acquisition enact it. Curiosity begets inquiry, which challenges established authority and propels the development of modernity according to Hans Blumenberg (1983). The Copernican dismantling of a geocentric understanding established curiosity as a virtue rather than the vice it had been when the world was thought to be limited under strict authority. This revolution in the way we imagine our place in the cosmos licensed us to observe and seek our own proof. Pursuit of the novel takes on fresh value beginning in the early modern era and continuing into the Enlightenment.[2] Indeed, modernity validates the eye's hunger for new and strange sights. An interest in the unusual, remote, and unexamined burgeoned, exemplified by Leonardo da Vinci in the fifteenth century. Curiosity prompted explorations, commencing the mobility that is a defining feature of modern era (Zacher 1976). The curiosity of a Columbus, Newton, or Franklin makes them heroic rather than presumptuous to the modern sensibility. As bold journeys into the unknown, inquiry conforms to modernity's orientation toward the future rather than the past. By the beginning of eighteenth century, Montesquieu asserts that curiosity is inherent in all men, naturalizing and authorizing the movement to expand limits of the known universe.

Not all were as sanguine about curiosity being a positive force for all people at all times. For some, it became a secular pleasure, distrusted as indulgence. Samuel Johnson's 1755 dictionary of English defined curiosity as an addiction to inquiry.[3] Associated with callow and reckless youth, "naive curiosity" was unproductive. A mature and proper "reflected curiosity," however, drove the rational, scientific inquiry that initiated modernity. Naive, natural curiosity matured, then, into the methods of scientific inquiry and rational analysis, which was an urge to go beyond mere visibility into "theoretical curiosity" (Blumenberg 1993, 226, 233–34). Modernity emancipated human curiosity from the constriction of external authority, legitimating and institutionalizing it as medical-scientific observation. Enlightenment rationality severed such decorous theoretical curiosity from a curiosity closely associated with the senses and passions (Daston and Park 1998). Yet, both a base and elite form of curiosity persist. Gossip and gawking get the bad name, while scientific observation remains untainted.

The goal of observation—of staring for the sake of knowing—is to make the unknown intelligible, to incorporate the unusual into our understandings of the usual. This process has a strong visual component. Accumulating knowledge has two visual aspects: observation and display. As the collection of knowledge, science relies on a spatial metaphor about proximity, about center and margin, about here and there. We can know that which is close because we experience it repeatedly; as it becomes familiar, we knit it into our explanatory schema. The unknown is unintelligible because it is far away from the quotidian. We must encounter something foreign regularly to make it native. The aim of science is to act from a distance, reaching out toward the strange to, in the words of Bruno Latour, collect it in "cycles of accumulation" and return it to the center, where we domesticate it into the ordinary (1987, 219). Knowledge is, then, "familiarity with events, places, and people seen many times over" (220).

The search for knowledge involves intense and sustained looking at unfamiliar objects—whether microbes, stars, or aboriginals—in order to corral them into the observer's arena of understanding. This domestication of the unknown takes the form of display, of visual reorganization into categories coherent to viewers. The tamed and transmuted objects of knowledge are displayed in collections such as early curiosity cabinets, museums, or encyclopedias, all of which proliferated between 1550–1750.[4] The collection stages a scene of staring that arrests time, erases particularity, and mutes origin in order to incorporate strange objects into familiar narratives of the world. Staring that leads to knowing thus requires the arduous visual work of reconciling the curious with the common.

Such staring is more than idle curiosity. It is theoretical curiosity aimed at mastering the unknown by making it known. This kind of looking is intense, focused, and asymmetrical. As what Michel Foucault calls the "clinical gaze," observation has been used to lasso the outlaw aspects of human variation into constricting categories and to diagnose differences as pathology.[5] According to this view, medical-scientific observation as diagnosis brings home the alien in chains, converting the unusual into the monstrous, sick, polluted, contagious, mad, queer, and deviant. Not only does it survey our exteriors to establish boundaries, but clinical observation invades our interiors to reckon the true relationship between inside and outside, between visible and invisible. Such practices as contemporary genetic testing, surgical procedures, and medical imaging technologies all rely on a Weberian rationalizing vision.[6] Despite these sharp critiques brought against the abuses of medical-scientific observation, the application of this knowledge collection has nonetheless profoundly sheltered those of us in modern, developed societies from suffering, pain, death, and hardship even while it has mastered us.

So while staring begins as an impulse, curiosity sustains it. The prolonged look becomes an expedition into unknown territory. What Michael T. Gilmore (2003) calls the "quest for legibility" that characterizes Western, in particular North American, culture is one of the shared conventions of possibility that determines how we see one another. To navigate the egalitarian, mobile, anonymous social landscape of modern life, we need to read others, to properly respond or ignore them. The intricate hierarchy of medical-scientific classification is just one axis of legibility that we depend upon to perceive each other. We enlist intense visual scrutiny to gather knowledge, answer questions, shape narratives, and explain dissonance. This visual voracity can transform our world-views. By the time stareable sights release their grip on us, the order of things may have changed for us.

BAROQUE STARING

Whether because of or in spite of suspicions about the visible and its human product, the image, we remain steadfastly compelled by what we see. And yet, propriety runs the show. Proper staring is decorous, selective looking, not just random gawking. In acceptable staring, an appropriate viewer synthesizes visual apprehension into knowledge that benefits the knower in carrying out cultural requirements. In contrast, what can be called "baroque staring" is flagrantly stimulus driven, the rogue looking that refuses to be corralled into acceptable attention. What might be called baroque staring is a giving over to the marvelous, to what Christine Buci-Glucksmann (1994) calls "the madness of vision."[7] Unconcerned with rationality, mastery, or coherence, baroque staring blatantly announces the states of being wonderstruck and confounded. It is gaping-mouthed, unapologetic staring.

This kind of staring overrides reason and restraint, revels in contradiction, and arouses fervor—much as does baroque art. Baroque furnishes a metaphor for such extravagant looking that draws from the seventeenth-century era in which Western arts were distinguished by dramatic complexity and evoked emotion by appealing to the senses. Deriving from the Portuguese word for unusually shaped pearls or from the Spanish medieval term for an obstacle in schematic logic, baroque portrays the irregular, bizarre, exaggerated, peculiar, and illogical. The contradiction and disorder of the baroque confound clarity. The baroque flies in the face of classical moderation and Cartesian rationality. It unsettles faith in legibility. Because the baroque distorts, it eludes logical narrative, defying the search for meaning inherent in the knowledge-producing human stare. Like a blank stare, a baroque stare bears witness to a failure of intelligibility. Neither accords with scientific observation or ordered Cartesian perspectivalism. Whereas a blank stare is an abdication of the looking process, a baroque stare is an overly intense engagement with looking. A baroque stare is unrepentant abandonment to the unruly, to that which refuses to conform to the dominant order of knowledge.

As such, baroqueness resides not in a visual object, but rather in the encounter between starer and staree. Baroque staring entangles viewer and viewed in an urgent exchange that redefines both. This overloading of the ocular apparatus is what provokes bewilderment and confusion in both parties.[8] The inexplicable captivates both baroque and scientific-medical starers, but the former remains in a state of wonderment, while the latter strives to vivisect the inexplicable to lay bare its secrets.[9] Baroque staring's renunciation of agency, whether as head-slapping astonishment or stunned fascination, is both threatening and exhilarating. The urgent question, "What is that?" stirs baroque starers. Such visual probing imposes illegibility on a staree. Singled out as alien, a staree is at once cornered and empowered. After all, the sight of a staree has brought a starer to his or her cognitive knees. Baroque staring thus exposes both its participants.

The Enlightenment turn toward the decorous and the staid banished wonder into the realm of vulgarity. Art, as well, trivialized the baroque by transforming it into rococo and eviscerated it with neo-classicism. Baroque staring at wonders became itself an oddity. Wonder evolved into proper looking.[10] Nonetheless, baroque staring can serve as a useful way to understand responses to startling sights in any period. Because baroque staring indicates wonder rather than mastery, it can lead to new insights. Mastery closes down knowledge; wonder opens up toward new knowledge. Mastery dominates starees; wonder places starer and staree in dynamic relation. As both verb and noun, *wonder* names the object and act of staring. To wonder means to want to know. A wonder is a source of knowledge. Baroque stares exceed, then, interested looking. A literally gripping sight provokes baroque stares even in our contemporary moment. In other words, we still wonder at wonders.

STARING AT OURSELVES

We stare to know, and often we stare to know ourselves. Perhaps, as Jacques Lacan (1977) suggests, our first baroque stares are at ourselves.[11] Being caught off guard by a surprising version of ourselves in some reflective surface is one of the primal scenes of staring. Visual self-regard is strange because of the limits of human perception. Our faces are the seat of the senses, the place from which we recognize the world, and also the location of recognition, differentiation, and affirmation from others. Our own faces are intimately familiar to us through the senses of smell, touch, hearing, taste, but never directly through sight. Paradoxically, we are denied the sight of our own faces, that most human, intimate sight of our particular self. We cannot directly recognize ourselves in a way that others know us. We experience ourselves as a body moving through the world that touches and is touched by our environment, as the philosopher Maurice Merleau-Ponty (1962) points out. But we can only see the very particular self that we are through the mediation of images or reflections, which reverse our appearance so that what we see is a slightly distorted mirror image of how we look to others. The person in the mirror or the photograph is not the person we experience ourselves to be; rather, that person is the one others see. This disjuncture between seeing and being ourselves encourages self-scrutiny. We learn to monitor ourselves and calculate our appearance through intently looking at these images, through staring at the surprising sight that we at once doubt and trust. Encountering ourselves face-to-face before the mirror, we become both subject and object of our stares. The work of self-scrutiny can be affirming or alienating, but always absorbing, often up against the edge of baroque staring.

The seduction of staring at ourselves has a long history. The classical myth of Narcissus, like that of Medusa, is a cautionary tale about the strange power of staring. So compelled was the young Narcissus by his own astonishing image in the pool that he plunged to the depths, drowning in a watery consummation of his misguided desire. Freud chose narcissism to describe the modern psyche's self-regard. Both the Medusa and Narcissus stories capture the power of visual fascination and its threat of trickery. Both myths are thick with irony. The upstart challenger Perseus takes up Medusa's awful power; Narcissus seeks love and finds death. These two stories admonish us about the dangers of baroque staring. *baroque*

We seem always to have been ambivalent about looking at ourselves. Preachers both early and late warned against the vanity of excessive self-regard and condemned the looks that incited lust. The vanity mirror is a symbol of frivolous femininity or foolish vanitas. Our reflected image could reveal our resemblance to God or incite dangerous "crazed stares" that were the devil's tool (Melchior-Bonnet 2001, 187). Despite these admonitions, we have turned with ever more fascination to reflections of ourselves.[12] Our forbearers looked at themselves in pools and polished stones. Mirrors, the human-made implement of self-regard, were present in ancient cultures, from Greece to China. Glass mirrors made Renaissance Venice rich. The Hall of Mirrors at Versailles, a monument to modern visual enchantment with self-staring, opened in 1682. By the end of the European eighteenth century, lucid, large, and relatively available mirrors made more people ardent self-surveyors. By the middle of the nineteenth century, small personal care looking glasses and household mirrors embedded in furniture and walls were ubiquitous.

Photographic portraits—which took hold of the Western world in the mid-nineteenth century—provided another venue for taking a hard look at ourselves.[13] These images offered both the curse and gift to literally—borrowing from Robert Burns—see ourselves as others see us.[14] This new capacity to stare at ourselves also yielded what Sabine Melchior-Bonnet calls the "democratization of narcissism" (Melchior-Bonnet 2001, 155). Christopher Lasch (1980) asserts, in fact, we live in a "culture of narcissism," that requires self-scrutiny through image management and makes us into preening, anxious, self-absorbed individuals.

These proliferating images of ourselves provide a flood of opportunities for baroque staring that is part of the "specular consciousness" typical of modern citizens. Despite our familiarity with our own images, we can still

staring @ us

be trapped into a baroque stare: the infant charmed by its surprising reflection, the partygoer confronted with a haggard face the next morning, the aging adult startled by the replication of his parent in his own face, or any of us wondering at our own unrecognizable expression captured in a staged holiday photo. All stare with fascination and incredulity at that stranger before them. These glimpses of what we might be are both deceptive and truthful. Reflections and photographs capture supposed reality, and yet that uncanny twin may not correspond with our felt version of who we are. Stares can be a response to clashing versions of the self.

That image we see is at once familiar and strange, the me and the not-me. We stare at ourselves to make sense of this other being that peers out as we brush our teeth, haunts our relations with others, ambushes us as we enter lighted rooms, scolds us for our inevitable lack of self-government, or enchants us when we get it right.

STARING AT DEATH

We stare not just to know ourselves but to know what we will become. Staring at dead bodies has historically been a highly structured public ritual as well as a spontaneous response. Like our own image, a dead body is both familiar and strange, recognizable as human but astonishingly inanimate. Dead bodies indicate an essential stasis in the natural world that challenges our own fragile animation. We can die randomly and kill purposely. Death borders familiar life, giving it shape and differentiating it from the strangeness of nothingness. Dead bodies also verify a terrifying contingency—the disorder of things and the impotence of humanity to change that. In looking death literally in the face, we can stare at our fate with awe, terror, sorrow, wonder, or simply vivid interest. Staring baroquely at death can be an attempt to absorb a knowledge that we can never truly master. *baroque*

In our contemporary moment in mainstream American culture, the sight of a dead body is unusual and often unexpected, a stimulus to eyes accustomed to the unequivocally alive. Staring at dead bodies—particularly at the moment of death or in full-blown decay—vanished for the most part from our experience by the first part of the twentieth century. The funeral industry and changing ideas of tastefulness have come between us and the raw evidence of our mortality (Laderman 2003). Until reform movements removed punishment, torture, and executions from the public eye, however, heads on pikes, criminals dangling at the ends of ropes, mutilated bodies, rotting corpses in gibbets, the boiled, burned, and the drawn and quartered were regular sights (Lofland 1973). Public executions were pageants of sin and salvation, corruption and justice, civil order and communal vengeance that engendered intense face-to-face looking. So potent, in fact, was staring between the witness and the executed that it was mitigated by the tradition of hooding the victims. Beginning in the seventeenth century in America, the concept of punishment and the practice of executions shifted from public warning to private internment, so that penitentiaries largely supplanted gallows and Panoptic surveillance took over the work of public torture (Masur 1989; Foucault 1979).[15] By the 1830s executions moved from the town square to inside the jailhouse walls.

Nonetheless, a number of death scenes that ritualized baroque staring endured into contemporary times. Lynching, the vigilante assertion of white supremacy that thrived in the United States into the twentieth century, was a public spectacle that persisted well past the time when legal public execution and torture had been removed from the sight of citizens (Brundage 1997). White men, women, and children gathered to gawk at hanged or burned victims. Although these violent displays might be attributed to a few vicious racists, throngs of ordinary white citizens stared at these horrific scenes as if they were petty amusements. Souvenir photographs and postcards, many scrawled with words such as "Negro Barbeque," document a drive to look (Allen 2000, 10).

An expanding commercialism continued to enlist the eye's apparent appetite for death. Sideshows and medical theater converged in American entrepreneurship, for instance, when P. T. Barnum held the public autopsy of Joice Heth, a "remarkable curiosity" first displayed live in 1835 (Barnum 1869, 82).[16] Billed as the 161-year-old nurse of George Washington, Heth was a blind, toothless, crippled slave woman who entertained a gawking public in both life and death. Barnum publicly staged her dissection in 1836 before doctors, medical students, clergy, and newsmen, charging fifty cents each and netting seven hundred dollars from zealous starers eager to look intently for truth her body might reveal (Reiss 2001).

In fin de siècle France, people flocked by the thousands to the Paris Morgue to stare at dead bodies displayed behind a glass window that divided the smell of the dead from the noses of the living. All the popular guidebooks of the day recommended the Paris Morgue, which stood in the shadow of Notre Dame, as a stop on a tour of the city (Schwartz 1998). The Morgue's purpose in presenting the dead was to aid in identifying unknown victims, but the practice clearly exceeded its original intent to become a public scene of staring. Urban residents looking for novelty in their newly found leisure ogled dead bodies similarly to appealing goods in a department store window.

The growing modern funeral industry interceded as well in the urge to stare at death. Where the Paris Morgue erected a window to separate the dead from the living, modern technology goes further to mediate encounters with dead bodies. The contemporary mortuary industry mitigates death's effects on the body so as to close the visual gap between them and us. With embalming and other "restorative arts" such as demi-surgery and make up, the funeral home offers up life-like dead to the stares of the living (Laderman 2003, 104). Perhaps the funeral home's frustration of the human impulse to stare at death has in part driven contemporary thrill-seekers to the endless screen spectacles of violent death. We feel its residual pull as well in random encounters with death's possibility, like the highway accident that snarls our otherwise dull daily commutes.

Photography—that modern way to see new things—can get between us and actual dead bodies, distancing them and bringing them closer at the same time. Memorial photography, for instance, sprang up along with photographic portraits as a way to preserve the newly dead in the transient moment before disintegration took them fully away (Burns 1990). Memorial photographs, like embalming, snatch death back toward life by flash freezing it in a stareable moment. Pictures move death away from actual experience, then, but they can also bring distant death before our eyes and hold it there. Whereas memorial photography is deliberate and posed, photojournalism, in contrast, can jump in spontaneously to capture the way death interrupts life.

The photojournalist Weegee caught unexpected death in his sensational pictures of 1940s Manhattan. More than that, however, Weegee exposed how urgently we stare at death. Working for tabloids and the Manhattan Police Headquarters, Weegee shot pictures of car crashes, murders, fires, and gangster liquidations. The focus in many of his gritty and raucous photos of New York life is not the gripping scene of death itself but rather the act of staring at it. Starers themselves are the center of interest in many of his pictures. A section entitled "The Curious Ones," from his 1945 book, *Naked City*, puts on view the wide-eyed spectators of his gruesome and enticing scenes. There, Weegee precisely sums up how baroque staring works: "These are men, women, and children on the sidewalks of New York . . . always rushing by . . . as if life itself depended on their reaching their destination . . . but always finding time to stop and look at a fire . . . a murder . . . a woman about to jump off a ledge. . . . When they have had their fill of the scene, they disappear as quickly as they came. . . ." (34). What Weegee documents is the stimulation and fascination glowing in the eyes of starers. The raw wonder on the gawkers' rapt faces gives the photos potency. In one picture we see a crowd intently watching a frantic crew trying to resuscitate a drowned swimmer at Coney Island in 1940. With eyes

[handwritten marginal note: Manhattan photojournalist]

fixed on the obscured body hardly visible at the edge of the picture, the expressions of the crowd range from concern, perplexity, horror, avoidance, to relish. Another photo from 1942 bares the twisted faces of a mother and daughter fixated in terror on the burning building in which another daughter is trapped. Several of his pictures show onlookers at the moment of last rites—one for covered fire victims, another for a tramp hit by a taxi on the Lower East Side. "Ambulance" from 1943 catches starers drawn abruptly from their routine into the unimaginable. In it, the white face of a cop looking at the lifeless face of a women being taken away emerges from the dark background of the night wide-eyed and slack jawed in astonishment at the wonder of death. Engrossed in watching the moment when life passes into death, Weegee's starers seem to stare to get the story as well. In "Killed in a Car Crash," for instance, starers are transfixed by an enormous wrecked vehicle, mangled and misshapen, that tells the story of this death more dramatically than the simple covered body by its side.

Figure 5.1. "Their First Murder." A crowd gathers in the Williamsburg section of Brooklyn, New York City, to see the corpse of Peter Mancuso, shot twice by an unknown gunman as he sat parked at a traffic light. The crying woman is Mancuso's aunt and the little boy tugging the hair of the girl in front of him is her son. (Photo by Weegee [Arthur Fellig]/International Centre of Photography/Getty Images.)

Weegee himself confessed to being "spellbound by the mystery of murder." His photos present less the murdered and more the fascination itself embodied in the spectators he framed with his camera (1996, 13). In his photos of watching crowds, Weegee often places his camera in the position of the spectacle—the fire, the dead body, or the wrecked car—in order to seize frontally the faces of the crowd mesmerized by the spectacle his picture never reveals. These photos frequently foreground the contorted faces of children elbowing up to the front for a better view. "Their First Murder," for example, shows a gang of children jockeying for position to stare at something in front of them but behind the camera (see figure 5.1). Their disturbed and disturbing expressions contrast with the generally more impassive stares of the adults around them. The caption under another group of eager children surrounding a weeping woman says, "A woman relative cried . . . but neighborhood dead-end kids enjoyed the show when a small-time racketeer was shot and killed" (1945, 86). Revealing children as the most eager starers seems to confirm that staring is a primal impulse not yet fully tempered in these children. Admonishments not to stare have thus far not overridden enthrallment and leashed them up with polite restraint. *[handwritten: curiosity]*

We might characterize what psychologists and physicians think of as the search for dopamine-induced pleasures of visual novelty as instead baroque stares of wonder. This is an impulse not just to look but also to know what happened, to get the story, to wonder about a wonder. Staring gratifies our craving for visual stimulation: it satisfies our hungry brains. Stareable sights such as our image in the mirror or a dead body offer urgent knowledge gathering expeditions. Yet staring at one another complicates the thrill of intense looking. Because we are vulnerable and exposed in interchanges of mutual looking, social order evolves toward regulating, even ritualizing, visual relationships, as we have seen. Staring among strangers, the very site of greatest potential for chancing upon human novelty, has in contemporary American culture come to be seen as untoward, a violation of the strict rules that govern social interaction. Baroque staring, then, gets us what we want but it also gets us into trouble when we direct it toward our fellow citizens. This contradiction makes staring compelling and fraught human behavior.

THE PERILS OF BAROQUE STARING

[handwritten: add to Baroque main idea section]

The staring encounter can be a tangle of desire and dread for starer and staree alike. Although we think of staring as an affront to starees, starers suffer a welter of psychological contradictions as well. Confrontations with illegible bodies interrupt our reveries on the mundane visual landscape. On the one hand, this can be a welcome opportunity to vivify dulled senses or even come to fresh understandings of our world. On the other hand, stareable sights can more than simply ruffle our predictable surroundings. The startling appearance of fellow humans with unexpected bodies or behaviors provokes psychological overstimulation. From the perspective of individual psychology, the intrusion of a potential staree can be what Adam Phillips (1993) calls a "radical besiegement" of the subject. In the Freudian model of the self, according to Phillips, the ego is ever vulnerable to and vigilant against "the experience of traumatic excitement; or rather, the seduction of one's own excitement" (42). The job of the ego is to compose the self, to guard the primal, overwhelming immediacy of desire. The ego must ceaselessly work to convert our childlike "original clamorousness" into the "calculated social poise" of mature adulthood that reflects self-mastery and displays appropriate patterns of excitement (42–43). A potential scene of staring risks overwhelming the fragile composure that the ego maintains over its inherent excitability, threatening to deluge us with uncontrolled desire. This besiegement menaces our brittle, if well-defended, egos. Even though we have collectively erected social regulations to protect us against staring, these conventions can further heighten our anxiety. Our inevitable excitability predestines us to violate social codes about appropriate eye behavior.

This appetite for profligate looking is a potential source of shame. Staring exposes our hunger to fasten our eyes upon novel sights, an urge as intractable perhaps as the drive to mate and eat. Recall Jean Paul Sartre's famous parable about the shame of staring. All staring in Sartre's account is illicit because it can be witnessed. "The Other *looks* at me," while I am staring. Caught peeping at the primal scene of sex through a keyhole, Sartre claims for his starer, "and as such he holds the secret of my being, he knows what I *am*. . . . The Other has the advantage over me" (1956, 473). All that Sartre's "Other" needs to know about "me" is that I stare. In this sense, all staring is furtive looking at lascivious sights. This triangulation of seeing and being seen exceeds a simple relationship of perpetrator and victim. In Sartre's version of staring, the visual hunger that drives us subjugates the starer more than the staree.

Another psychological dread that staring ignites in the starer is an unsettling awareness of our own embodiment. The denial of death and vulnerability that the ego relies upon to get us through our days depends upon the disappearance of our own bodies to ourselves (Leder 1990). In the kind of engagement that staring at unusual bodies begets, the starer is forced out of what Phillips calls the "benign forgetting of the body that takes care of itself" (40). A stareable body ambushes our attention, demanding acknowledgment of both its embodiment and our own. This claim on our awareness disturbs the taken-for-grantedness of our own bodies, waking us up to a body relentlessly subject to the disturbances of desire, illness, and mortality.[17] Bodies that insist on our notice hold us thrall. Being subject to the stare—rather than the subject of the stare—bears out our inability to resist the excited impulse to stare, in spite of our vigilant super-egos or internalized parental prohibitions. Staring is a form of fascination confirming the intransigence of our own bodies.

For the staree, being the object of someone's visual scrutiny is more complicated than being a victim of our fellow human's bad manners. To be sure, unwanted stares can be annoying or tedious. Stares can also seem like accusations. The visual harassment of being stared at is a perversion of the our need to be seen, to be held in the sustaining visual regard of an attentive other, the requirement D. W. Winnicott (1960) tells us is fundamental to the development of the self.[18] Being seen is recognition, a validation of our existence from the primary person who keeps us alive. The poet Audre Lorde captures the paradox of the staree in remarking that "[W]e fear the visibility without which we cannot truly live" (1984, 42). We both need and dread the intense recognition that staring accords us. To be the object of the stare is to be exposed to judgment, appropriation, or abrupt dismissal. Yet the visual embrace of a stare is a validation of our being, the relational registering that we matter to another, even if it perhaps exposes our deepest vulnerabilities. Staring, then, has the power to sustain or demolish us. This power the other holds over us vivifies the staring relationship. Our hunger for and horror of the stare demands containment. The primal need to look and to be looked at are human urges potent enough that we have surrounded them with a fortress of edicts to control or even eliminate staring.

main ideas
_____

curiosity
baroque
staring @ us
death

PART III

Don't Stare

6

Regulating Our Looks

Don't stare.
—Everybody's mother

Never laugh audibly nor stare at people.
—L. G. Abell, *Woman in Her Various Relations* (1851)

AGAINST CURIOSITY

Everybody knows that curiosity killed the cat. As an enactment of curiosity, staring is risky business. As we have seen, a long-standing wariness about curiosity pervades the Western tradition, underpinning America's prohibitions against staring.[1] To those who condemn it, the curiosity launched by the impulse to stare at inexplicable sights is a grab for unauthorized knowledge, a presumptuous overreaching. As the desiring mind following the desiring eye, curiosity can bespeak discontent and breed iconoclasm. A poke in the eye of the gods, curiosity puts us in charge of the story, trouncing obedience and risking sound punishment. Eve, Prometheus, Icarus, Oedipus, and Frankenstein warn us against the hubris of curiosity, of wanting to know more than is good for you. To understand our contemporary proscriptions against staring, we need to explore more fully the distrust of curious looking in the Western tradition.

So voracious and potentially dangerous is curious looking that only a respectable goal rescues it from our uneasiness. Curiosity is a transitive concept that demands an object. Because the object of curiosity is by definition unknown, this lurch toward knowing can thrust us into either good or evil,

Figure 6.1. Dan Reynolds, "'Whatever you do, don't stare at my father's glass eye,'" February 6, 2007. Courtesy of www.Cartoonstock.Com.

the profound or the trivial. Proper scientific curiosity wins Nobel Prizes. Idle curiosity makes us busy bodies. Salacious curiosity induces us read the *National Enquirer*. A blunt instrument, curiosity overtakes; it mows down and gobbles up the object of its contemplation. Curiosity recontextualizes its object. Curiosity in the service of mastery tames the extraordinary. But its ardent focus can also elaborate the mundane into the exotic, the ordinary into the rare. Like *wonder*, the word *curiosity* names both the desire to render the strange familiar and the strange thing itself. The force of curiosity makes something into a curiosity (figure 6.1).

Staring, as we saw, is curiosity's vehicle. Disobedient looking at a forbidden sight especially gets you into trouble. Pandora loosed the afflictions of the world because she could not resist peeking in at them. Lot's wife turned into a pillar of salt because she had to have one more look at the gruesome wreck of her home. An anxious over-the-shoulder double-check cost Orpheus his beloved Eurydice. Seven murdered previous wives assailed the curious eyes of Bluebeard's new wife as she entered the forbidden castle chamber. Eyes that will not behave seem to be our undoing. Seneca warns rightly that curiosity is an affliction in which the eyes run away with the mind. Plutarch's officious Lamia stores her eyes in a jar at night and puts them in again by day to gawk at the affairs of others. Staring is evidence of temptation in Christian thought. For Augustine curiosity is the sin of lusting with the eyes and the first move toward the deadly sin of pride. Evil, he speculates, might be avoided simply by shutting "the doors of his eye," but perpetually the eyes fly open anew, overwhelmed by curiosity. Erotic or pornographic books were known as "Curiosa" in late nineteenth and twentieth-century England.[2] In this tradition, staring is a visual vice, a defiant delinquency met with harsh censure.

Curious looking may be a path to noble discovery, as we have seen, but equally so it seems to be a route to catastrophe or triviality. What makes inquisitive looking threatening or heroic is also what makes it feckless. Staring is the opposite of keeping your nose to the grindstone. As a craving for stimulation in search of a target, staring is at once purposeless and purposeful, at one moment intrusion and the next idleness. One person's remarkable scene is another person's mundane landscape. To stare, then, is to barge into someone's place. As such, curious looking is meddlesome, prying into someone else's life. Staring is visual snooping.

CIVILITY AND DECENT BEHAVIOR

Staring puts us in one another's faces. Contemporary America has responded to this uncomfortable exposure in part by fortifying the bulwark against staring bequeathed to us by the Western tradition. A web of regulations aimed at mitigating staring's interpersonal and social threat arose in American culture from its beginnings. Codes of propriety abound that attempt to spare us from being both starers and starees. Our mothers' emphatic importuning against staring gets its authority from a long line of conduct manuals that detail proper behavior for looking at one another. George Washington inaugurates these cautions in his collection of "Rules of Civility and Decent Behavior in Company and Conversation," in which he admonishes his fellow Americans to control their eyes. Washington counsels people not to look at "men of quality . . . full in the face" when speaking to them (2000 [c. 1744–1748], 12). Besides this gesture of deference, our first president warns as well against "looking everywhere about you" to anxiously assess your own status in comparison to others (19). Washington's strongest prohibition against staring, however, is a directive to "gaze not on the marks or blemishes of others and ask not how they came" (23). Washington's pronouncement against intrusive, questioning stares that demand an account of our fellows' "blemishes" gets at the heart of our mothers' scoldings. Our urge to explain the visual novelty that attracts us merits a firm hand slap from the Father of Our Country. By decreeing that inquisitive eyes threaten "civility" among our fellow citizens, Washington endorses a national ban on staring.

A gush of conduct manuals appeared in nineteenth-century America that unanimously affirm Washington's declaration that we must not stare at one another. The manuals extend uniform admonitions to readers seeking social propriety: "Never stare at people. It is a mark of ill-breeding, and rightly gives offense," a book entitled *Manners that Win* proclaims (1883, 24). In short, the manuals conclude that to "stare is odiously vulgar" (Howard and Roberts 1868, 77). Many of these etiquette guides also offer clues as to why staring is improper in America. Considering the larger cultural context of these books suggests that prohibitions against public staring at one another arises from a convergence of several historical phenomena.

Perhaps the major influences making staring "vulgar" were the emergence of the middle class and the accompanying ascendance of anonymity in public culture.[3] During the nineteenth century, America unevenly but decisively transformed from a face-to-face traditional, agrarian society where people were born, lived, and died in the same community into an individualistic, industrial, wage-labor, mass society in which most interaction occurred among strangers in an urban, public setting (Lofland 1973). This enormous shift in human social relations required new rituals of interaction and spatial choreographies that differed greatly from those of a collective village setting organized around established status and kinship relations. This modern world demanded a new urgency of looking that allowed us to recognize and respond appropriately to one another. Awash in all kinds of unfamiliar sights, Americans were increasingly surrounded by people whom they had never laid eyes on before. Confronted by this new alien landscape, people needed to know what to do with their eyes.

At the same time, an emerging middle class, armed with capitalism and egalitarianism, firmly renounced the old aristocratic order that new America so distrusted. Part of that required inventing new ways of looking at one another. The stable hierarchy of the old aristocratic order required its subjects to display their status and position through elaborately legible costumes and uniforms that announced who they were to everyone who looked at them. Citizens of democracy, in contrast, supposedly had the opportunity to change their status at any time. Appearance needed to reflect this ideal of equality. To realize this promised social fluidity, people's appearances should not lock them into a particular status but should accommodate aspirations toward social mobility. Nevertheless, a person's social position at a given moment needed to be proclaimed. What you looked like, then, should suggest who you were to your anonymous visual interlocutors but not reveal enough information to trap you into any particular fixed identity. Aspiring Americans were on the move—socially, economically, and geographically. They displayed that mobility in the appearance of being busily headed somewhere else. To be pinned down by a stare made them wiggle with anxiety.

An illegible appearance gives Americans room to travel; inconspicuous looks let you make yourself up. Nonetheless, social interaction also requires that we be able to recognize one another. The confidence man and the humbug, for example, must be distinguishable from the genuine thing.[4] Spectacles of hierarchical status such as royal crowns and robes, heraldry, coronations, and elaborate insignia encourage obeisant staring. In contrast, middle-class status repudiates flamboyance, demanding instead the stealth signification of gray flannel suits and briefcases that now mark undifferentiated proper democratic attire. So while accruing middle-class status benefited Americans, conspicuously displaying status was considered inappropriate. The dandy, for instance, who attracted attention with expressive costuming and behavior, was a residually aristocratic figure especially targeted for social approbation (Kasson 1990, 118–28).[5] The egalitarian ethic of appearance contained contradictions that staring troubled. Middle-class men were doers not lookers. You wanted to appear comfortably middle-class without flaunting it.[6] Even aspirations toward middle-class status needed to be muted so as not to disclose any vulnerability. The trick was knowing how to declare yourself without revealing too much of yourself. The strict visual conduct detailed in the popular etiquette guides suggests that staring led to Edenic forbidden knowledge—too dangerous for everybody's own good.

GENTLEMANLY LOOKING

Gentlemen do not stare. As unmoved movers, middle-class men should strive to be self-possessed agents of their own futures. The vulnerable openness or intrusive presumption of staring violates a hands-off ethic among citizens uneasily scrambling to appear both equal and aspiring at the same time. This visual leaving each other alone accommodates a new reciprocity amongst citizens based on an awareness of fellow feeling and mutual according of status. This relational complex is encoded in visual etiquette. A "stony stare," the gentleman learned, for example, "is discourteous" to other gentlemen (*Manners That Win* 1883, 282). A dominance and subordination ritual, staring among gentleman of the same class threatens to upset the delicate balance of power that the premise of equality promises. Thus, to stare at a peer is "impertinent," a failure to "show equal courtesy" that causes a staree "shame and anger" (Howard and Roberts 1868, 93; 251; 77). Eyes must simultaneously affirm and assert; they must acknowledge without challenging. Eye behavior is at once a subtle act that confirms your own social station and a mannerly bestowal of status upon the other. The stare is far too blunt a visual instrument for such a delicate operation.

Properly looking at your inferiors is an indication of gentlemanly rank as well. As crucial as recognizing peers, sorting through pretenders and subordinates requires visual vigilance. To stare at someone beneath you, however, is a failure of sympathy, a sentiment crucial to middle-class decorum.[7] To scorn inferiors, particularly those meek enough not to challenge your position, violates the spirit of benevolence that was essential to middle-class identity. Sentimentality, fine feeling, and a sense of social stewardship marked the nineteenth-century American well-bred man (Kasson 1990). A gentleman who aspires to be "manly-hearted, upright, and true," a poem called "Good Manners" counsels, will suffer "deserved disgrace" from untoward behavior, such as staring. Staring is a crude mannerism that betrays proper behavior toward our lessers. One adage counsels readers never "The lame or the deformed to shock, By heartless laugh or cruel mock; God's simple ones to tease and jeer, Or at the ignorant poor to sneer" (Howard and Roberts 1868, 251). A gentleman with true social grace spares the beggar, cripple, or physically unsettling unfortunate the embarrassing attention brought by a stare of curiosity or revulsion, as Washington declared. More than this, your inferior could be your peer at any moment. The tentative nature of all social positions bred both anxiety and optimism—and a new way of visually relating to our fellow Americans.

Gentlemen were not to stare at one another, but perhaps even more so, they were not to stare at women. *The American Gentleman's Guide To Politeness and Fashion* inveighs against the "too-frequent rudeness of men" that indulge in "staring [at] every modest woman."[8] The author insists that, "No one possessed of true good breeding will indulge in a practice so at variance with propriety" (Lunettes 1857, 132). A man staring at a woman threatens other men, perhaps more than women. One book asks rhetorically, "if you saw your sisters stared at in such a way, would not the hot angry blood rush to your face? A young man who respects his own mother will never stare at any woman, with his mouth open, like a gawk rooted to the ground" (Howard and Roberts 1868, 77). Leering at women is strictly proscribed for gentleman for two reasons. First, staring at women who belong to other men threatens the stable economy in which men have legal and economic ownership of women; second, staring reveals a sexual hunger that puts a man in the vulnerable position of seeming, even being, enthralled by women. If Samson had never looked at Delilah, he might still have his locks. The rule that gentlemen should not ogle women does not reflect simple prudery, then, but rather signals their respect for the property of fellow gentleman and their independence from the siren charms that would deplete their wills, leaving them wide-eyed, open-mouthed, and "rooted to the ground."

Staring, then, is a class marker. Lower orders stare with abandon; gentlemen restrain themselves, including their eyes. Staring was "the mark of a ruffian," according to one etiquette book, a particularly egregious violation of proper decorum that cast you in with the lower social orders (Howard and Roberts 1868, 92). Rigorous command over our bodily functions makes us civilized.[9] For gentleman, the rule against staring, the conduct books instruct, is part of a larger regimen of ascetic self-control that includes forbearance against whistling, swearing, loud talking, tilting in one's chair, jingling loose change, telling overlong stories, or other raucous activity. Genteel refinement required scrupulous governance of expressiveness itself, especially any form of personal discomfort. Mannered gentlemen and ladies never betrayed their "mere physique" through indecorous gestures such as sneezing, sniffing, coughing, yawning, scratching, picking, clearing nose or throat, and certainly never hinting at functions that occur below the waist (Kasson 1990, 126). Loss of self-government was projected onto the lower classes and questionable women, from whom staring was expected. The sociologist Georg Simmel reflects in 1901 on the meaning of undisciplined surrenders to embodiment, concluding that "gaping and staring" are "particularly unaesthetic" expressions because they indicate "spiritual paralysis, the momentary absence of spiritual control" (1965, 278). Staring is a failure of will over flesh. The properly manly do not succumb. Staring attests to a shameful "paralysis," as Sartre's keyhole peeper felt so keenly, that discloses abdication of intentionality. Losing command of one's eyes risks losing the status that many Americans worked hard to achieve and demonstrate through exquisite self-control.

LOOKING LADYLIKE

Ladies must never stare, either, but the ethic of restraint operated differently for women's eye behavior than for men's. Whereas the male stare is a potentially hostile instrument to be mastered, the female stare compromises a woman's virtue, which is the ultimate threat to her position as a lady. A gentleman's stare damages others; a lady's stare damages herself. A conduct book subtitled, "Practical Rules for American Females," cautions women repeatedly against staring. In public, women are told they should "never laugh audibly nor stare at people" (Abell 1851, 163). In church, the guide instructs its readers, to "not allow your eyes to rove" and "not gaze and stare at anyone" (165). Another manual warns that at the theater for "a lady to stare at people in the audience through the opera glass" violates her "modest dignity" and indicates that she is "ill-bred" (Howard and Roberts 1868, 331). In sum, women continually learn that "it is rude to gaze at people and shows a great want of cultivation" (161).

More than indicating the ill breeding of low status, however, staring imperils a lady by opening her up to engagement with the world. Always suspected of weak wills and a predilection for the flesh, all women are imagined as naturally given to reckless looking. Ladies must cultivate "that self-control, and power to ignore by not seeming to hear or see unpleasant things" (*Manners That Win* 1883, 265). As fastidious viewers, proper ladies never exhibit the curiosity, desire, or voyeurism that staring suggests. The intensely appetitive, acquisitional, or knowledge-gathering stare is a masculine tool to be judiciously monitored by its owners and scrupulously forbidden to their women. Ladies, as inviolable possessions of certain gentlemen, are best ensconced in a private domestic sphere. When she is outside her master's house, a lady's behavior should extend her exclusion from the interactional public realm so as to never risk drawing herself into relations with other men. This isolationist decorum demands that, "A lady walks quietly and unobtrusively along the street, hearing nothing that she ought not to hear, and seeing nothing that she ought not to see," as one etiquette manual pronounces (265). Staring provides a clear signal of unsavory qualities in women. This cautionary doggerel from the nineteenth-century called "The Saucy Wench" suggests that a woman's stare brands her as insolent, insensitive, faithless, and foolish:

> Your knowing wink and brazen stare,
> Are just the signs that do declare,
> Howe'er you think conceal'd by art,
> An empty head and callous heart.[10]

Not only must ladies refrain from staring, they must never draw the stare upon themselves. They must rein in laughter, conversation, expression, comportment, or any "peculiarity" such as "nervous twitching, cross eyes, stammering, lisping" that might draw a stare to them (Abell 1851, 238). If you fail such strict self-governance, you have "drawn the gaze upon yourself" and "betrayed" your position as a lady (132). To freely look and be looked upon shift from privilege to threat for women. Whereas interrogative looks are untoward behavior for men and women alike, women were more vulnerable to the consequences of violations of decorum because their social status derived from the men to which they were attached.[11] One rulebook unequivocally warns, "no lady, young or old, forms the acquaintance of a stranger upon the streets, or seeks in any way to attract the attention of the other sex. To do so is to waive all claims to consideration as a lady, to say nothing of reputation as a virtuous woman" (*Manners That Win* 1883, 265). To stare or be stared at is not simply bad form, then, it is the loss of ladyhood.

THE CULTURAL CONTRADICTIONS OF STARING

There is much more at stake, then, in the staring encounter than meets the eye. Far exceeding simple rudeness such as wiping your nose on the table-cloth or belching, staring is as inauspicious to starers as it is to starees, both of whom stand to lose status in the exchange. Staring shamefully bares a staree's peculiarities to the prying eyes of a stranger at the same time that it shamefully exposes a starer's intractable curiosity, as Simmel and Sartre suggest. Both starer and staree have failed to properly control themselves. In this way, staring violates the civilizing process. What we think of as manners, as we have seen, attempt to protect us from being either starers or starees. Even well into the twentieth century, American etiquette books recognized both the necessity and privilege of visual anonymity. A 1925 manual called *Standard Etiquette,* instructed businessmen never to make themselves "conspicuous" (Brant, 85). A 1944 etiquette book advocated that people in general should cultivate "inconspicuousness [as] is the keynote to well bred behavior in public"; well beyond the era of Victorian prudery, visual discretion is achieved by never calling attention to "the body or its functions" (Lofland 1973, 117). To draw the stare through any eccentric behavior or appearance is to violate social decorum just as surely as does the act of staring. Both starers and starees risk the untoward conspicuousness against which these guides warn. This strict social proscription drenches natural curiosity and the human urge toward visual outreach in mutual embarrassment. The child not yet socialized into this enforced ethic of mutual inconspicuousness is a frequent concern of contemporary etiquette manuals. Several "guides to contemporary living" from the late twentieth century explicitly charge mothers with monitoring their children's embarrassing staring behavior toward people who are "different" (Baldrige 1978, 10). In a section called "Relating to People with

Disabilities" from *365 Manners Kids Should Know*, for example, parents are advised that their child should not stare or "blurt out" questions about other people's disabilities (Ederly 2001, 299). What is hidden in our mothers' admonitions not to stare is also the warning never to incite the stare of others (figure 6.2).

Even laws protect us against staring. Manners extended their authority into legal policies decreeing how strangers should look at one another. A wide range of U.S. state and municipal codes aimed primarily at preventing street begging make it illegal for people considered unsightly to appear in public. For example, a Michigan municipal ordinance established in 1957 outlaws staring—termed as improper ogling—along with "profane language, obscene conduct, begging, wrongful molestation, fighting, and loitering" in any public space (Lofland 1973, 70–71). A subset of these public conduct codes has been called "ugly laws."[12] The first of these American ugly laws, enacted in San Francisco in 1867, prohibited street begging by specifically preventing certain people from appearing in public places. Ugly laws continued to proliferate in the codebooks of American cities and states through the first two decades of the twentieth century. An 1881 Chicago City Code, which stood for almost 100 years, captures the spirit of these laws: "Any person who is diseased, maimed, mutilated, or in any way deformed, so as to be an unsightly or disgusting object, or an improper person to be allowed in or on the streets, highways, thoroughfares, or public places in this city, shall not therein or thereon expose himself to public view, under the penalty of a fine of $1 (about $20 today) for each offense" (Schweik 2009, 1–2). While these laws try to limit the nuisance of beggars, a stronger concern seems to be to rid public

Figure 6.2. "The Bus," Archer Coe. http://www.flickr.com/photos/45936529@N00/.

places of people who will incite staring. People with unusual comportment, surprising shapes, or shocking features become here "unsightly" and "improper person[s]" who the law orders to refrain from exposing themselves to the public view. Less about the act of begging than the act of viewing, the law does not forbid giving them money; it forbids looking at them.

These ordinances bar "unsightly" citizens from public places because they are in fact too sightly. Both the rules of courtesy in the etiquette books and the rules of law in the code books serve the same end: protecting us against our own urge to stare. The language of the etiquette manuals disallows staring by appealing to the genteel sensitivity that ladies and gentlemen should cultivate toward those who are imagined as less fortunate or different from them. The language of the law, in contrast, forbids staring by invoking a harsher logic of turning interest into "disgust." The sharp words describing potential starees as "disgusting object[s]" suggest that the law does not intend to protect starees from the shame of severe visual scrutiny but rather to shield potential starers from objectionable sights. Implied in the language of this ordinance as well is that our vividly stareable fellow humans—those who display marks of disease, vulnerability, or the vagaries of other chance encounters that shape our bodies—compel our eyes and interest. If there was no danger that one's eyes would be drawn to such sights, there would be no need for the law. Ugly laws aid ladies and gentlemen in the job of monitoring their own impulses and bodily functions by preventing them from embarrassing evidence of their own visual stimulation. An 1890 ordinance in Columbus and Omaha, for example, prohibited starees from exposing themselves for the purpose of "exciting sympathy, interest or curiosity" (Schweik 2009, 10). The laws protect people in public spaces from what John Kasson (1990) calls "agoraphobic anxiety," the fear of being seen seeing, of not being able to overcome their urge to stare (113). The worry is that our capacity to turn away from such sights is not secure enough that we can resist the temptation to violate the American social code against staring. Like anti-prostitution laws, ugly laws are intended to save us from ourselves. These ordinances against staring further the common good, then, by banning irresistible sights.

This armature of prohibitions is so sturdy that any advocacy for staring requires an apologia. Staring is a bold move that demands defensive justification or fetches sharp rebukes. In the mid-nineteenth century, for example, Walt Whitman's scandalous poetry celebrated staring. His poem "Crossing Brooklyn Ferry" (1856) urges public looking as it dismisses the mannerly by celebrating visual curiosity: "I see you face-to-face!" he proclaims of his fellow passengers; "Crowds of men and women attired in the usual costumes, how/curious you are to me!/On the ferry boats the hundreds and hundreds that cross, returning home, are more curious to me than you suppose" (lines

1, 4–7).[13] Staring is the rogue poet's conduit to the reckless vitality at the American core. Repudiating the fastidious and proper, Whitman seizes the blunt rudeness of staring as the perfect instrument of fervid connection. Putting staring to similar use, the American writer Walker Evans recalls un-learning not to stare:

> I remember my first experience as a café center in Europe. *There* is staring that startles the American. I tried to analyze it and came out with the realization that the European is *really* interested in just ordinary people and makes a study of man with his eyes in public. What pleasure and an art it is to study back, and a relief to me as a young more or less educated American, with still echoing in the mind his mother's "Don't stare!" . . . but I stare and stare at people, shamelessly. I got my license at the Deux Magots . . . where one escaped one's mother in several other senses, all good, too. (Rathbone 1995, 29; italics in original)

Both Whitman and Evans must counter psychological shame and fussy motherly nagging in order to assert staring as an expansive right of the manly citizen loosed in a world of compelling curiosities. Evans, especially, captures the tension between his innate desire to stare and the command "Don't stare" that echoes "in his mind." For the American-bred Evans, the "license" to stare he finds in Paris café culture is a "relief" from the rule bound ways of looking, enforced by the now far-off mother, all of which he has "escaped." Like our American hero, Huckleberry Finn, Evans flees the socializing matron by lighting out for the territories in search of adventure. Out of the suffocating domestic trap of the familiar, these boys head out in search of manhood into a thrilling world of unfamiliar sights. The particu-lar quest for Evans is the dopamine-drenched "pleasure" of staring "shame-lessly" at his fellow humans, of "mak[ing] a study of man with his eyes in public." Whitman and Evans both need to work themselves up with visual ardor to overcome the barriers of social etiquette. Staring flings them into a space of face-to-face interpersonal possibility where they might come to know something meaningful about those strangers who surround them.

Staring encounters stir up anxiety and call for rules because they make public several cultural contradictions. The first is the paradox at the heart of the civil inattention that staring violates. As we have seen, to both cultivate visual anonymity for ourselves and grant it to others is a rite of American culture. Yet, this ethic of inconspicuousness contradicts claims to the value of the unique individual as a model for citizenship. Our understanding of ourselves as autonomous, distinct individuals is a fundamental political principle of democracy (Arieli 1964). At the same time, democracy premises that each individual is equal to any other. The need to have our individuality validated through civic recognition of our uniqueness is in conflict with our need to be similar to our fellow citizens, as the philosopher Charles Taylor (1994) points out. To be accorded the equal respect that democracy promises, we need to be wholly ourselves and at the same time just like everyone else. Staring is the social flash point where these competing demands for distinction and homogeneity collide. As a recognition of human variation, staring validates our individuality, calls out our differences from others. Sameness does not merit stares. But even though stares affirm our distinctiveness, we can never be sure of the meaning attributed to our personal idiosyncrasies by our visual inquisitors. So our belief in pliable appearances becomes a dilemma about whether to hide or display our differences. This communal worry about seeing and not seeing, being seen and not being seen, rises to a new intensity under the scrutiny of stares.

Despite our uneasiness about looking at each other too keenly, we gawk relentlessly at the myriad spectacles American life began abundantly providing by the late nineteenth century.[14] Today, we navigate a daily avalanche of reiterated images that at once stimulate and enervate us. The surging demands that we produce and consume bid us insistently to look at products and expect the life they promised. Indeed, Walt Whitman, the poetic voice of nineteenth-century America, exalted public viewing as our national virtue and right: ". . . what I am," writes Whitman in *Song of Myself* (1900), "Stands, amused, complacent, compassionating, idle, unitary, / . . . Looks with its side curved head curious what will come next, / Both in and out of the game, and watching and wondering at it" (lines 74–78). The rapidly changing world Americans were gaping at was filled with new things to see and new ways to see them. Nights were aglow with new artificial light. Gas street lamps and electric home lighting dazzled the eye. Civic celebrations of progress and nationalism flourished. The World's Columbian Exhibition of 1893, for instance, drew 716,881 people on a single day and the 1927 ticker tape parade for Charles Lindbergh in New York City attracted four million spectators. Even ladies, if properly accompanied, might risk this kind of staring. Most novel to Americans out on the street and looking around was merchandise. The burgeoning commercial culture and the beginnings of consumerism demanded display and desirous looking. Ladies, especially, could shop in order to fill their role as ornaments that displayed the status of the men on whose arms they gracefully leaned. Spectacles such as the Macy's Thanksgiving Day Parade, begun in the 1920s, fused commercialism with traditional forms of spectacle such as religious carnivals and processions. Ersatz tableau vivants behind department store windows allowed Americans to look at new goods and imagine them as indispensable.[15] This appetite for the new animated American eyes.

All of this excited looking occurred at the same time that the prohibition against staring at one another was being codified in conduct manuals and public codes. Astonishing sights competed for the citizen's eye. Staring at supposed Wild Men or Genuine Indians trotted out at World Exhibitions or even straining to glimpse decorated heroes at parades offered a safe social distance that face-to-face encounters on the street with fellow citizens did not. Ladies and gentlemen were not to stare or be stared at by people with whom they might strike up a relationship. The visual intimacy of staring at possible equals upsets the fragile coherence of our route to recognizing one another, to understanding precisely who it is we face in this jumble of strangers through which we must navigate. Here, then, is a paradox of staring: beginning with the era of Whitman and the emergence of the Great American Spectacles, public life demands that citizens stare at the new and changing worlds we live in, while at the same time staring at one another risks intrusions far too familiar for everyone's comfort. The result was a contradictory cultural edict that Americans should always see a spectacle but never be a spectacle.

PART IV

Starers and Starees

7

Looking Away, Staring Back

The first problem is where to direct your eyes.
—medical sociologist, Fred Davis, "Deviance Disavowal"(1961)

LOOKING AWAY

The contradictions among our desire to stare, the abundant offering of stareable sights, and the perpetual admonitions of our mothers make public staring a furtive pleasure at best for many Americans. Few of us get the unambivalent license to stare that the writer Walker Evans found, as we saw in the last chapter, in Parisian café society. Consequently, our eager stares often quickly shift to uncomfortable looking away. Our ocular id, in other words, jerks our eyes toward a stimulating sight and our ocular super-ego guiltily retracts them. We may withdraw a stare in simple deference to propriety or parental prohibition. Charges of rudeness further encourage us to cut and run. Sometimes, however, truncated stares come from our distress at witnessing fellow humans so unusual that we cannot accord them a look of acknowledgment. To be suddenly confronted with a person extraordinary enough to provoke our most baroque stares withers our ready curiosity and we turn away, snuffing out the possibility for mutual recognition. If the knowledge that staring delivers is unbearable, the expected elasticity of human connection that mutual looking offers becomes brittle. When we suddenly find ourselves face to face with some momento mori or our most dreaded fate—we look away.

The turmoil that looking away brings has led several artists to ponder staring relationships in their work. In 2005, the portrait painter Doug Auld created ten paintings of young people significantly disabled by burn injuries. His portrait series, "State of Grace," explores the "visual reality" of his subjects and reaches to express "who they really are at their core" (Auld 2005–08). Auld uses the familiar conventions of traditional portraiture—such as realism, texture, color, pose, and likeness—to portray very unconventional subjects. The jolt of these portraits of burn survivors comes from showing us a kind of person we rarely see. As portraits, the paintings announce that their subjects are worthy of public commemoration, important enough to look at, even beautiful. These pictures force us to make sense of faces patterned with vivid colors, limbs sculpted into surprising shapes, and bodies deeply etched with intricate swirls. They lure our curiosity, invite us to stare. As the realism of portraiture does its work of making a likeness, we come to recognize the effects of burning on flesh. Auld's portraits translate what we think of as disfigurement into pictures of "beauty and courage." They confront us with "our fear and our repulsion of the unknown," converting it into appreciation for their subjects' "unique disarming beauty." (Auld 2005-08).

Auld undertakes more, however, than making people who are hard to look at presentable. He intends these paintings to let us stare without having to look away. "I hope," says Auld, "the viewer will look" (Auld 2005-08). The motivation for the series of portraits came from a scene of staring Auld experienced thirty years before he began to paint burn survivors. Ambling

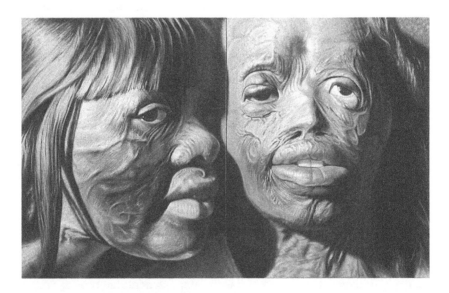

Figure 7.1. Doug Auld, "Rebecca and Louise." Diptych/oil on canvas, 50 in × 80 in © doug auld (2005) from his series "State of Grace" (portraits of burn survivors). www.dougauld.com.

through an outdoor market, the young Auld encountered a vision he was not "prepared for," he told a *New York Times* reporter in 2006. He caught sight of a young girl who was significantly burned. Her face shocked him into staring, imprinting a vivid image that stayed with him over the years. "She was literally melted—no ears, no nose, just holes. Slits for eyes. Her neck was like a long, drawn thing." His description captures his struggle to make sense of her strange face. So challenging was this task and so unprepared was Auld that he withdrew his stare, short-circuiting his inquiry into her humanity. When the girl looked back at the man whose eyes were locked on her face, he lost his voice and did "what everybody else did. I turned my head away" (Newman 2006, 1.25). Haunted for years by this broken connection, Auld decided to address his regret with his art. He approached the Burn Center at St. Barnabas Medical Center in Livingston, New Jersey, in order to contact former patients to seek permission and cooperation in painting their portraits.

"So go ahead and stare," the open faces and direct looks in Auld's portraits seem to say. In fact, one of the subjects, Alvaro Llanos, explains his willingness to participate in the project by saying: "I'd rather people be staring at a painting than at me" (Newman 2006, 1.25). Another subject, Louise Benoit, appears in a double portrait along with her sister, Rebecca (figure 7.1). Instead of the conventional double portrait of aristocratic couples or monarchs, however, this picture shows sisters who acquired their distinctive looks together in a fire that killed five other family members. Auld means his pictures to sustain our stares, to give starers "the chance to gaze without voyeuristic guilt at the disfigured, [so] they may be more likely to accept them as fellow human beings, rather than as grotesques to be gawked at or turned away from." In staring at the portrait of herself and her sister, Louise Benoit wonders however whether the arresting close-up views of their burned faces will disgust people or encourage them to "see more than scars" (Newman 2006, 1.25). What happens in the delicate transaction of looking and looking away is unpredictable.

The artist Chris Rush also grants us "Permission to Stare" in his portrait series of "unusual children and adults," most of whom are people with disabilities, that was exhibited at a Brooklyn gallery in 2006.[1] Rush's drawings are studies from life done at a facility for disabled people where he volunteers. Like Auld's paintings, Rush's portraits gain their aesthetic punch by putting unusual faces in our faces. Whereas Auld uses bold texture and color to render scarred flesh less shocking but still compelling, Rush gets between his subjects and our discomfort by softening their differences with the medium of conte crayon and posing them with great dignity. Rush's pictures navigate between us and them, attending carefully to the visual relationship by gratifying our "deep curiosity" while at the same time inviting "empathy" and "sensitivity." The exhibition narrative explains that the portraits invite us "to draw close to their strangeness and see something of ourselves waiting there." They show what to many of us is the "strangeness" of disability in the familiar frame of a portrait.

One of Rush's most arresting drawings presents a young woman in the regal profile pose we know from the familiar commemorative portraits of the Italian Renaissance (figure 7.2). Her likeness emerges from the sharp line her stately features form against the background; her nose and chin lift imperially; her eyes gaze impassively down on the world beneath her. Her head is turbaned with a richly colored and ornately patterned aristocratic headdress, and her shoulders reveal a simple but elegant gown. On first

Figure 7.2. Chris Rush, "Swim II." Conte crayon on paper. Portraits are life size in scale.

glance, she looks like a modern Florentine lady. On second glance, however, we recognize a face we have never seen in a portrait. We see the distinct features of a person with Down syndrome, her hair wrapped in a bright beach towel, her face in a faraway reverie, and a simple heart tattooed on her shoulder below her bathing suit strap. The portrait invites us to stare, engrossed perhaps less with the "strangeness" of this woman's disability and more with the strangeness of witnessing such dignity in a face that marks a life we have learned to imagine as unlivable and unworthy, as the kind of person we routinely detect in advance through medical technology and eliminate from our human community.

In *The Body Silent* (1987), anthropologist Robert Murphy, who conducted fieldwork on his own experience of quadriplegia, points out that looking away from people who make us uncomfortable differs from granting them visual anonymity. Looking away is an active denial of acknowledgment rather than the tacit tipping of one's hat to ordinary fellow citizens expressed in simply not noticing one another. Looking away is for Murphy a deliberate obliteration of his personhood. "[A] wheelchair cannot be hidden," he notes, "it is brutally visible" (93). People refuse to look at Murphy, he concludes, partly because they know that they are not supposed to stare at him and have no easy way to relate to him. Having been on both sides of stares, Murphy writes of his own "selective blindness" before becoming disabled, contending that a disabled person entering his "field of vision" would not register in his consciousness. After he began using a wheelchair, however, he saw that sociality between nondisabled and disabled people is "tense, awkward, and problematic," and that this is often expressed through ocular evasion. The newly quadriplegic Murphy found that acquaintances "did not look [his] way" and that he was "virtually ignored in crowds for long periods, broken by short bursts of patronization" (91). This "pattern of avoidance" begets feelings of shame and guilt which initially erode Murphy's dignity and self-esteem (91). Murphy's subtle analysis of the social message that looking and looking away sends to starees suggests that recuperating the dignity lost in such exchanges is a demanding task for people with disabilities.

Conferring dignity on people whose differences draw stares is the challenge to which these portraits of disabled people rise. These portraits intervene between starees and starers to offer respectful, even beautiful, pictures of people we have not learned to look at in this way. They revalue devalued people, the kinds of people most of us have only glimpsed in institutions or in medical pictures with black boxes over the eyes. This anonymity that medical photographs impose on a staree also prevents the person pictured from staring back at the viewer. Auld's and Rush's portraits rework the way we usually stare, however. They keep us looking rather than looking away. They grant us more than permission to stare; they use the clout of high art to transform our staring from a breach of etiquette or an offensive intrusion into an act of appreciation. These portraits enable visual pilgrimages of deliberate contemplation that might be scuttled in a face-to-face encounter on the street. The invitation to look that a portrait offers precludes our skittish staring and instead allows us to look deep and long into these unfamiliar faces made strangely familiar.

STARING BACK

Staring is a high-stakes social interaction for everybody involved. The struggle for starers is whether to look or look away. The struggle for starees is how to look back. Stareable people have a good deal of work to do to assert their own dignity or avoid an uncomfortable scene. People with unusual looks come to understand this and develop relational strategies to ameliorate the damage staring can inflict. Rather than passively wilting under intrusive and discomforting stares, a staree can take charge of a staring situation, using charm, friendliness, humor, formidability, or perspicacity to reduce interpersonal tension and enact a positive self-representation.

In her memoir, *Autobiography of a Face* (1984), Lucy Grealy writes about discovering as a young girl the possibilities that staring back might hold for her. Grealy spent a lifetime as a staree after her multiple surgeries for jaw cancer, starting when she was eight years old. Having to navigate the world outside her family soon showed Grealy that she "possessed a certain power" because people "noticed" her. "Wherever I went, even just to the store with my mother, I was never overlooked," writes Grealy, "I could count on some sort of attention, and I discovered that people were embarrassed when I caught them looking at me. I stared right back at the strangers. . . . They always looked away quickly, trying to pretend they hadn't been staring" (Grealy 1984, 101). What practiced starees come to understand, Grealy suggests, is that stares are to be engaged rather than avoided. Some take up this engagement with the relish and others with dread. Nevertheless, whether they are a challenge or a burden, stares do not necessarily make one a victim; rather, they can make one a master of social interaction.

Accounts from starees such as Lucy Grealy about staring back find support in the portraits of people with disabilities by Doug Auld and Chris Rush. These portraits show rather than tell how starees stare back. Portraits can provide their subjects with an opportunity to deliberately engage their viewers through the conventional poses of traditional portraiture. Eye comportment is one of the most important elements through which portraits define their subjects. Intense eye-to-eye engagement with the viewer can make a subject seem to reach out of the picture to stare down the viewer. A pose of outstaring one's starer confers an authority that people like the ones that Auld and Rush portray can have trouble maintaining in facing social stigma. We expect such an imperial gaze to come from a monarch but not from people we have learned to see as pitiable or even repugnant. One burn survivor who saw Auld's pictures, Dan Gropper, thinks these portraits work against what he calls the tiresome "poor Dan" attitude he gets along with the stares (Newman 2006, 1.25). Taking a good look at these portraits can show viewers that people who look like Gropper or Auld's subjects can and do "have a very good life."

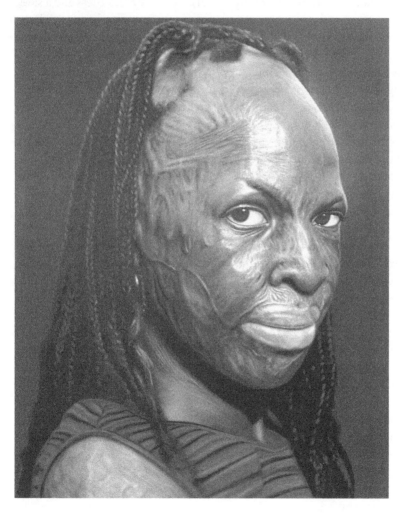

Figure 7.3. Doug Auld, "Shayla." Oil on canvas, 40 in × 50 in © doug auld (2005) from his series "State of Grace" (portraits of burn survivors); www.dougauld.com.

Refusing to wilt under another's stare is a way to insist on one's dignity and worth. Shayla, for instance, one young African-American woman Auld portrays, stares back with a particularly penetrating look (figure 7.3). In a three-quarter profile pose and bedecked with African-style braids scattered across her scarred scalp, Shayla's eyes are steady on us, emerging from beneath furrowed brows out of a stern face textured with intricate brushstrokes and colors that announce the residues of burning. Shayla is staring hard at us staring at her. Her look refuses even a shred of the poor victim role. She has caught us and we cannot look away. In another example of looking back, one of Rush's most striking subjects stares at us with a look that approaches an ironic smirk (figure 7.4). In a little black dress and a sleek hairstyle, a young woman named Gwen elegantly fans out a hand with long, beautiful fingers just beneath her chin, accentuating her face. Her eyes stare directly at us from a most unusual face, one we'd consider disfigured. As a vamp, the ever-desirable woman playing hard to get, she stares openly at us staring at her. This vamp's self-presentation suggests a womanly confidence and sophistication that contradicts what we have learned about people with so-called facial deformities.

Portraits, of course, show only half of a staring exchange. Because they are static representations of starees, the portraits of Shayla and Gwen allow us to consider how starees can use comportment, expression, and even costuming to stare back. In other words, these portraits pull the staree out of a live encounter in order to deliberately stage a staree's self-presentation. Face-to-face staring encounters, in contrast, are living communications filled with complex and dynamic interrelations. Many starees take the lead in these interactions. Uninvited attention is something that people generally do not put up with for very long without developing a set of effective responses. Sometimes starees rise to the occasion with deliberateness, grace, and generosity. Sometimes, however, the stare-weary have crankier responses. One man with restricted growth who has been stared at his entire life reports that he reacts to gawkers with "avoidance" or "disengagement," and often "flips them the bird" (anonymous, 2006 interview).[2] Part of the "embattled" nature of having a stareable disability, Robert Murphy (1987) observes, is managing the patterns of attention, avoidance, and awkwardness. Murphy concludes that the visual presence of disability "robs the encounter of firm cultural guidelines, traumatizing it and leaving the people involved wholly uncertain about what to expect from each other" (87). As many of the interviews for this book suggest, the work demanded of ultra-noticeable people to deal with this uncertainty can be taxing, tedious, or even tormenting.

Nonetheless, starees also suggest that managing staring exchanges can generate creative interpersonal skills that are psychologically sustaining.

Figure 7.4. Chris Rush, "Vamp." Conte crayon on paper. Portraits are life size in scale.

A vigilant staree assesses the precise attitude of the starer, measuring intentions and attitudes so as to respond in the most effective way. Accomplished
starees can help starers maintain face by relieving them of anxiety, understanding their motivations, working with them to overcome their limited
understanding of human variation, and indulging their social awkwardness.
A seasoned staree evaluates when to turn away, stare back, or further extend
the stare. Some allow the staring to go on in order for the starer to get a good
look. Others find it most effective to use eye contact and body language to
terminate the stare as soon as possible, although this risks being interpreted as
hostile. Another option is to redirect the stare. For example, one staree reports
connecting her own eyes to those of the immobilized starer and guiding
them away from the feature of her own body upon which the starer's eyes
have fixed. By taking over the stare, this staree adeptly rescues the hapless
fellow from the embarrassment of the stuck stare and restores the ease of
typical face-to-face encounters.

Starees develop fluent staring management routines that are more
sophisticated than simple defensive reactions. The psychologist Len

Sawisch (2006 interview) explains the process he uses to steer staring interactions the way he wants them to go:

> Staring by itself is not usually noticed unless I "see" the starer staring. When I do, I acknowledge the stare non-verbally with eye contact and a slight nod, a faint smile, or other gesture. This then "requires" the starer to either signal back or to look away. If they don't look away, I can exaggerate my acknowledgement (point, bug my eyes, mock bow, etc) or I can choose to look away. If I don't look away, I am challenging the other party to a confrontation escalation—which I am not usually interested in doing. If the person is close enough, it is easier to go "verbal" and acknowledge their presence generally with my most masculine but non-threatening voice tone and a situation appropriate greeting, like "How you doin'?" I may use a honorific ("sir" or "ma'am") but with no hint that I am of lower caste (i.e., "awarding" the other my social status).

For Sawisch, staring is an artful preamble to regularized face-to-face social interactions, conducted adroitly only by the experienced staree. Judiciously selected gestures, words, tone, and comportment acknowledge or establish social status. Accomplished starees agree that different starers require different responses. The adult starer, who has been acculturated against gawking, most often stares furtively, for example, which can make it difficult for a staree to directly take charge of the encounter. Adult starers sometimes exercise looking as a form of intrusive entitlement, which can require starees to use aggressive measures such as callouts or, as we saw earlier, middle fingers. Sometimes this curiosity appears as unwanted aid, as when starers try to lift limbless people or wheelchair users who have not asked for assistance (Frank 2000; Linton 2005). Entitlement sometimes occurs in the form of inappropriately familiar questions about how people with unusual bodies accomplish physical tasks that ordinary people cannot imagine them doing. One woman, who has congenital amputation of all four limbs, for instance, reports being accosted while waiting at the bus stop by a man who demanded to know the logistics of how she goes to the bathroom, eats, and sleeps (anonymous, 2006 interview). Such tacit or explicit demands to account for oneself ultimately require starees to prepare sets of responses to dispatch, engage, or defuse their starers.

Sometimes starees develop different strategies for managing children than they use for adults. Children not yet fully socialized can stare with an innocent curiosity that starees often indulge, but which sometimes swells into taunting or aggression. For example, several starees identified what one called the "persistent stare" often enacted by children who simply will not let go of you with their eyes. This is curious staring gone baroque, free from ameliorating restraint that comes from socialization. The asymmetry in maturity and authority between an adult staree and a child starer complicates things. Starees are often more likely to feel responsible for educating a child about tolerating human differences or indulging a child who does not yet know not to stare. While many starees are critical of parents who allow their children to taunt, one staree tells of how terrible she felt when a mother slapped her child across the face for staring and pointing gleefully to the innocent discovery of her first one-legged person. The same staree regretfully recalls her own response to a child starer against whom she used semi-hostile humor rather than patient educating: "In the past I have responded quite unfairly to staring people. One tiny child once asked me where my leg was, and I (sort of fed up that day) looked down and FREAKED OUT! 'Oh my God!' I exclaimed, 'I had it this morning!' Now I simply tell them I was sick and the doctor took it off and wait to see if they have any other questions" (anonymous, 2006 interview). This staree is quick to acknowledge her leadership in directing the staring encounter and the generous seriousness she brings to that responsibility. "I know," she affirms, "I haven't seen the end of that little devil inside me who now and then likes to play with people's fear and disgust factor."

The staree Kevin Connolly has taken the staring management techniques he has learned over a lifetime into the realm of documentary photography (figure 7.5). Connolly, who was born legless and gets around mostly on a skateboard wearing a "boot" not unlike a strapless Birkenstock around his hips, draws baroque stares wherever he goes (Brown 2007). A professional skier and photographer who travels the world widely, Connolly decided in 2005 to start capturing his staring interactions with his camera. Having snapped over three thousand starers in his travels, Connolly has become a canny observer of people observing him out on the street (figures 7.6–7.8). His point in photographing starers is not to humiliate them in any way, but rather to make a study of what staring is about and how it works. Ordinary starers hold as much interest for Connolly as his surprising appearance holds for them. He has come to understand staring as a universal reaction, what he terms "more reflex than conscious action." He himself stares and says that he would stare at someone like himself if he were to see him on the street. Connolly sums up the physiological impulse to stare, the way it precedes understanding and interrupts quotidian life: "Before any of us can ponder or speculate," he writes, "we stare. Whether it is a glance or a neck twisting ogle, we look at that which does not seem to fit in our day to day lives" (Connolly 2007).

The photographs along with Connolly's explanation of the project not only document startled looks but also offer a fuller description of the staring exchange than we have seen before. First of all, because the faces Connolly portrays come from all over the world, we see a wide variation in age, sex, race,

Figure 7.5. Chris Toalson, "Portrait."

ethnicity, individual features, and cultural contexts. At the same time, these faces pull together tightly into a uniform community whose membership we see through their remarkable unanimity of intensely attentive expressions. As such, Connolly's photographic project constitutes a visual catalog of starers. Looking at Connolly's pictures shows us what we look like when we stare. Seeing how befuddled they look is disconcerting. But his project goes beyond the immediate affective exchange of staring and extends into the interpersonal relationship that staring often begets. If staring bears witness to an interruption in our mundane visual field, as both Connolly and cognitive psychologists have suggested, it creates at the same time an urgency to stabilize the ordinary world again through finding a coherent explanation for the inexplicable sight.

Figure 7.6. Kevin Connolly, "Man and Girl; Reykjavik, Iceland."

In other words, Connolly's starers often engage him in composing a story for themselves that explains his leglessness. In Bosnia, someone thought he was a landmine victim; in Romania, a gypsy vagabond; in Ukraine, a beggar; in New Zealand, a shark attack survivor; in the United States, a wounded Iraq war veteran. Starers' curiosity often extends beyond explanations for Connolly's leglessness into wonder as well regarding how he does quotidian tasks such as going to the bathroom, cooking, reaching places built for the fully legged—and especially about his girlfriend. People work to fit him into what they do know already in an effort to figure out something that is quite new to them. Apparently they need to know how someone who seems so much like themselves can at the same time be so different.[3] Whereas some starees find

Figure 7.7. Kevin Connolly, "Woman and Children; Sarajevo, Bosnia."

such curiosity inappropriate, Connolly seems to relish the opportunity to help them imagine his life as livable and fully human.

As Kevin Connolly's remarkable archive of starers demonstrates, the most potentially generative staring situation is one that produces mutual interest. Rather than turning away his starers, Connolly engages them, if nothing else by surprising them with his camera. He moves many of them, however, beyond the startle he catches in his viewfinder into a relation of empathetic exchange. They begin to imagine what it is like to be him. In this way, the narrative that staring begets can lead to the kind of empathetic identification Walt Whitman calls for in his poetic celebration of hearty staring. Connolly nurtures this relationship with some of his starers, perhaps out of generosity,

Figure 7.8. Kevin Connolly, "Woman and Man; Tokyo, Japan."

ennui, pragmatism, or his own need to reknit himself into the human community away from which stares push him. Starees may also elect to invite empathy as a counter to pity, the diminishing, too frequent response to disability. Pity is an emotional cul-de-sac that ultimately distances starer and alienates staree. A block to mutuality, pity is repugnance refined into genteel condescension.[4] Empathy, in contrast, bonds in a mutual recognition of shared humanity. Anthropologist Robert Murphy (1987) explains transformative staring encounters that brought him new knowledge and realigned solidarities. After becoming a wheelchair user with a literally diminished social status, Murphy, a white man, finds that women and Blacks look at him differently and more openly than before. Blacks, he finds, recognize and greet him as "fellow Outsiders" (127). Before he used a wheelchair, women with whom he established eye contact would typically look away, but when he becomes disabled, women continue the eye contact, nod, or smile, which he interprets as "an opening of the self, an acknowledgment of the other, a meeting without closure" (127). Disability, he concludes, feminizes men, making them socially equal to women and people of color. This feminizing does not make Murphy feel further diminished, but rather seems to him an affirming recognition that gives him a new set of potential interpersonal relations within which he can develop a stronger sense of self. Murphy's wheelchair dissolves his previous status, creating an opportunity for new relational equality.

If an arc of empathy is to leap across the breach opened up by staring, persistence and generosity must prevail on both sides. Starees must insist on recognition as fellow humans by wielding an array of interpersonal techniques that the commonly embodied need not acquire.[5] One staree explains this interactive process as an opportunity to "transform an uncomfortable and annoying inevitability into a positive reflection of myself as a example of a person with a disability who is a proud and functioning member of society" (anonymous, 2006 interview). She understands her role in the staring encounter as one of "defiance." Her aim in that defiance is to "reflect back to them that (1) they are staring at someone, (2) that someone KNOWS they are staring at them, and (3) that person they are staring at is an amazing person. Then they walk on with something to think about . . . they MIGHT be thinking that . . . we're not so different after all." When this woman stares back—much like Shayla, the burn survivor who peers starkly at us out of her portrait—her returned stare is not a plea, but rather an assertive outreach toward mutual recognition across difference. The returned stare from the starees both on the street and in the portraits instructs the wide-eyed that they are amazed by an "amazing person." The starer—whether stunned, tentative, or hostile—responds to the staree, who guides her visual interlocutor toward the self-representation of her choice. An amazing person, the eyes explain, is what you see.

PART V

SCENES OF STARING

> [W]e fear the visibility without which we cannot truly live. . . .
> And that visibility which makes us most vulnerable is that
> which also is the source of our greatest strength.
> —Audre Lorde, *Sister Outsider* (1984, 42)

Scenes of staring can help us understand our impulse to look hard and our responses to being looked at hard. Staring begins as our brain's search for novelty, a desire for visual stimulation amid a landscape flattened by familiarity. If an encounter can be sustained, staring asks questions. And those questions open up into stories. To stare is to ask, "Why are you different from me?" and "What happened to you?" To observe the stare is to ask "Why is she looking at that?" and "What is his interest?" To undergo the stare is to ask "What is attracting her?" or "What is wrong with me?" Each of these implicit questions is the nub of a narrative about who we are, how we fit into the human community, or how we understand each other. As such, scenes of staring can generate new stories.

Starees, as we have seen, usually take the lead in directing staring encounters. People with stareable traits come to expect starers and often develop a range of strategies to manage the awkward responses. Staring at one another has a geography. What counts as stareable leaps out of an otherwise unremarkable body, seeming an abrupt invitation to an exotic ocular destination. Certain bodily sites inherently draw more attention than others because they are thick with cultural meaning. Our faces, for example, are the first territory our eyes inhabit when we encounter one another. Our hands, as well, are places of recognition telling us whom we are approaching. The scale of others is the vast setting from where we visit local spots such as faces, hands, and breasts. These sights are sites from which interactions arise that can be thought of as scenes of staring. The scenes of staring selected in the following chapters cluster around particularly stareable aspects of human anatomy: faces, hands, breasts, bodies. The scenes gathered together here are largely deliberately choreographed staring encounters rather than the spontaneous, unstructured ones that generally characterize our everyday lives. Some are actually staged as performances or mediated through films or narrative accounts. They provide an illustrative set of case studies that magnify the dynamics and amplify the possibilities of staring. In doing so, they necessarily highlight the potentially artful and productive roles starees take in the interactive meaning-making of staring.

8

FACES

> ... the basic motivating factor for all human beings is not self
> preservation or sex or love. It is the desire not to be embarrassed.
> —David Roche, *The Church of 80% Sincerity* (2008, 61)

FACEDNESS

We stare with and at faces. The face is the "focus of human interaction," apprehending the world and revealing us to it (Yu 2001, 1). Faces are the first part of a human embryo to differentiate. By eight weeks we have lips and eyelids; by five months come eyebrows, tiny ears, and a distinct face ready to recognize and be recognized (Sims 2003, 48–49). Newborns prefer to look at faces more than any other object, and infants of a few months will smile while gazing at another face (McNeill 1998, 205; Johnson and Morton 1991). Children draw stick figure bodies attached to huge animated faces. We recognize each other through facial distinctiveness captured in mug shots, classic portraits, picture IDs, or exaggerated cartoon caricatures. We see faces even where they are not—in the moon, the clouds, the mountains. The face is the most usually unclothed part of human bodies, ready to look and be looked at. Alert to the dynamics of communication and recognition, we are perhaps most alive to one another when we are face-to-face.

Our faces engage in many information-gathering activities. Our eyes stare; our ears hear; our noses sniff; our tongues taste. All of these likely evolved in order to eat. At the face's center, our mouths mediate between us and our environment as we taste, suck, eat, kiss, talk, bite, smile, nourish, grimace, sneer, and laugh our way through the world. The cluster of sensory features that evolved to keep us fed also make us known to the world. Faces

[handwritten margin note: babies always staring!]

express emotions, thoughts, and character. Brows knit, mouths gape, lips grin, cheeks blush, jaws clench, eyes weep, and pupils dilate with libidinal enthusiasm. Acts of perception are gestures. Eyes wink, gleam, glitter, twinkle, glaze over, cut, make contact, pierce, penetrate, and assist the mouth in fashioning a frown or smile. Our agile eyebrows are "active little flagmen of mind-state" (McNeill 1998, 199).

Faces often reveal our roots and histories, as well. The shape of eye, nose, and lips, the texture of hair, and the pigmentation of skin are cues to racial and ethnic identity. Features are also tokens of our character or heritage. Noses are social emblems in stock figures such as Cyrano de Bergerac, Pinocchio, W. C. Fields, or the Jew. Ear shape, like that of noses, is taken as an index of character. Pitcher ears supposedly mark fools. Cesare Lombroso believed that criminals and prostitutes could be identified by the contours of the ear (Lombroso-Ferrero and Lombroso 1972). Moreover, we wear our years, habits, and locations on our faces. Vestiges of age, drink, sun, diet, stress, illness, and hard looking brand our noses, cheeks, foreheads, teeth, or eyes. Faces also bespeak our interiors. Characteristic facial features announce a Down syndrome perspective. Widely spaced eyes correlate with schizophrenia. Bald men have more heart disease than the hirsutely headed. People who get polio tend to have large central incisor teeth (Zebrowitz 1997).

So essential is the face to human interaction that it anchors much of our language. Because humans turn to their own bodies to understand the world, our facedness provides a rich source of collective meaning. We call on the face to summarize complex ideas. Long, straight, poker, or iron faces express affect. An insult is a slap in the face; futility renders us blue in the face; failed endeavors blow up in our face; defiance flies in the face; repentance is saving face; a betrayer is two-faced; the anonymous are faceless; friends and loved ones are familiar faces; the humiliated lose face; the embarrassed are shame-faced; the angry are in your face, the rejected must get out of our face; to enter the social world is to show our face; to object we make a face. The orienting aspect of the face spins out into expressive verbs as well. Punishment is facing the music; honesty is facing up to it; confronting is facing it down; disagreements are face offs; damage is defacement. Individual facial features yield vivid and succinct expressions. We eye something we want, get an earful, nose around, keep our chins up, and put our noses to the grindstone. We can be cheeky, mouthy, or nosy. How our face looks is who we are.

READING FACES

Faces are consequential texts that we read attentively. Many of our enduring cultural icons are faces. Helen's visage launched the thousand ships that began the Trojan War. Medusa's face turned men to stone. The enigmatic features of the Sphinx held the secret that propelled Oedipus's terrible journey toward self-knowledge. The placid countenance of the Virgin Mary consoles and redeems. The expression of the Mona Lisa beguiles. Understanding what Vicki Bruce (1988) calls "facial speech" is vital to human relations (27). We seek knowledge by staring at faces and learn to read very minor variations with great accuracy.

Our impulse to stare at faces, to search the countenance for revelation, has a long history in human thought and practice. Physiognomy, the art and science of face reading has its roots in ancient thought. Ancient Chinese, Persians, and Romans believed that faces revealed a person's essence. Aristotle's *Historia Animalium* has six sections on physiognomy. In describing the form and function of the human head, for example, Aristotle claims uniqueness for the human face on the basis of its physiognomic properties. People with large foreheads are sluggish, small ones fickle, broad ones excitable, bulging ones quick-tempered (Aristotle and Peck 1965, II, VII–IX, 39; McNeill 1988, 165–168). Although the general idea that the face reveals character persisted widely, the practice was codified as a science and named in the late eighteenth century by Johann Caspar Lavater, who made great claims for its revelatory truth value. Lavater's physiognomy fused the emerging concept of science with the ancient spiritual practice of reading the appearances of things in the material world as an index of the divine world or a physical manifestation of hidden truths. Whereas the older practices read the appearances of exceptional physical phenomena such as monstrous births, comets, earthquakes, and entrails of sacrificed animals to disclose divine will and augur the future, physiognomy posited that common appearances—the ordinary human countenance—revealed its own hidden character (Friedman 1981).

Like democratic thought, physiognomic thought universalized people by offering a generalizable taxonomy by which all could intuitively judge the value of our fellow human beings. Lucy Hartley (2001) suggests that while physiognomy is often classed with discredited pseudo-sciences such as phrenology and mesmerism, it in fact transformed from the eighteenth through the nineteenth century as it was inflected by the developing scientific theories of evolution, physiology, and eugenics (Hartley 2001). As modernity's will to know increasingly became a will to control, reading human bodies as a means of evaluating them logically extended into using that evaluation to produce the kinds of bodies that the social order values. Once Lavater's physiognomy merged with Darwinian natural selection, interpreting the body gave way to molding the body. Ought trumps is; the descriptive yields to the prescriptive. We thus take up the alternatively progressive and dubious idea of shaping the population and the individual into what we collectively want them to be. Our conviction that the manifest body reveals the hidden soul (in religious terms) or the character (in secular terms) underpins both the eugenic extermination by which the Nazis sought to improve the race and the current medical enhancement practices we employ for individual self-improvement and collective progress.

Physiognomy, then, evolved as a way to limit human particularity—as manifest in the face—by submitting it to a scheme of predictable interpretation. This form of generalizing the act of human recognition advanced the modern inclination to categorize individuals under the authoritative rubric of science into groups that could be evaluated and ultimately manipulated. A residue of physiognomic thought undergirds the modern idea that the face that does not conform to social standards should and can be remade. While humans have always decorated and augmented their faces, in contemporary societies we actually remold the contours of noncompliant faces through aesthetic surgery.[1] Rather than simply *seeing* the meaning of a given face, as in the physiognomic model, we now *master* the meaning of a given face through technological alteration. A postmodern model of the face understands it—as well as our entire body—as what Susan Bordo calls "cultural plastic" that can be reformed at will. The idea that shape determines story has shifted to the conviction that story determines shape (1993, 246).

How we look at and to one another is a symbol for human relationships in religious and philosophical thought. The theologian Martin Buber, for instance, understands human face-to-face interaction as key to divine knowledge. In his formulation of the "I and Thou" dyad through which God is enacted, to be in the presence of the human face is to create an obligation between persons and to experience "the profound belonging to the world before the Face of God" (Buber 1958, 108). Our facedness anthropomorphically gives God a face, making that figure accessible to humankind. By investing God with a countenance, Buber's theology posits face-to-face encounters as fundamentally benevolent and essential to our spirituality.

Buber offers a theology of the face, while the philosopher Emmanuel Levinas provides an ethics of the face. To Levinas, the face is an expression of the person and a moral signifier, as it is within physiognomy. Levinas is concerned, however, not with the revelatory nature of the face, but rather with its effect on the viewer. Levinas posits that the face makes demands on its viewer. The immanent "visitation of the face" incurs an obligation, an "epiphany" commanding one to serve the other (Levinas et al. 1996, 53). Levinas tells us that "the face is the other who asks me not to let him die alone." Moreover, "to be in relation with the other face to face is to be unable to kill" (quoted in Butler 2006, 138).[2] Buber's face of the other is liberatory, while Levinas' face of the other invokes a prohibition: "the face says to me: you shall not kill" (R. Cohen 1986, 24). Whereas the physiognomic face is particular, Levinas's and Buber's faces are universalized: any and every face will make an equal claim. In these readings, staring at a face creates a responsibility arising from our shared humanity.

For other modern thinkers, however, face-to-face relations imperil us. In the tradition of human relations laid out in Hobbes, Machiavelli, and Hegel, Sartre sees faces as threats to be read. "The body advances," he writes in his essay on faces, "bearing the sacred object between its shoulders on its neck" (Sartre 1956, 159). All staring is domination in which "our faces rule" and reveal "our darker passions" (159). The fleshly materiality of the other's face—its immanence—is disturbing, even repulsive. Faces have "voracity" and are "pierced with greedy holes" and make "objects leap backwards" (161). Faces of other people diminish the self in Sartre's account of face-to-face interaction, in which our own visage is puny, stuck in a narcissistic moment and unable to realize all the potency it witnesses in another face. The "I" is intimidated and resentful in the presence of another's face, limited because "I do not see my own face" (159). "I carry [my face] in front of me like a secret which I have not fathomed," Sartre begrudgingly observes, "and it is the faces of others, instead, which teach me what mine is like" (159). As we saw in chapter 5, one's own face then is an epistemological problem, solved only by analogy.

This anxiety of facedness intensifies in the modernist literature of alienation. In 1962, for example, the Polish émigré writer Witold Gombrowicz characterized human interaction as "a relentless duel of face-making, face-wearing, face-imposing" (Newton 1998, 244). In this grim mutuality of facial fashioning, the sufficiency of our own face is forever compromised by the intrusive face of another, always demanding a reckoning. Such "facial claustrophobia" is defensive posturing seemingly specific to modern urban anonymity, where we are assaulted by alien faces at intimate range—as anyone who has taken a subway at peak hours knows all too well (248). With their relentless particularities, the faces of others engulf us with pleas for recognition, what one critic calls "the ordeal of intersubjectivity as physiognomy" (249).

RECOGNIZING FACES

Faces, then, are texts we engage or resist, opportunities for revelation or refusal. For Buber and Levinas, the faces of others beckon and bond us to one another. For Sartre and Gombrowicz, faces confront and alienate us from one another. We stare at faces to differentiate friend from foe, familiar from strange, invitation from rejection, anger from adoration, comic from tragic. The ability to recognize faces is essential in human interaction, indeed to our survival. Much of the entire brain as well as specialized areas recognize and make sense of faces. As newborns, we learn very early to recognize our mother's face. Adults can discriminate among thousands of faces. Our capacity to stare interpretively at faces is a fundamental form of social capital that enables human flourishing. People adapt facial recognition strategies to fit their situations. African Americans, for example, tend to develop superior emotion recognition compared to whites (Zebrowitz 1997, 28). The supposed intuition and emotional fluency of women may develop from their traditionally subordinated status. Blindness or low vision asks us to rely on alternative sensory clues that staring provides to the sighted. In contrast, certain brain injuries or conditions such as autism may inhibit people from recognizing emotion on another's face, creating social disability. Prosopagnosia, a brain injury causing the inability to recognize faces, often prevents people from knowing they are being stared at and leaves them unable to sustain human relationships (McNeill 1988, 86). The staring relationship is, then, a central arena in which we recognize the inner lives of one another and are recognized in turn.

The visual architecture of recognition—of distinguishing among faces and their meanings—abounds with challenges. Constancy and homogeneity pose problems for visual perception of faces. What cognitive psychologists call the "object constancy problem" involves the difficulties in recognizing objects as perspective, lighting, distance, and other contextual factors change over time (Rhodes and Tremewan 1994). In other words, how do I know my mother both when I am at her breast and when she is across the room chatting with her friends? Moreover, how can I know my mother both when she is laughing and frowning? The "homogeneity problem" arises in visual cognition when objects share a configuration. The visual patterning of faces is very similar. What makes a face a face is its regularity, its predictable shape, allocation, and arrangement of features. In philosophical terms, homogeneity determines the face's essence. Our cognitive task is to differentiate among similar configurations, to recognize a face as a face but also as a specific face. Reading and recognizing faces demands negotiating between the universal and the particular, between the parts and the whole. The problem of the typical face is recognizing it as a particular face. The problem of the distinctive face is recognizing it as a face. The problem of the distinctive feature is how it affects perception of the whole. The problem of the facial gestalt is how to find the nuances of individual features. The intense visual work of staring at faces is then both a cognitive and an epistemological undertaking. When we look at another person, we seek to know much. Is this a face? Do I know this face? Whose face is this? Does this face know me? What is this face's response to me? What does this face mean? Does this face matter to me? What relation do I have to this face now and what will it be in the future?

Familiarity determines our ability to know faces. All people, for example, are poorer at recognizing faces from races other than their own. Experiments that distort photos of faces by changing the spatial relations among components confuse face perception. We also have trouble recognizing inverted faces but not inverted objects. Visual perception studies suggest that we recognize faces as undifferentiated wholes rather than by way of their constituent parts (Peterson and Rhodes 2003). Such research suggests that competent, efficient facial recognition depends on encountering faces that meet certain visual expectations. In other words, an internalized facial norm shaped by culture—what psychologists call "norm based coding"—determines facial legibility (Rhodes and Tremewan 1994, 279). As long as we are seeing the kinds of faces we are accustomed to coming across, visual cognition and the social relations that accompany them go smoothly. The unexpected face confounds us, presses us—and thus makes us stare. This visual indeterminacy is more than a cognitive problem, however. Illegible faces are a social problem, too.

FACE-WORK

What sociologist Erving Goffman calls "face-work" demands staring. Face-work extends both reading and recognizing faces into an interactive social drama of self-management and status negotiation. Face-work is an exacting interchange of mutual scrutiny, adjustment, call, and response in which visual vigilance is crucial. Because we recognize ourselves in the faces of others, we often seek out faces we suspect will tell us what we want or need to know about who we are in the social world. In this process, we first visually identify a face with which we want to engage and then stare at it intently to discern its response to the face we have put forward. Goffman's work emphasizes that such face-work is more than simple individualized communication; rather, the ways that we stare at one another are highly ritualized ceremonies of regard acted out anew in each staring encounter (Goffman et al. 1988).

Face-work is exacting and potentially perilous. We can be "out of face" if we are unprepared to perform according to expected conventions (Goffman 1982, 8). We are in the "wrong face" when information surfaces that threatens the face we put forward. We try to use the social tool Goffman calls "poise" to conceal any shamefacedness that comes from having the wrong face or being out of face. Failures of poise can be, for example, faltering conversational fluency like forgetting someone's name, the emergence of unflattering information such as a lost job, or breaches of class etiquette such as using the wrong utensil; these failures damage the faces we offer up to another's scrutiny. Such unwariness or exposure can make us "shamefaced" (8). Staring at someone's actual face can signal that their status is in danger, that their metaphorical face is wrong. Sometimes the damage is so severe that a starer pretends not to see or refuses to meet the staree's eyes—as did the repentant artist Doug Auld when he faced the burn survivor—causing a scene of mutual embarrassment. Face-work is a staring encounter through which we perpetually renegotiate our self-esteem and status, making us exceedingly vulnerable to one another.

Levinas and Buber consider the ethical and theological implications of encounters between any two faces, whereas Goffman examines relations between two very particular faces. Goffman's face-work is a dynamic social interaction in which one puts a particular face before a hostile world judge, much more like the Other that Sartre and Gombrowicz propose. For Levinas other faces ask us not to kill them; for Goffman other faces ask us to spare them from embarrassment. Our faces are for Goffman images of our own and others' appraisals of us. In contrast to Buber's understanding of faces as sites for intersubjective flourishing, Goffman puts forward an adversarial model of public mutual staring in terms of victory and defeat. For Goffman, face-work occurs in a combat zone.

The complex maneuvering of staring and being stared at in our everyday face-to-face encounters depends, perhaps more than anything else, on everyone accurately following the rules. The conventions of comportment and conversation that govern such encounters are, as we saw in chapter 3, handed down to us as part of a routine acculturation process. The degree to which we are able to conform our bodies and behaviors to expected standards of these rituals of recognition will determine how successfully such exchanges proceed. Because our faces are the most particularized and finely read part of our bodies, facial legibility rests upon a narrow set of expectations and tolerates a limited range of variations. The rituals of public face-work are most successfully performed when nothing diverges from expected patterns, when everyone involved knows exactly the meaning of each feature and gesture. This security of signification is exactly what a typical face guarantees. The sociologist Georg Simmel suggests that successful faces rely on formal symmetry. For this unity to be "aesthetically effective, it is essential that the spatial relation among the facial elements be allowed to shift only within very narrow limits," Simmel asserts (Wolff 1965, 277). The atypical face is a failed face, perhaps an improperly human, irrationally organized face. Simmel's analysis anticipates cognitive psychology's conclusion that being judged attractive and typical gives us an advantage in almost every aspect of our lives. Studies repeatedly show that people whose faces conform to expected standards earn more money, accrue more respect, and appear smarter and nicer than those with unorthodox faces (Patzer 1985).[3]

Unorthodox faces also throw easy recognition rituals into chaos. A face that cannot conform to expectations is illegible, seeming to withhold both the hoped-for affirmation or dreaded condemnation the viewer seeks in another's face, neither confirming nor denying status. Face-work thus goes awry. More than just interpretive collapse occurs. Thwarted understanding can intensify into urgent staring as a starer grasps toward legibility. An interpretive crisis quickly can become an etiquette disaster as both members of the face-working dyad accumulate uneasiness and mutual embarrassment.[4] Staring engages such starees in uninvited face-work, robbing them of comfortable "civil inattention" the typical are accorded in public (Goffman 1980), as we saw in chapter 4. Moreover, Goffman suggests that people with inappropriate facial demeanor—including those with unusual faces—are stranded in face-work without the tools of typicality to build valued versions of themselves (Goffman 1956). While Goffman is in some sense right about the status compromise of an unorthodox face, there is often more to a staring encounter than meets the eye.

SAVING FACES

People with unorthodox faces must work hard in a staring interaction to save face, both for themselves and for their starers. Because these starees have much experience in being targets of stares and also have much to lose in face-work rituals, they often learn to be adept at managing staring situations in ways that save face for all. What sociologist and pioneer researcher on facial plastic surgery, Frances Cooke Macgregor (1974), calls "face saving stratagems" can be a subtext in many studies and stories about what is generally called facial deformity or disfigurement, a characteristic that Macgregor concludes is the "most devastating of social handicaps" (25–26).

In response to this "aesthetic rejection" Macgregor finds people use three techniques: "withdrawal, aggression, and active responses" (xxiii, 64). While withdrawal and aggression are stereotypical responses—think of One-Eyed Jack or the Phantom of the Opera—the "active responses" Macgregor documents are more interesting and innovative. Macgregor's starees developed techniques to control an interactional dynamic by introducing rather than avoiding the issue of their appearance, by preempting staring, or by controlling an ensuing demand for explanations. One woman with an unusual face, for example, was not able to maintain face because people looked over her shoulder, avoiding staring at her face when they talked to her. Her active response was getting people to look directly at her without staring. In another instance, a young man with a cleft palate, who had a "pretty tough" first few days of tormenting in the navy, told Macgregor, "Then I took over," and began humiliating in return any man who had embarrassed him, until the "wisecracks" stopped (61). Another man had a practice of giving any one of a variety of "one complete sentence" answers to the intrusive questions that accompany staring, such as "I was in the war" or "I was in a ring wrestling with a bear." "That stops them," he says (61). A more gentle face-saving strategy came from a young earless man who commented that "talking to people fast about their own interests keeps them from noticing my ears so much or asking me questions" (62). Yet another man structured encounters so as to be seen by his interlocutors well before an actual conversation needed to begin. A woman with facial scarring entered rooms and conversations with a wry, "Please excuse the case of leprosy!" Such preemption averted intrusive questions, established her credentials as fully human, and endowed her with wit. If she did not take her appearance as grim, so might not others. Finally, one woman whose face was altered considerably by cancer treatments told Macgregor frankly, "I can't blame them [for staring] because they've never seen anything like me. Anyone like me is dead! . . . By classifying them as weak I classify myself as strong and am therefore able to cope with them" (62).

A closer examination of staring relationships between typically faced and unusually faced people raises questions about whose face is being saved in these delicately negotiated interactions. When the perspective shifts from that of a typically faced to a startlingly faced person, a different story can emerge. In what he calls the challenge of "changing faces," James Partridge (1990) explains the potential for exercising agency, enacting a positive representation of oneself, and commanding the other that can come from staring encounters. Partridge, who himself has a significantly unusual face, offers an account of face-work from a staree's perspective. He begins his practical advice to people newly enfaced, usually by accident or illness, with straightforward acknowledgment that an atypical face catapults both sympathetic and hostile viewers into wide-eyed stares. Starers, Partridge acknowledges, will be unable "to hide their shock and concern" (1990, 9). It is the staree's job to help them overcome this.

The face being saved in these staring encounters is not a staree's, but a starer's. Having a face that violates appearance standards may elicit stares, but a loss of self-possession and an inadvertent breach of social etiquette make a starer vulnerable. Recall that Georg Simmel observes that gaping and staring are "particularly unaesthetic" expressions (Simmel and Wolff 1964, 278). Staring makes starers unattractive objects whose good face at least momentarily sags. The staree, then, has the opportunity for generosity by allowing a starer to maintain face. Partridge sagely describes an interpersonal dynamic between starer and staree: "They have usually come to help you, but you may well find that you have to help them" (Partridge 1990, 17). The active agent here is the staree who saves the face of a starer lost in a muddle of "shock and concern," attraction and avoidance, identification and differentiation.

STAREES AT WORK

Partridge explains that the first element in taking control of a staring encounter is for starees to sense the stare. This preparedness arms a staree with proper relational tools to manage expected staring encounters with great effectiveness. The second element in this process is to decide how to oversee the dynamics of the stare itself when it inevitably arrives. The third element is manipulating the eyes of the starer to end, extend, or relocate the stare. Finally, a staree can and often must engage in conversation to manage the encounter. Partridge offers: "You will have to keep up the conversation until you judge it right to help them ask the big question: What happened to you?" (Partridge 1990, 89). Of course, a staree will have a variety of ready and fluent answers to "this inquisition"–like Macgregor's interviewee who said he was in the war—so the encounter can move forward (Partridge 1990, 90). Managed properly by the staree, staring can be an intentional prelude leading to mutually affirmative face-to-face social interactions.

In addition to maintaining the starer's face, staring encounters can provide unusually faced people with an opportunity for self-development. Since face-work is more exacting for them, they must learn to develop ways of presenting themselves to others, as Partridge suggests. Rather than causing narcissism or self pity, having an unorthodox face can take one out of one's self because of the responsibility to the other that comes from having to justify one's looks to the world. Since staring violates often unquestioned social conventions, a productive unruliness can ensue when the predictable structure of face-work gives way. Partridge posits, for instance, that the starer is actually frightened by the staree, by the influence a stare has over a starer's eyes. To enlist the potency bestowed by someone's fear and convert it into a form of personal authority inflected by either generosity or command can enlarge the self in ways that are psychologically beneficial and socially effective. What Partridge calls "successfully bring[ing] some people back from their recoil" or "turn[ing] the sympathy to constructive uses" requires substantial psychological acuity and facility (Partridge 1990, 93, 94). Having a stareable face can shape one in more profoundly positive and productive ways as well. The philosopher Jurgen Habermas (2004) recently wrote, for example, that his experience of having a cleft palate and the accompanying multiple surgeries positively shaped his intellectual development. Habermas explains that the impetus for his important life work analyzing public space and the political public sphere arose in large part from being the object of public scrutiny because of his unusual face. So while distressed face-work and uninvited attention are certainly tiresome or even troubling, the staring process for starees can nevertheless be a generative arena from which creative interpersonal skills and deep wells of sustenance emerge, as we will see.

WORKING STAREES

The humorist and storyteller David Roche makes his living from his face (figure 8.1). Roche turns face-work into a performance and a paycheck by deliberately invoking stares and crafting the ensuing encounters on his own terms and for his own purposes. There is a resourcefulness in his work that not only makes a virtue from necessity but turns trauma into generosity. Roche's body of work offers a more subtle understanding of staring than do studies on the topic of receiving stares. His "message" is the perspectives and experiences of human beings with extraordinary features or forms can in fact be ordinary. "His stories reveal," his Web site tells us, "that his face is unique, but his experiences and message are universal" and that his "warm humor" comes from his "deep understanding of human frailty" (D. Roche, "About David" 1999–2006). The frailty, we come to understand through his stories, is not that of his unique countenance but rather of his viewers' imaginations.

Roche's public performances stage staring, anticipating its predictable patterns and intensifying them for dramatic effect. He tells audiences, "I am a one-man show, both on stage and off." "When I walk on stage," Roche writes, "the audience says with one voice: 'What happened to your face?' I have encouraged them to say this, so I then explain...." (D. Roche). Enthralled, the audience is all his, their eagerness to comprehend such novelty so acute that no one can turn away. Roche is orchestrating group face-work here, skillfully maintaining his own face while amply providing his audience the narrative their stares demand. Humor—what Roche calls "the most subversive of the arts"—has the effect of transforming a predictable staring encounter replete with mutual discomfort, surprise, or horror into a didactic opportunity for Roche. Roche's humor never partakes of the slapstick or melodrama often associated with clowning or blackface minstrelsy, two other performances that use hyperbolic faces as rhetorical tools. Wit and generosity aim to dispel

Figure 8.1. "David Looking Up." www.davidroche.com.

his starers' anxieties as he offers a story about finding his own inner beauty and strength from what seems to be a flaw. He claims his own dignity and humanity as well by asserting, "I am proud to be part of the emerging culture of disability" and recounts stories that politely let starers know he is sexually active and attractive (D. Roche, "About David"; figure 8.2).

Roche's most incisive and detailed account of staring comes in a longer written piece called "Finding My Voice." Here, Roche suggestively recounts his experience of undergoing what Michel Foucault (1975) calls "the clinical gaze". Roche's story begins in the medical waiting room, which collects people together as facially pathological. This diagnostic gathering sets everyone on edge by muting their individuality and highlighting their

Figure 8.2. Vince Maggiora, *San Francisco Chronicle*. David Roche talks to seventh- and eighth-grade students after an assembly at White Hill Middle School in Fairfax, California (1999).

supposedly grim and dire commonality. Of the waiting room, Roche avows, "I was never more conscious of my disfigurement." The waiting room leads to the medical theater, which isolates Roche from even his supposed fellow sufferers. In the interest of scientific progress and in exchange for excellent medical treatment, Roche has made a Faustian bargain by agreeing to display his face as a pathological specimen before a team of doctors. The exposure in the medical amphitheater and the photographs made in the examination room generate "conflicting feelings" of "shame mixed with a bit of exhibitionism." He has seen faces in medical photographs before, recognizing in them a "look of dissociation and fear, helplessness and resignation" but also "the glow of anger." "They are the eyes," he tells us, "of people like me, who also were specimens on display." In the actual medical theater where Roche is presented before a team of diagnosticians, a flurry of looks and expressions are exchanged. Upon entering the amphitheater full of starers, Roche stares back to "observe and classify them according to facial expression and posture." Staring at them staring at him, he notes: "Physicians and dentists are drawn back, more objective and assessing. Social workers nod to convey their understanding and warmth. They seek eye contact. Surgeons have the least emotional affect. They peer more closely, with narrowed eyes that search incessantly, not for eye contact but for incision sites. A couple of the younger ones flushed slightly when I look at them; they have not yet learned to mask their faces well" (D. Roche, "Finding My Voice").

But Roche's capacity to stare back gives way as the medical examination intensifies. The clinic director reads Roche's medical history, answering all questions about Roche's face. The reading of Roche's face as pathological trumps all of his other histories. "My role was to be observed," he concludes. "This was where I received my medical education, where I learned about my condition." As the doctors proceed to scrutinize Roche's face, his subjectivity and humanity shrink. "Their territory had been established," he writes, "if our eyes met, it was only for a nanosecond before theirs turned away with an easy, practiced avoidance. My face no longer belonged to me" (D. Roche, "Finding My Voice").

Roche, however, conducts the final scene of the staring drama, taking it back from his starers. When the clinic director pronounces at the end of the examination that Mr. Roche has made "an excellent adjustment," the heretofore mute and compliant face finds its voice, seizing the narrative of his face back from the doctors. A "short bark erupted from [his] throat" and with tight chest and roaring ears, he explodes to his own surprise at the wide-eyed director, "don't talk to me about adjustment! You don't know! You don't know! You never . . . you never talk about feelings . . . or anything!" The astonished doctors gape, but Roche's all too human outburst transforms their earlier clinical stare. Now they are "locked into a combination of shock and scientific observation." While the staring encounter belonged to Roche for a moment, the doctor quickly regains medical authority by looking directly at him, pronouncing yet another pathology—"perhaps you would like a referral to a psychiatrist, Mr. Roche?" This resort to diagnosis briskly terminates the drama, resolves the tension, restores the status quo, and dismisses the patient (D. Roche, "Finding My Voice").

And yet, Roche gets the last word. At that moment, he says, "I began my career as a performer and public speaker." Roche carries his face maintenance strategies of insistent self-definition beyond the Hemangioma Clinic and out into the world to a different set of starers. The face he lost in the clinic is restored on the stage and the Internet. Roche begins staging staring encounters that reach toward the visual interrelation of mutual recognition described by Martin Buber. This claiming of the "I" allows him to offer the position of "Thou" to his starers. Roche's extraordinary face inspires baroque staring that will not easily yield forth the kind of human obligation that Levinas predicts in encounters between the typically faced. Roche's is not the generic universal face of philosophers and theologians. At first glance, Roche's face is an exaggerated version of the truculent, even monstrous, countenance that threatens Sartre and Gombrowicz. Because Roche's face is so stareable in its striking individuality, it is a physiognomic face in its literal sense, one that asks for interpretation, one that challenges a starer's proficiency at recognizing this face as fully human. One of his starers, the writer Ann Lamott (2008), gives us an example of reading Roche's face that works against a pathological understanding. "Telling his stories through a crazy mouth, a jumble of teeth, only one lip and a too-large tongue," writes Lamott, "David's voice did not sound garbled but strangely like a brogue; like that of a Scottish person who just had a shot of Novocain" (Lamott 2008, xi). Lamott's description humanizes the countenance that starers initially view with alarm and confusion. Her reading of Roche's face is physiognomic in its detail, honoring its unusual aspects without rendering it either monstrous or threatening in its otherness. Roche's greatest generosity, then, is presenting his starers with the quandary of his face. He is, to use James Partridge's terms, "helping them" to get beyond their "shock and concern" and to move toward an expanded appreciation of the wide range of human variation.[5]

FACE TO FACE

The 1999 documentary film, *Face to Face: The Schappell Twins,* offers a look at relations between starees and their starers. The announced subject of Ellen Weissbrod's modest film is the conjoined twin sisters, Lori and Reba Schappell. But the film is less about Lori and Reba's unusual enface- ment and more about a way of being in the world that comes from sharing a face. *Face to Face* concerns the sisters' debut into the public world in their late thirties.[6] Emerging from twenty-four years of institutionalization into a world of people shaped quite differently from them, Lori and Reba draw baroque stares wherever they go. The twins are conjoined so that their faces and perhaps a quarter of their skulls are merged at and above Reba's left eye and Lori's left eye. Each has about three quarters of her own separate face, and each shares one eye and the quadrant above it with her sister. This quite extraordinary configuration requires the sisters to always be face-to-face. The angle of their conjoinment, however, precludes them from actually ever seeing the other's face, an elaborate version of the shared irony that all humans are denied direct knowledge of their own faces. Lori and Reba relate to one another, then, more through touch than sight. Their perpetual contiguity invites an almost constant embrace between them that encourages much tender mutual grooming and petting, as well as an alternately sweet and sassy girlyness toward one another. They giggle, bicker, snipe, encourage, and whisper loving prompts to one another. Mutual support is literally the mode of their relationship.

Although they are genetically identical, as are all conjoined twins, Reba is significantly smaller and does not walk as a result of spina bifida. One of the resourceful adaptations they have devised to live together in a world built for other embodiments is for Reba to sit on a kind of rolling bar stool that is propelled by the sturdier Lori as she moves along. Attached and identical as they are, Reba and Lori have quite different temperaments, aspirations, and tastes. Reba, the feistier of the sisters, is a redheaded country and western singer with a fierce sense of independence, although not from Lori. Lori, with her simple brown haircut and sensible shoes, wants to work in a hospital and have a family. Although they imagine different careers, lifestyles, and pleasures, neither woman questions their fleshly or familial attachment to one another. There is not a hint of drama here about the question of surgical separation. They are committed to accommodating one another in ways that go beyond the imagination of any pair of ordinary singleton partners.[7] Their conjoinment is an opportunity for resourceful adaptability that those of us for whom the world is conveniently structured could hardly imagine.

Lori and Reba do extreme face-work in the film. The twins cruise through the public realm with great poise, confidence, and good cheer, narrating their own lives, experience, and opinions. Their myriads of first-time viewers, however, are awestruck, stopped in their tracks with mouths agape and eyes out of control. The twins are virtuosos of every face-work strategy that Partridge or Goffman describe. They anticipate and maneuver staring encounters, often instructing starers how to handle themselves appropriately. The twins seldom adopt the didactic largess of David Roche, but instead they save face for their gawkers by pragmatically easing them away from frozen astonishment or maudlin sentiments, which always end in mutual embarrassment. Reba, for instance, brandishes a tourist's camera that she uses to stare back at her visual interlocutors, but at the same time she firmly informs people who try to take pictures of her and Lori that they must obtain Lori's permission to be photographed, then adds that because she is a country singer, they are free to photograph her as if she were a celebrity.[8] With some indulgence and often strained patience, the twins let us know that they understand their starers' loss of composure and social grace as simply ignorance about the intricacies of human variation and of alternative ways of being in the world. *like Abby & Brittany*

The film's project is to make the viewers—like the starers it shows—comfortable with the Schappell twins by presenting them as regular people getting through their day (figure 8.3). The twins relish being a spectacle, making a virtue out of necessity as does Roche. All three cultivate a certain celebrity that comes to them from transforming unwanted attention into effective face-work. Reba and Lori maintain face by taking pleasure in

Figure 8.3. Tona Lewis, left, of Brick, N.J., shakes hands with conjoined twins Lori and Reba Schappell during the grand opening celebration of Ripley's Believe It or Not Odditorium, Thursday, June 21, 2007, in New York's Times Square (AP Photo/Mary Altaffer).

dressing up, working out the logistics of putting on eye makeup and refining a style for themselves. In one scene, for example, the twins ham it up at the hairdresser's while a star-struck stylist lovingly colors, cuts, and fashions with precise differentiation their shared head of hair—one red and poofy, the other auburn and sleek. By showing us they care about their looks, Reba and Lori announce to viewers that theirs is a substantial and pleasurable life, worthy of respect rather than pity. The effect is to make the film's singleton viewers accustomed to and charmed by the twins so that, when the many interviewed starers reveal their own prejudices and lack of imagination in their comments about the twins, initiated viewers find themselves smirking at such naïveté and bias because, like the twins' long-term friends, they have come to find Reba and Lori unexceptional and indeed lovable. The film documents the clear disadvantage of the poor, tiresome singletons in staring encounters and shows the spunky conjoins working the crowd with measured equanimity and dignity. Generosity overrides bitterness for Reba and Lori. Despite twenty-four years of forced institutionalization, they are in many ways more worldly and psychologically sophisticated than their starers.

WAYS OF STARING

The stares that faces such as David Roche and Reba and Lori Schappell summon up are particularly intense. Starers respond with baroque staring, the kind of indecorous, wonderstruck, unapologetic staring that we have all been warned against. The film *Face to Face* repeatedly captures awestruck faces of starers whose composure has been hijacked by Reba's and Lori's faces. Photos of David Roche surrounded by his audiences reveal the same stunned faces. Baroque staring, we saw earlier, is a manifestation of wonder, of being transfixed in the presence of something beyond our understanding. It is whole body staring in which our eyes drag our faces and bodies along with them as they reach toward comprehending a sight that upsets the way we—up to this moment—thought things were and ought to be. This stopped-dead-in-your-tracks-rooted-to-the-spot look also appears in the photographs of Kevin Connolly, the legless young man who snapped more than thirty-two thousand pictures of his starers as he traveled around the world. Faced with what appears to be a visual conundrum, such as what appears to be half a person, starers express astonishment and confusion through arrested comportment. This kind of failure to command one's body violates the rules of social interaction and, as we saw, is one reason why staring counts as unseemly behavior. A spellbound starer becomes a baroque figure, overwrought with looking, eyes askance, demeanor amok, and mission derailed—dazed, and confused before an extraordinary face.

Baroque staring can lead to trouble for both starer and staree, as we saw earlier. Yet even though encounters between typically faced and unusually faced people begin with startled, riveted starers, those frozen moments of interpersonal connection often cannot endure. Because neither starer nor staree can sustain the tension staring produces, the staring dynamic must move forward. An arrested starer may quickly be able to regain enough composure to withdraw a stare. Roche terms these kinds of end stops to a looking relationship "separated" staring. Separated staring is more than simply looking away out of civil inattention. It is visual fleeing, often the wide-eyed, looking-over-one's-shoulder retreat of the fearful. In separated staring, discomfort overwhelms both attention and curiosity so that baroque staring collapses under its own weight. Roche confronts his audiences about their urge to separate by identifying their fear. "You are afraid," he accuses, "because our faces stir that deep fear that comes lurching out of your unconscious, the raw fear that you are disfigured perhaps" ("Finding My Voice"). He goes on to refocus them onto themselves: "When you step out of the shower and stand naked in front of the mirror, where does your gaze fall? Do you notice body parts that may be unattractive, even disgusting to others? Do you turn away from your own image? Or perhaps your disfigurement is internal—some character flaw, some habit. Or perhaps something was done to you. Something you feel ashamed of" ("Finding my Voice"). Roche provides a kind of psychic service for his audience: "That's my job, to carry the weight of that fear for you, so that you can pretend that you are normal" ("Finding My Voice"). By calling into question their own pretended status, Roche performs some intricate face-work by inviting them to question the fragility of their status as "normal" and perhaps to consider the costs of maintaining that status, of having that "face." Speaking for a larger community of starees, Roche puts forth a pronouncement about spectatorship: "We know that you turn away, not from our faces, but from your selves, from your own fears" ("Finding My Voice"). So by accepting their stares, Roche artfully turns them back on themselves.

Sometimes separated staring is born of fastidiousness. It is a visual pushing away by those who cannot bear the surprising particularities of stark human embodiment and perhaps the unwelcome reminder that their own bodies are or will be disabled, too. These are the easily repulsed, the people who blanch at the purplish scar, the cataract-clouded eye, or the vivid and intricate birthmark. This is the "aesthetic rejection" Frances Macgregor identifies (1974, xxiii). In its most virulent form, this kind of separated staring expands from repulsion into revulsion. In *Face to Face*, some viewers of the Schappell twins found the women's presence in violation of their right not to look at something they find unpleasant. More than offended, they declare their holiday ruined by Lori and Reba's entry into it. Apparently these fastidious starers prefer the comfortable dulling of perception that looking at normalcy begets rather than the magnetism of spectacular novelty and the unsettling pleasures of baroque staring.

The most malignant form of separated staring is hostile spectatorship, which is similar to dominance staring in its attempt to overwhelm the staree with its aggression. One staree—this one with a wisdom gained from years of managing stares—tells of being spit upon, screamed at, and accused of being "the ugliest thing he had ever seen" by a very young man on the street in San Francisco. Although stunned, the target of this attack concluded that insecurity and lack of self-esteem led to such raw cruelty. This is a variety of separated staring stemming from puerile vengeance and a deficiency of empathy, a deep failure of human connection resulting from inner torment. Many stareable people pronounce children to be the most distressing starers, which is contrary to conventional wisdom about the charming innocence and inherent gentleness of children. One staree reports that children about the ages of seven or eight are by far the most likely starers to taunt. In her memoir about surviving disfiguring cancer of the jaw, *Autobiography of a Face*, Lucy Grealy agrees that, "the cruelty of children is immense, almost startling in its precision" (1994, 7).

Sometimes, however, the initial baroque stare persists for such an uncom-
fortably long period that the staree needs to take action to release everyone
from the uneasily arrested situation. The Schappell twins, for example, often
speak directly to their rapt lookers by reminding them that staring is not
polite or kindly and usually firmly instructing their onlookers that the "problem" is not their faces, but rather one that belongs to the "world." One twin
sums it up: "They have to get used to it." Their faces, she explains to the film's
viewers, are only "an abnormality from the way they are used to living" (*Face
to Face* 1999). In this scene, the spoken intervention unsticks the stare and
allows everyone to move back into their proper spaces of civil inattention.

Alternately, sometimes a baroque stare shifts not to civil inattention but
to a look that is enlivened with interest. David Roche calls this "engaged"
staring. To describe such looking in spatial terms, engaged staring draws
the viewer toward the object of the stare, rather than either transfixing or
repelling the starer. In engaged staring, an initial startle response gives way
to curiosity and attention. Instead of fleeing, the starer sticks with the staree
to get to know more. The interrogative potential of all staring proceeds pro-
ductively in engaged staring, enabling people to convert the extraordinary
and unknown into the familiar and expected and stimulus-driven to goal-
driven stares. David Roche's on-stage performances hasten his starers from
the initial grip of his face toward engaged staring by encouraging them to
keep staring and then revealing himself as a person like them, as a nice guy.
One of his stories describes the trajectory from arrested to engaged staring
this way: "The parents of children in the waiting room of the Hemangioma
Clinic scrutinized me surreptitiously . . . glancing fearfully again and again
and again, seeking to divine the future of their own children's faces in mine.
Their gaze held an intensity and intimacy. Their sidelong glances sought to
take me in fully to simultaneously record my physical characteristics and the
wholeness of my being, doing this with some degree of furtiveness, trying
to absorb another human being with a sidelong glance. Their stares were
not separated but engaged" ("Finding My Voice"). Their fear of staring or
of Roche's face derails their eyes from their quest for knowledge or reassur-
ance. But the broken off stare returns, driven by a need to "record" Roche's
very particular face. This is a stare of connection rather than separation. It
meets rather than dismisses. It intrudes benevolently out of an urgent mission to know. Through the contours of Roche's face, they see their children.
This face-to-face engagement is an "intimacy" akin to the I and Thou relation described by Martin Buber as the fundamental human connection.
But these starers are engaged with a face that differs so drastically from a
proper face as to call into question our shared understanding of humanity.
Yet their own children may have such a face, and so the starers empathize
with Roche. To "absorb another human being" through this kind of engaged

baroque staring is to know themselves through the other. This is the kind of visual engagement that the great defender of staring, the writer Walker Evans, urged on his fellow Americans: "Stare," he advised, "It is the only way to educate your eye, and more. Stare, pry, listen, eavesdrop. Die knowing something. You are not here long" (Rathbone and Evans 1995, 28). For Evans and other ardent lookers, engaged staring is a way of being in the world; it is an urgent quest for knowledge of what is human. To hold the stare along with someone so stareable as Roche or Lori and Reba Schappell, to be open to the interactions they invite, to do some face-work with them, promises knowing something new.

Though Roche's concepts of separated and engaged stares, and our discussion of them, emerged from a context of staring at faces, they apply to stares directed at other body parts. As we will discover when analyzing stares at the hands, breasts, and body, however, starees in such encounters must deal with the additional challenge of making starers' eyes meet their own.

9

Hands

I'm a sock in the eye with gnarled fist.
—Cheryl Marie Wade, "I Am Not One of The" (1988)

HANDEDNESS

Hands make us human, or so we are told. Our opposable thumbs, the pre-hensile utility, agile fingers, exquisite sensitivity, sleek hairlessness, and pro-tective nails distinguish our hands. We grasp tools, partners, enemies, and food with more accuracy and grace than our hoofed, pawed, or finned fellow creatures. Uprightness frees our hands, providing us with the evolutionary advantage denied to our knuckle-walking cousins. Poised for action at the ends of generous and flexible arms, our hands are implements of our wills. Civilization sprung from the marriage of our capable hands to our prodi-gious brains (Wilson 1998). The devoted teamwork between brain and hand outstrip the utility of our legs. In this technological age, hands ensure our survival the way that legs did for hunters, gatherers, and farmers. We do not need to flee on legs from predators and toward food; we need to manipulate keyboards, cell phones, pens, and paper to survive.

Hands do things. Aristotle called hands "the instrument of instruments" (Zandy 2004, xi). As such, hands are witnesses to human endeavor and de-sire. We look to the physiology of hands for meaning. Anatomists, for exam-ple, named fingers for their utility. In medieval Latin, the index finger was "Demonstratorius," the digit for demonstrating or pointing. The middle or third finger was "Impudicus" or "Obscenus," the digit for assigning derision or blame. The fourth or ring finger was "Goldfinger" in Anglo-Saxon and "medicus" in Latin, possibly because doctors wore gold rings on their fourth fingers. Finally, in medieval Latin our little finger was the "Auricularis," the digit for extracting ear wax (Napier 1980, 37–38). Hands appear to help us conceptualize our world. Available items are on hand, handy, or in hand. Remarks can be made offhand. Disordered things are out of hand. Powerful people have the upper hand. Unscrupulous people are underhanded. Used things are secondhand. A disingenuous complement is left-handed. Guilty people are caught red handed. Awkward people are all thumbs. Ineffectual people sit on their hands. Human labor itself is signified by the hand. Workers are "hands." Fate is "the hand of God." The universe is "God's handiwork." Hands do the work of humanity, but they also serve us as visual emblems.

SPEAKING HANDS

Hands doing their jobs commonly do not draw stares. The expressive work of hands, in contrast, demands scrupulous watching. We talk with our hands as much as with our mouths. Our faces may be the command centers of communication, but our hands speak a more common language. Hands are our harbingers, announcing us and our intentions to the eyes of others. Pointing is a visible grammar. Babies point before they speak. An open, extended hand is a congenial greeting, a clenched fist a hostile warning. Thumbs up or down signal assent or decline. A handshake seals agreements. A raised right hand swears oaths; over the heart, the same hand pledges allegiance. Wringing our hands expresses worry or confusion. Ancient Greeks prayed by turning their palms upward toward heaven. Christians pray with their palms together. On the street, the upturned palm pleads for coins; the extended thumb requests a lift. We clap our hands together or soundlessly wag them above our heads to signal approval or appreciation. Sign language and classical rhetoric involve a complex syntax of meaning-laden gestures. An extended middle finger expresses scorn. The raised pinkie speaks femininity just as the firm handshake confirms masculinity. Fathers give their daughter's hands to husbands to gesture transfer of ownership. Differences in hand comportment are observable social distinctions, as well. Northern Europeans, for instance, historically have considered vulgar the vigorous and abundant gesticulating of Southern Europeans (Bremmer and Roodenburg 1992). The handshake expresses greeting between equals, whereas a bow or curtsy indicates deference to social superiors (Roodenburg 1992, 152–89).

Hands attract intense looking when they act as instruments of linguistic intercourse. The art of oratory extends the word from mouth to hand and bonds hand to eye. Our hand's extended range of motion and malleable form enables subtle gestures requiring close reading, making hands the center of visual interest in gesturing. A tradition of codifying gestural systems str-etches from early classical rhetoricians, such as Aristotle and Quintilian, through the contemporary disciplines of kinesics, which studies commu-nicative body movements, and to linguistics, which regards gesture as a form of language. Quintilian elaborated the theatrical gestures that speakers could use to secure their arguments. He describes wonder, or *admiratio*, as a manual gesture. The intricate bodily expression of wonder for Romans was a movement in which "the right hand turns slightly upwards and the fingers are brought in to the palm, one after the other, beginning with the little finger; the hand is then reopened and turned round by a reversal of this motion" (Graf 1992, 41). The more fundamental, if more subtle, bodily ex-pression of wonder, however, is staring. The wide-eyed, fixed baroque stare that is the hallmark of admiration or astonishment is enhanced in the rhe-torical tradition with Quintilian's hand gesture that intensifies and clarifies the meaning of a stare that registers wonder.

A more extravagant, and thus more stareable, gestural system of commu-nication are the sign languages used by Deaf communities.[1] Sign languages are distinct from the manual gesturing systems such as classical oratory because they do all the work of communication rather than augmenting speech. Best understood as the indigenous languages of Deaf peoples, sign languages have a complex syntax and semantics that extends beyond the simple one-on-one correspondence of rhetorical gestures. This nonvocal, unwritten, kinesic language was developed by and for the Deaf, who count themselves as a linguistic minority, something like Francophone Canadi-ans.[2] Staring is fundamental to Deaf cultures. In 1912, a Deaf man named George Veditz described his community as "the people of the eye" (Padden and Humphries 2005, 2). One listens to speakers; one stares at signers. This kind of visual listening can exceed the range of hearing communication, as when a Deaf person "overhears" a conversation across a room or chats with signers far out of auditory range. Because both lip-reading and manual gestures are integral to Deaf communication, Deaf people are starers. One Deaf signer reports, for example, that hands hold more visual interests than faces for her. She always stares at people's hands, whether they are signing or not. She adds that she stares a great deal in general, certainly too much she thinks, at least by hearing standards. "I stare," she says, "to 'hear' and understand better" (anonymous, 2006 interview).

The lively flying hands of signers are a staring occasion for anyone within visual range. Hearing people often stare at signing because sign language seems novel to the unaccustomed eye. So Deaf signers are often starees. One Deaf woman explains, for example, that in cosmopolitan areas she seldom draws stares from hearing people except from fascinated children, who often come forward encouraged by parents to show her that they have learned to fingerspell their names in school, something she finds alternately cute and wearisome. On the other hand, in small towns with less linguistic diversity, she often gets more visual attention than she prefers. One way she manages intrusive stares is to wave and say "hello" loudly, a move that confuses hearing starers by introducing spoken language into what they assume is the total silence of Deaf people, many of whom speak with Deaf accents. A bolder move she uses is walking over and asking a starer what they are staring at. For her, this strategy of outing a starer deflects back onto them the unwanted attention (anonymous, 2006 interview). Another Deaf signer reports: "I'm leafing through a magazine while standing in line at the grocery store and suddenly I realize all eyes are on me because someone is telling me, even hollering at me, to go to a different register" (anonymous, 2006 interview). Because her starers assume she is hearing, that she is part of the majority culture, they read her as rudely ignoring her fellow shoppers. Their stares of censure are in fact a failure of recognition on their part. Because Deaf people are an unexpected part of the social landscape, they often forfeit the visual anonymity on which hearing people can comfortably count.

READING HANDS

When hands function as legible rather than tactile instruments, we look at them differently. Gesturing, as we saw, demands visual interpretation of hand movements. Sometimes however, we read the hand itself. In the ancient practice of palmistry, for example, meaning lies not in a hand's actions but in its actual flesh. Palmists are masters of attentive staring, regarding hands as archives of the past and narratives of the future that call for intense focus to yield up this knowledge. Staring at hands in this way predates recorded history. Aristotle esteemed it; Julius Caesar and Alexander the Great were hand readers. The art of divination from observing the hand understands the body as a sign of character and a fleshly version of the soul. In classic palmistry, the thumb indicates willfulness, discipline, and personal drive. Jupiter, the index finger, signifies leadership and influence over others. Saturn, the middle finger, shows an ability to impose order and executed detail. Apollo, the third finger, demonstrates creative drives and public persona. The creases on our palms tell the stories of our hearts, deep secrets, and the moment of our deaths, none of which are revealed without careful stares.

Although palmistry now seems like superstition or tawdry exoticism, it persists today in practices that read hands through surveillance techniques such as fingerprinting. The science of dermatoglyphics, sometimes known as dactyloscopy, applies the positive impressions of the papillary ridges for a forensic, archaeological, and medical identification. Every person's finger-prints, even those of identical twins, are wholly individual and immutable. Our distinctive papillary ridges can be temporarily obliterated but will even-tually return, making fingerprinting an ideal way to classify and identify people. Inaugurated by Scotland Yard in 1901, whole towns and entire classes of people were fingerprinted by mid-century (Napier 1990). The most re-cent version of reading about a person from looking at their hands is bio-metric technologies. Electronic finger scanners and machines that register hand geometry have replaced the familiar ink smudges on birth certificates and police records. Automatic scanning has begun to target our faces, reti-nas, ears, gaits, and even body odor. These scanners as well as surveillance cameras or even photo IDs are examples of technological staring in which machines come between starer and staree. This kind of impersonal staring is a form of inspection not open to the interpersonal dynamics of face-to-face staring.

ABSENT HANDS

The gesturing hand occasions a scene of staring in which hands are vividly present. The fingerprint or biometric scanner, in contrast, effaces the ac-tual hand, focusing the stare on the trace an absent hand has left of itself. Staring at an absent hand occurs as well in the spectacle of the hand that is not there. When hands enter our visual field, we expect them to look and function in typical ways. Seeing a vanished hand violates the visual expecta-tions of bilateral symmetry that is an organizing principle of handedness.[3] An assumption of matching sidedness, which occurs in many other living natural forms, shapes our visual sense of proper handedness. The sociologist Georg Simmel claimed that the twoness of hands compose their "organic character" so that "one hand always refers to the other; only the two together realize the idea, as it were, of 'hand'" (Simmel 1965, 276–77). The coop-erative interlaced functioning of agile, compatible, decadigital, prehensile hands is a symbol of human capability. This romance of double-handedness is expressed perhaps most fully in Albercht Durer's iconic drawing, "Praying Hands," in which corresponding palms and aligned fingertips suggest the harmony, grace, and mutuality of profound interconnection.

This primacy of double-handedness makes singleton hands unexpected enough to draw stares. Musical performances by one-handed pianists pro-vide an interesting case of staring at hands. The unusual presence of an absent hand in such performances changes them from a primarily aural ex-perience accompanied by a visual component into a performance in which

Figure 9.1. Paul Wittgenstein, c. 1920. Photo by D'Ora Photos, Vienna, Carlsbad. Signed by Paul Wittgenstein. © Wittgenstein Archive, Cambridge, UK

eyes play a much larger role.[4] By far, the most famous single-handed pianist was Paul Wittgenstein (figure 9.1). A well-known Austrian pianist, Wittgenstein lost his right arm in World War I and continued to play the piano. "I immediately determined upon the plan of training myself to become a one armed pianist, at least to attempt it," he wrote in October 1915 (Flindell 1971, 112). Wittgenstein sought out, commissioned, and professionally performed left-handed piano works from 1915 until his death in 1961.[5]

Professionally performing at the piano with one hand distinguished Wittgenstein from ordinary accomplished pianists, influencing the interpretation of his work and the reception of his artistic persona: people attended his concerts as much to stare at him as to hear him play. In a 1959 interview, one critic set the terms for Wittgenstein's performance thus, "it takes double the talent and energy for a left-hand pianist to convey the impression of a musician with two arms" (Flindell 1971, 113).

The spectacle of a one-handed pianist reveals the difference between viewing and staring. A one-handed pianist elicits staring because we expect to see paired hands at the keys. Indeed, performing with two hands and ten fingers is fundamental to the accepted idea of piano playing. The distinctiveness of the one-handed performance calls attention to our fundamental conceptions of piano performance, confounding it and making us stare. A student of Wittgenstein's, for instance, recalled attending his performance for her first time with her father when she was twelve years old. After the concert, her father asked if she had noticed anything unusual about the pianist, which she had not. When her father informed her that the pianist had played with only his left hand, she could not believe it (Flindell 1971, 113). This story suggests that full comprehension of this musical form requires intense visual engagement.[6] The present hand, which dazzles with its solo performance, eclipses the absent hand. Even the empty sleeve, which is the concert costume of an absent hand, decorously discourages staring. This dynamic moderates pity or shock that might distract from the performance. Although an extended period of visual contemplation may lead a viewer to notice the pianist's single-handedness, the scene encourages admiration for the achievement of technical skill against what are imagined as great odds. Startled as the starer might be by one rather than two hands playing the piano, the sleight-of-hand, so to speak, of one-handed piano performances is that the present hand obscures with its spectacular dexterity the absent hand, rescuing viewers from lurching into full-blown baroque stares.

AMPUTATED HANDS

The causes, character, and consequences of staring differ when the context is not a performance. Images of amputated hands offer a useful instance of how staring gets enlisted as a political plea. The visual assault of amputated hands figured as a potent political tactic used by both sides during Sierra Leone's nine-year civil war. Although much brutality occurred during this civil struggle, mass amputation was one of the most disturbing forms of terror inflicted upon civilians.[7] The terrible signature of the rebels was amputation by machete, usually of the hands: the rebel forces systematically amputated the limbs of more than twenty thousand Sierra Leonean civilians, many of whom died. The intention, however, was to maim rather than kill. The victims were randomly chosen, often from the same villages as the perpetrators, and many were children. These amputations were public spectacles.

Like any public spectacle of deliberate mutilation, amputation in the Sierra Leone civil war was a form of communication. The rebels used the hands of their victims to deliver messages to their communities, the government, and the international community (Carey 2006). The severed hands themselves were part of the semantics of commitment within the rebel military order. Warriors collected hands in bags to display as evidence for promotion and as tokens of performance. The amputations delivered the message that the rebels could seize the symbol for self-sufficiency at will and did so in a manner calculated to draw the most stares. The rebels carried out the actual limb cutting on the public, communal pounding blocks used to prepare rice and used the implements of food production and land clearing such as machetes or cutlasses to sever hands. This language of hand amputation bespoke who had the power to determine who could participate in the life of the community. In the language and culture of the Loma, which is the larger region from which the new nation of Sierra Leone was carved, ideas of power, capacity, and personhood referred to the hand/arm, a continuous body unit called *ze*. The fundamental life activities of Loma culture—such as clearing the forest, planting and harvesting rice, building and thatching huts, and preparing food—require strong and capable hands. Thus, though the amputated hands drew stares from both local and international starers, the local nuances of the amputations were an alien gestural speech that no translator could render comprehensible to foreigners.

Amputation spoke most effectively through the display of its aftermath. The violent semantics of amputation, in other words, had to be seen to be heard. All sides in the conflict emphasized the visual message of amputation by staging dramatic scenes of staring. The rebels with machetes sent the handless back to their terrified villages and their horrified government as embodied exclamation points. Soon the international community and the legitimate Sierra Leonean government also arranged spectacles of staring as political strategies against the rebels. The amputees became living symbols of war's brutality and the catalysts that forced the various factions to work together. The widely circulated, shocking spectacle of their raw and exposed handlessness before the astonished eyes of the world eventually forced the intransigent parties to the negotiation table.

In the United States, scenes of staring directed public attention to the conflict in Sierra Leone and gathered support for its victims. On September 26, 2000, the U.S. House of Representatives Africa Subcommittee held a public hearing entitled "Sierra Leone's Youngest Victims: We Can't Ignore."

A group of eight refugee amputees from the Amputee Camp in Freetown, the capital of Sierra Leone, who came to the United States to appear at the hearings (figure 9.2). The refugees were to get surgery, be fitted with prosthetics, and be trained in their use—all free of charge. An organization called "The Gift of Limbs Project" donated medical care and living expenses. The congressional investigation centered on the appearance of these eight amputees, six of whom were children, whose presence was a call for justice. They were to tell their stories with words; but more important, they were to tell their stories by being seen. The amputees testified with their bodies, their handlessness punctuating their stories for the American eyes. The sight of stumps where hands are expected shocked viewers. An appalled Senator John Kerry said: "every American should take note of what is taking place here today" so that the sight would "steer everyone to work to bring [the barbarism] to an end" (Fisher-Thompson 2006).

The Americans carefully orchestrated many staring encounters to ensure that starers understood the purpose of their stares and their expected

Figure 9.2. Children from Sierra Leone arrive at Dulles Airport. Damba Koroma, eight years old (left), holds a balloon as Memunatu Mansaray, four years old, has her balloon tied to the wrist of her one arm by Milly Terry of Friends of Sierra Leone. They are in the United States for orthopedic surgery and prosthetic fitting in New York. © 2008, *The Washington Post*. Photograph by Carol Guzy. Reprinted with permission.

response. The vanished limbs and all too visible stumps brought forward in photographs, media, and public appearances demanded intense looking and equally intense responses. The stareable refugees appeared before the New York City Council, marched in a protest down Fifth Avenue, attended dozens of fundraisers, and went to a celebrity picnic with the Clintons. A Sierra Leonean émigré named Etta Touré who worked with Americans summed up the role of these the amputees, as "visual evidence." She noted that while the dead are eventually forgotten, the sight of stumps and vanished limbs "is going to be around us forever" (Packer 2003, 55). House International Relations Committee Chairman Ben Gilman explained that seeing the handless refugees was an opportunity to "recognize the horror" of war (Fisher-Thompson 2006, n.p.). And he was right. "I saw those children, and all I could do was cry," said one woman at a Washington, D.C., fundraiser for the amputees (Frazier 2000, M02).

The shocking sight of handless stumps paraded before astonished audiences first invited staring and then justified it. To do this, the scenes grant permission to stare and refuse to let starers look away. They appropriate the social blunder of staring, converting it to a proper, even praiseworthy, social act. To use the terminology of cognitive psychology, this strategy seizes stimulus-driven visual exploratory behavior and transforms it into proper goal-driven visual focus. In other words, the context surrounding these scenes draws baroque stares for the ultimate purpose of paying intense attention.

MECHANICAL HANDS

Amputee war victims shock viewers into attentiveness, which we have seen can be politically productive when stares are channeled into action. A baroque stare in such cases becomes a proper, socially sanctioned stare. A mechanical hand that stands in for an absent hand invites a different kind of staring, however. A prosthetic hand eases the startling sight of a stump. But the hybrid of machine and flesh also violates our visual expectations. In other words, a mechanical hand is an unexpected presence in the place of an unexpected absence. Of an alien shape and substance, a prosthesis does the work of a hand but is a visually improper one. Such an ersatz hand confuses our eyes, making us stare. Regardless of how functionally proper it may be to its user, the visually improper hand demands an explanation. Every mechanical hand invokes a drama that ordinary appendages lack. As with the stareable faces considered in the previous chapter, we stare seeking clues to this story. The drama of the mechanical hand usually has two acts: Act one is how-did-you-lose-it?; act two is how-do-you-use it? All amputees appear in the one act drama, but the prosthetic wearer stars in the full two-act production.

One readily available story a prosthetic hand calls forth is that of the combat veteran. From Captain Hook to Lord Nelson, our received stories about prosthetic hands in public view are often about military heroes. Historically, war itself produces large numbers of amputees, which in turn produces significant advances in prosthetic technology. This gruesome circuit of cause-and-effect turns loss into restitution and victims into heroes. Media coverage of the second Iraq War has featured many upbeat stories about technologically amazing artificial limbs. In this kind of story, war provides the script for the first act in the drama of the absent hand and prosthetics provides the script for the second act. Battle takes away the fleshly hand and technology supplies a serviceable replacement. In replicating living hands, these artificial limbs accomplish the dual job of enhancing function and appearance, although doing this equally well is difficult. A hand that looks almost alive, for instance, is less functional than an obviously mechanical hand that grasps and manipulates most effectively.

A mechanical hand answers the needs of its wearer, whereas a cosmetic hand answers the needs of its starer. A news article from the *Washington Post* about a disabled veteran recently returned from Iraq demonstrates how staring contributes to this contradiction between appearance and function. The story of Sergeant Brian Doyne's relationship between staring and his new hand is subtitled: "With Lifelike Prosthesis, No Stares" (Williams 2005, B1; figure 9.3). This tale of soldiering, wounding, and healing features one of the primal scenes of staring. Sergeant Doyne's story begins with the typical kind of visual cruising that takes place at a Starbucks counter, where an "attractive blonde waiting nearby for her coffee sizes him up." Her "eyes stop for a vanishing moment" on some traces on his face remaining from the explosion that blew off his left hand. She does not even notice his absent hand, however. In fact, "No one seems to think anything of it," the story assures. Doyne's stump goes unremarked at Starbucks and elsewhere, we are astonished to learn, because he has nine prosthetic hands. The one he wears to Starbucks secures something for him that the others do not: it gives him the "shining possibility" of visual anonymity that restores the civil inattention that amputation revoked. This cosmetic high-tech metal hand enclosed in a plastic sleeve is painstakingly sculpted and painted to replicate its matching fleshly hand. This hand delivers Sergeant Doyne a respite from stares so that "for some moments, at least, he will not stand out in a crowd, or in a Starbucks line." The "highest purpose the hand serves is to shield him from the prying eyes of strangers, to protect the privacy he cherishes." The function of this mechanical hand is not to work but to

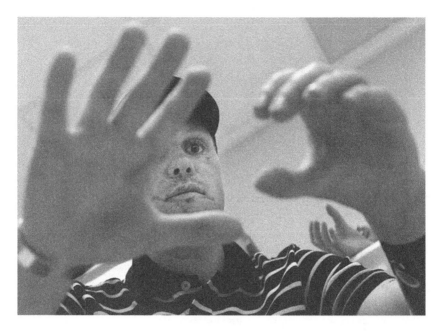

Figure 9.3. Army sergeant Brian Doyne, twenty-six, checks out his newly completed prosthetic at Walter Reed Army Medical Center in Washington, D.C. Doyne, whose left hand was blown off by an improvised explosive device (IED) just outside Tikrit, Iraq, is having a life-like prosthetic made by artisan Michael Curtain. © 2008, *The Washington Post*. Photograph by Jahi Chikwendiu. Reprinted with permission.

be viewed, to be seen without being the object of stares. The reprieve the mechanical hand offers is "a chance to get away from those questions" the inquiring stares demand.

Ironically, the news story itself offers Doyne no relief from "those questions." Weary as he may be from the inquisition of stares, he presents his story to the readers of the *Washington Post*. After being drafted into what he calls the "fraternity of the disabled," he explains, his nine mechanical hands give him "some more normalcy in the way we're perceived." He only occasionally wears his "normal" cosmetic hand, the one painted with freckles and matching skin tone, for special occasions: job interviews, Starbucks, visits to the local tavern, in situations where he thinks his more functional hands, or certainly his handlessness, would draw the unwanted stares that keep him from passing for a regular guy. The price for this kind of passing, however, is that Doyne can not do much of the work he needs to do with his "normal" hand, like retrieve parking tickets from a machine or repair cars. The work of this stareless hand, Doyne says, is the task of "making other people feel more comfortable." He makes an important distinction here: he wears his cosmetic hand not so much to protect himself from stares but rather to spare his viewers the discomfort of being starers. In other words, Sergeant Doyne extends to his starers a face-saving strategy that ultimately benefits him by regularizing the social encounter, by readmitting him into the realm of the ordinary.

As Doyne's story suggests, the differentness of his hands and what that means comes into being through stares. The intended purpose of devices such as Doyne's "normal" prosthetic hand is to rescue stareable people from stigma. The manifestation of stigma in the social world is being stared at, for it is then that people register another's status and reflect it back to them. Looking normal, then, is fundamentally a stigma-dodging maneuver. The cosmetic hand works simultaneously, however, to save the starer from the social stigma of staring. So when Sergeant Doyne uses the most functional of his mechanical hands as an efficient implement, the look of his hand draws stares that stigmatize staree and starer. When he gets the best function from his hand, he also gets the most stares. When he chooses the fewest stares, he chooses the least function. Managing to negotiate this conflict between appearance and function is precisely the task of the newly disabled. What is best for starers is not always what is best for starees.

Sergeant Doyne has only recently learned how to manage old tasks with his new hand. In contrast, he has been well-instructed for his entire life about the consequences of looking unusual, of having a body that draws stares. He probably learned the lessons of staring in the same way as the rest of us: from a mother who in hushed and anxious whispers told him not to stare, and from television, movies, and books that provide cautionary tales about the consequences of staring at a body gone wrong. The classic 1946 movie, *The Best Years of Our Lives*, is just one of many examples. The movie recruits the anxiety of staring and being stared at, telling the compelling story of war veterans returning to civilian life by featuring the story of the double amputee, Homer Parrish. Homer is played by the actual bilateral hand amputee, Harold Russell.[8] The film offers up intimate views of Homer's absent arms and presents prostheses to the viewers, capitalizing on the discomfort that such an unrestrained staring experience coaxes from the unsettled viewer. What might be called this staring tension builds toward a dramatic climax in which all the stifled staring energy erupts in a confrontation between Homer and a group of neighborhood children who have been unable to keep their urge to stare in proper check; their "separated stares" have turn hostile. Homer is no longer able to tolerate their giggles and gawks, which are safely situated outside the family garage where he has retreated from the stresses of the mutual uneasiness his disability prompts. In a dramatic response to their muted stares, Homer menacingly thrusts his prosthetic hooks through the glass window toward the horrified children, who are at once frightened and awestruck by his power to shatter the glass without injuring his "hands." As he smashes his hooks through the window, the previously soft-spoken and depressive Homer shrieks "You want to see how these hooks work? You want to see the freak? All right, I'll show you. Take a good look!" This climactic scene dramatizes the visual difference between Homer and those with unnoticeable bodies. This scene functions as a kind of training film not just for those marching off to the risks of war but to all of us as we live in environments that change the form of our bodies to make them stareable. Staring announces the well-kept secret that simply being in the world over time reshapes our bodies. The kind of passing Sergeant Doyne reasonably seeks with his "normal" hand reveals our collective reluctance to accept disability or to accommodate the bodies that life bestows upon us.

UNORTHODOX HANDS

Many people with stareable hands know what Sergeant Doyne learned about presenting hands to the public view. Unorthodox hands, whether mechanical or fleshly, often fascinate eyes most fully when they are at work. A typical working hand is unremarkable, whereas an unorthodox hand puts on a show whenever it undertakes even common tasks. Ordinary activities such as eating, drinking, grooming, or manipulating objects become spectacles of interest when unusual hands accomplish them. A wine glass deftly handled by a split hook prosthesis, for example, can amaze an entire cocktail party. People with paralyzed hands use heads or mouths to operate keyboards, and what might be called minority prosthetic devices such as Velcro cuffs or mouth sticks call attention in a way that majority prosthetic devices such as hammers or screwdrivers held by the standardly handed do not. With their differences animated, unusual hands leap forward out of a routine visual landscape. As we have seen, surprise might initiate a stare, but in the case of unusual hands encountering a usual task, curiosity about human ingenuity often sustains this visual inquiry. Unsure of just what they are seeing, starers focus an engaged stare on the novel manual innovation before their eyes because they have never before seen such a relationship between body and task.

The single-handed or the handless also often practice an eye-catching manualization of the whole body that the standardly handed never develop. A one-handed person, for example, reports using her rib cage to supply the grasping capability needed to operate a manual can opener, creating stares of amazement from friends in the kitchen. The handless draw eyes with a range of alternative solutions to manual tasks. They transport items by nestling them in armpits rather than palms, grip things with teeth instead of fingers, clutch stuff between shoulder and jaw rather than between thumb and fingers, and nudge along what they need with their knees instead of their hands. An armless person smoking a cigarette with her toes after dinner enraptures an entire dining room. Even minor variations in expected hand behavior attract eyes. A woman with rheumatoid arthritis, for example, finds that simply feeding herself with two hands at the same time, rather than lifting food and drink to her mouth in a polite single-handed fashion, causes people to stare at her. Another one, with inflexible hands, holds utensils with a Velcro cuff (anonymous, 2006 interviews).

For all these people, just going about their business creates quite a spectacle. Even more eye-catching are congenitally armless people, especially those who do not use prostheses. Without prostheses, armless people perform typically manual tasks with their toes and feet, much to the fascination and amazement of those who use hands for such jobs. So compelling are these handless performances that historically many armless people have made a living by displaying to the typically handed the ways they accomplished quotidian tasks.

A rich record of testimonies, reports, advertisements, and images documents the wonder such sights inspired. A 1726 handbill, for example, proclaimed Matthias Buchinger, the celebrated "Little Man of Nuremberg," to be "the greatest living German" (Jay 2005). Born handless and legless, Buchinger was twenty-nine inches high. The famous calligrapher, juggler, swordsman, trick bowler, and magician married at least twice and fathered several children. One of his many renowned digitless feats included making an eight-inch high Whimsey Bottle, inside of which he constructed a miniature scene of miners digging ore, complete with tiny intricate implements. In turn-of-the-century American freak shows, "Armless Wonders" were amongst the most spectacular and well-paid performers. Armless Wonders such as Charles Tripp and Anna Leake Thompson never simply displayed themselves; instead, they worked wondrous feats with their toes. They drank gracefully from tea cups, wrote beautiful calligraphic script, cut out intricate paper dolls, and sewed elaborate needlework before their starers. Armless Wonder Charles Tripp collaborated with Legless Wonder Eli Bowen riding a tandem bike; Bowen occupied the front seat grasping the handlebars while Tripp rode on the back seat pushing the pedals with his feet. This scene presents starable bodies as less surprising in themselves but rather most novel in their mutual cooperation and innovation in doing something their bodies are ill-suited to achieve.[9]

In an era of disability rights, armless people have other employment options besides freak show entertainers. For example, Theresia Degener, whose photo we saw in chapter one, is a congenitally armless woman, an attorney, professor, and disability rights leader in Germany. In Degener's public appearances, rather than penning calligraphy or cutting out paper dolls with her toes, she delivers lectures or press conferences while holding a microphone with one foot and making rhetorical gestures with the other one (figure 9.4).

An important plank in Degener's political platform is her refusal to normalize her body with prosthetic arms. Wearing elegantly tailored professional suits fitted to her armlessness, she insists on presenting herself as she

Figure 9.4. Brigitte Faber, portrait of Dr. Theresia Degener.

was born and using her body in ways that work best for her. In contrast to Degener, American attorney and nonprofit CEO John Kemp, an armless and legless disability rights leader, uses prosthetic arms, legs, and hands to enhance functioning. Like Degener's nimble toes, Kemp's agile hooks are sources of amazement for the ordinarily handed. As the master of ceremonies for the 2002 Ms. Wheelchair America Pageant, Kemp cut quite a figure with his tuxedo, silver hair, movie star face, power scooter, and prosthetic hooks. Their self-presentation—not unlike that of David Roche or the portraits we have seen—conveys great dignity and personal authority. Whether living people or artistic images, they decorously refuse pity, tragedy, or victimhood. Like Buchinger, Tripp, and Leak-Thompson, Degener and Kemp use the visual pull of their stareable bodies as public announcements that people with significant disabilities have good lives and make valuable contributions.

Whereas armless people such as Degener and Kemp make use of their stares on the political stage, other armless people capitalize on their stares on the dramatic stage. Performance artist Mary Duffy, for example, turns being a staree into art. In her stage performances, the armless Duffy presents herself in a startling tableau vivant of the Venus de Milo, assuming the pose of this classic armless female nude. This reference to the icon of female beauty invites Duffy's starers to consider armlessness as a proper form of beauty rather than insufficiency or disfigurement. Duffy's performance as Venus, in other words, asks her audience to convert the baroque stares they bring with them off the street into the reverential stares they would bring to the Louvre. By presenting herself as a work of art, Duffy repudiates the reading of her body as a pathological specimen. She instructs her starers how to stare at her, then delivers a soliloquy instructing them how to think of her. She tells them simply that she is "whole, complete and functional."[10]

PERFORMING HANDS

Like Duffy and fellow stage performer David Roche, the poets Cheryl Marie Wade and Lezlie Frye invoke stares to make audiences see differently. Where Duffy offers up a Venus-like armless body to her starers, Wade and Frye brandish their all-too-present hands. Wade and Frye offer no conventional poetry reading where the poet's body is a proper but unremarkable delivery vehicle for spoken words. This poetry engages the eye as much as the ear. It is poetry of the hands, the unorthodox hands. Indeed, the point of their performance is to get their hands in your face.

Their poetic performance unveils hands that usually remain discreetly covered, tucked away from view so as not to attract tedious awkward looks. Wade and Frye violate the taboo against staring, refusing audiences the escapes of furtive looking or looking away. In the tradition of armless wonders of early freak shows, they offer working hands rather than static displays. The work of their hands is the craft of poetry rather than scissor, quill, or needle. These performances fuse the cultural authority wielded by the high art of poetry with the extravagance of freak show display. Wade and Frye invite stares, validate them with poems, and then tell their stories.

Figure 9.5. Brenda Prager, portrait of Cheryl Marie Wade.

In performing her poem, "My Hands," Wade taunts her starers. From her wheelchair, she flaunts the hands that polite society prefers she hide (figure 9.5). She grabs deprecating words for her hands, fiercely claims them as her own, and hurls them back:

> Mine are the hands of your bad dreams.
> Booga booga from behind the black curtain.
> Claw hands.
> The ivory girl's hands after a decade of roughing it.
> Crinkled, puckered, sweaty, scarred,
> a young woman's dwarf knobby hands
> that ache for moonlight—that tremble, that struggle.
> Hands that make your eyes tear.
> My hands. My hands. My hands
> that could grace your brow, your thigh.
> My hands! Yeah!

Calling up "your bad dreams" with a truculent "booga booga," Wade takes on the monster role that has traditionally thrilled and titillated viewers. Her stareable hands become threatening "claws" that she is not only going to show to her starers but show them what those claws do. Wade's hands "make your eyes tear," perhaps with shock or repugnance, but never sympathy. Although they may look incapable, Wade's hands do things. They "ache," "tremble," and "struggle." They are evidence of a life of "roughing it." No passive feminine "ivory girl's hands," Wade's hands are sexual predators that "could grace your brow, your thigh." Threatening for the squeamish or alluring for the adventuresome, the sexual proposition is the real "booga, booga" of Wade's performance. The poem's closing withdraws Wade's hands from her audience and focuses her own approving gaze upon them. "My hands! Yeah!" she sighs, with a sound of satisfaction reminiscent of sexual release. With this, she releases her audience from the looks of horror she demanded and leaves them viewing her self-love, not as narcissistic regard but rather as an affirmation of these hands as whole and right. By making them stare, she has guided her audience to see her hands as she experiences them, as "My Hands."

Lezlie Frye gets her hands in your face too. Using the familiar tone and gestures of hip-hop performance, Frye demands that her audience stare at her hands while she tells them about what it's like to be a staree. In poetic terms, Frye merges form and content. Costumed in alternative black, with a deliberately tight sleeveless top that exposes her contrasting white arms, she struts to the rhythm of her words, gesturing emphatically with her distinctive, asymmetrical hands. In one rap-style poem called "Don't Dis- My

Ability," Frye follows Wade by taunting her viewers to take a good look at her hands but then retracts that offer, redirecting their stares to where she wants them to go:

> Don't stare here
> Fix your eyes on your fear
> Check yourself
> Inspect yourself for
> Whatever it is that's so alarming
> That you won't look me in the eyes stop
> Telling me lies
> About who I am[11]

Frye uses here a visual call and response to manipulate the staring encounter. Like our mothers, she commands her starers to "check yourself." Her starers' eyes are going to the wrong place for them to learn anything about her or themselves. If they stare at her hands, they can not look her "in the eyes," in order to affirm her personhood. She continues by narrating her version of this staring encounter to her starers:

> Look I can feel it when we meet
> Inside, discomfort
> Outside, grin
> It's confusing these two faces
> Digesting my image . . .
> And how I feel is tired.

The tension between her starer's "discomfort" and the "grin" that glosses over their anxiety accounts for her weariness. Frye is "tired" of unwanted attention, of being denied the civil inattention that typically handed people enjoy. The genre of rap poetry fits well her purpose of violating social decorum to signal social dissent. She calls up stares to protest stares. She makes more to say she has had enough.

Frye finishes this poem with a coda called "Imagine," in which she instructs her starers how to see her. "I'm sick of doin' time for abnormality, anomaly, deformity, defect," she insists. Exorcising this litany of aberration and lack, she insists on a new way to see her. With her hands brought forward in a gesture of communal witnessing, she avers to them, herself, and to her starers: "I'm a person in a body and I am whole."

Mary Duffy, Cheryl Marie Wade, and Lezlie Frye use performance similarly as a ritual of redefinition, an assertion of self on their own terms. The performances of all three women recognize and repudiate the idea that

stares could make them internalize alienated images of themselves. Like Sergeant Doyne, the amputee war veteran in Starbucks, these women struggle
against absorbing a view of themselves that the uncomfortable stares of
strangers enforce every day. In a poem entitled, "Things You Don't Think
about When You've Got Ten Fingers," Frye recounts that a lifetime of stares
has trained her "into submission into/ Wishin' I was someone who looked
a different way in this / Ten finger world / Ten fingers swirl around me as I
learn to say, Wait for me / You can wait while I see what I can do with my
body, with my hands." Here she refuses the normalization that Doyne sometimes seeks, searching instead like the armless Theresia Degener for her own
distinctive way of doing tasks and being in the world. Going for full visual
disclosure is a liberation not from stares themselves, but from an internal
image of herself as deficient. By using public performance to determine the
terms on which they are seen, these women remake their own images. At
the end of their performances, they expect their audiences to be seeing them
differently. Frye describes this ceremonial act of revelation as "Making room
for the look at myself / That's missing from my body's vocabulary." Of this
new image, she says, "I want to know what my hand looked like in the womb
/ Before I knew what it means to live in a body classified as dis-abled."

These women's performances demonstrate, then, how a staring encounter can be an opportunity for a staree to reimagine herself rather than simply
reeducate the starer. In staging staring Duffy, Wade, and Frye manipulate
staring to draw out its productive potential. As active agents in staring encounters, they expand the opportunity for political statement that staring
enacted in the images and appearances of the Sierra Leone amputees. They
are not victims in these performances, but intentional meaning makers.
Their performances of what Rebecca Schneider (1997) calls "the explicit
body" unleash and realign the power inherent in staring by merging body
and word in an act of self-making. This is the same task writ large that all
disabled people face. Duffy, Wade, and Frye make serious art from the quotidian stuff of the daily stigma management people with disabilities must
master to get through the stares and, more than that, present to the world a
life worth living. In short, these women generate new ways of seeing and of
understanding what it means to be human.

10

BREASTS

You Can't Look Away Any More
—*New York Times Magazine* headline about Matuschka (1993)

ICONIC BREASTS

Breasts are ubiquitous cultural icons.[1] From the sacred fount of the Maria Lactans, the titillating cleavage of Miss America, the ample bosom of Mammy, to the erotic blast of the Playboy centerfold, the sight of breasts signifies woman. As both symbol and flesh, no other bodily mark of sexual identity is so routinely or ritualistically offered up to the public eye. Even though the penis and vagina carry perhaps equal cultural significance, representations tend to finesse the way we see these parts of our bodies. The penis stands in for phallic power but seldom shows itself in public.[2] Michelangelo's famous statue, for example, expresses David's masculinity through his commanding demeanor and musculature, not the incidental bit of flesh between his potent thighs. Phallic forums, such as the Washington Monument, are stylized rather than mimetic representations of penises. Vaginas appear even less often in respectable representations. Artists such as Georgia O'Keeffe, Judy Chicago, or Eve Ensler rework the vagina's image as a dark, secret snare into flamboyant flowers, dinner plates, or storytellers.[3] Symbolic hotspots as they are, penises and vaginas for the most part demurely decline stares. Breasts, by contrast, are in your face.

Maternal breasts have been on view from prehistory through the beginning of the modern era. The Venuses of the prehistoric fertility cults are enormous bosoms with vestigial limbs attached. Over twenty globular imbricated breasts adorn the elegant torso of the pre-classical Artemis of Ephesus. The bountiful, fertile breast takes on the human scale with the ever-lactating madonnas, reaching an apotheosis in the Madonna-del-latte of the Italian Renaissance. The Dutch Golden Age domesticated the lactating breast as a symbol of secular comfort. The new French Republic of the late eighteenth century offered images of maternal breasts to its new citizenry. People even see breasts where they are not. A long tradition of projecting the maternal breast onto the landscape exists as well, from the Virgin Land to the Grand Tetons, named by a trapper after the French slang for *breasts*.[4] In 1498, Christopher Columbus likened the newly sighted South America to an Edenic nipple projecting out from a mammary globe (Yalom 1997). In our contemporary era, the maternal breast has vanished, however, and the erotic breast has proliferated (87), responding in part to consumerism's more-and-bigger ethic. The comely pinup with her 36-24-36 measurements and the plastic, perky, rocket-titted Barbie figure have obliterated the sturdy fertility goddesses as the breasts we see.[5]

HIDDEN BREASTS

The maternal breast has almost entirely receded from view in our day. Museums or a few churches are the only remaining public spaces where maternal breasts can be seen, safely contained there as aesthetic or sacred relics. The sight of an actual fleshly maternal breast in modern America raises controversy and even legal clashes. A particular flashpoint is breastfeeding in public. In 2004, for example, thirty mothers with infants held a "nurse-in" at a local Starbucks in a Washington, D.C., suburb to protest after a nursing mother was asked to cover up or move to the restroom. Amid the gush of rancorous public responses, one editorial called this sight of breastfeeding, "the latest assault on the right to a peaceful cup of [coffee]" (Roberts 2004, C01). The *Washington Post* writer, herself a former nursing mother, explained her complaint as being "about the slippery and ever-changing slope of social standards" (Roberts 2004, C01). Such skirmishes about which breasts we ought and ought not to stare at ended up in local courts, where breast feeding advocates argued, in short, that nursing women should be accorded civil inattention in public.

Confrontations about public breastfeeding are less about the merits of bottles versus breasts and more about monitoring staring. For the miffed editorial writer who wanted to drink her latte in peace, the issue apparently was not protecting the rights of breastfeeding mothers but rather protecting starers from the lure of starees. Her complaint was that the nursing mother "expects me to avert my eyes" (Roberts 2004, C01). In other words, she wanted to be shielded from her own impulse to stare. Perhaps more, she wanted to spare her fellow patrons from staring. Her plea to the nursing mother, "Please, please, please. Just don't," suggests moreover that she sought to protect her fellow mother from being a staree. The latte lament tells us something about social anxieties over what and how we see in public spaces. We expect maternal breasts to be sequestered in private spaces whereas erotic breasts are unremarkable staples of public visual culture. This moves the nursing breast from a space of simple looking into the territory of staring. Seeing maternal breasts where erotic breasts are expected makes people starers and nursing mothers starees. The social violation that provokes most anxiety, then, may not be breastfeeding in public but rather staring at it.

EXPOSED BREASTS

The naked breast before the naked eye holds a potential charge, both in the past and today. Exposed breasts bespeak varying ideas of womanhood. Deep, inviting cleavage modestly promises sexual thrills. The bountiful maternal breast, whether Mommy or Mammy, whispers comfort to the child. The pierced breast of a rock star shouts down feminine modesty. The Madonna's breast intercedes for souls. The bikinied breast teases and withholds. The pert, pushed-up breast sells everything from lettuce, cars, drinks, dolls, to wars. The pastied breast of the go-go dancer goes almost all the way.[6] The appearance of breasts makes women legible as women; but—perhaps more important—staring at breasts supposedly tells us who a woman *really* is. The choreography and comportment of women's breasts, more than any other part of her body, are an index of her person. Although a woman's understanding of herself may differ wildly from the message that her breasts convey to the eyes of the world, her breasts nevertheless announce the essence of her womanliness.

The visual magnetism of breasts can make both starers and starees anxious. Women often feel self-conscious about their breasted appearance. Too much breast means too much femininity; too little breast means not enough. Flat-chested women may hide behind bulky sweaters or compensate with padded bras. Buxom women may defend against ogling with baggy clothes. One big-breasted woman says, "If a man stares at my breasts, I just don't give him a chance. I wish just once a man would look into my eyes with the same interest that he looks at my breasts" (Latteier 1998, 21). Men too can be wary of visually crossing into forbidden territory if they stare at women's breasts.

Breast starers can be thought rude, insensitive, or lascivious. The staring scene at Starbucks worried people, in part, because staring—or not—at nursing breasts is unfamiliar visual territory.

Even though breasts entice stares, the border between what can and cannot be seen gets cautiously negotiated. The tensions between hiding and exposing breasts, between who should look when, fuel fierce debates. Moralists rage against immodest breast display while breasts doing sex work shout

Figure 10.1. Marc Tyler Nobleman, "Does my resume mention my breasts somewhere? I can't think of any other reason you would continue to stare at them." November 8, 2001. Courtesy of www.cartoonstock.com.

out from street corners. Big breasts sell products while breastless cancer survivors display their scars in protests. Mothers get arrested for nursing babies in public while public health advocates promote extended breastfeeding. Mothers and adolescent daughters struggle over necklines while commercialism makes children into sex pots. The surgical shaping of breasts escalates while implants are deemed dangerous. This deep cultural ambivalence turns the female breast into a perpetual peep show (figure 10.1).

Proper looking gets complicated, then, when breasts are the object of stares. One perspective on anxiety about who should and should not stare at breasts comes from a person who was born intersexed. After living for twenty-four years as a woman, this person transitioned to being a man, an identity with which he felt more comfortable. In addition to comportment and costuming adjustments, testosterone treatments accomplished his transition into manhood.[7] Testosterone provided some of the visible marks of manhood such as facial hair, a more manly body, and a lower voice. Hormonally becoming a male, much to his surprise, affected his staring behavior. He reports that after taking testosterone for several weeks, he began noticing women's bodies differently from before, when he had mostly only looked at people's bodies to simply note differences. Now that he is hormonally a man, he says when he first sees women in public he finds that he rarely looks at their faces anymore but begins his visual acquaintance with them by staring at their breasts. Having lived as a woman, he finds it mortifying to have developed what he calls "guy's eyes" and become a "breast man." Nonetheless, even when his brain tells him not to stare at breasts, he has difficulty not doing so. Despite his initial resistance, he now says that he accepts and even relishes this stereotypical looking practice as part of everyday life as a man (anonymous, 2006 interview). His new social position as a male, in other words, grants him permission to stare at breasts. Here then, the privileges of proper masculinity override the social proscription against staring.

When the expected meanings of a woman's breasts are not clearly decipherable, the sight of them can escalate to visual frenzy. Add to the controversy over public breastfeeding the fury over pop superstar Janet Jackson's fleetingly exposed nipple that 140,000,000 Americans gaped at during the halftime entertainment at the 2004 Super Bowl. The so-called Nipplegate controversy swirled around whether people were supposed to see Jackson's breast. It was an American spectacle: the public was outraged; the FCC launched an investigation; Jackson publicly asked for forgiveness for her inadvertent wardrobe malfunction; Viacom stock went way up. People debated the meaning, not so much of Jackson's nipple, but of our collective, momentary, astonished peek. Moreover, that startled stare defined the mythic cultural spectacle that is the Super Bowl. Those who argued that the Super Bowl is a wholesome American ritual that families share together were irate about Jackson's nipple while complacent about her edgy bump-and-grind performance. Jackson's apology reassured the public that nipples should remain a private resource in the patriarchal family, not a titillating girlie show.

By slipping into view, Jackson's nipple startled her viewers because it went too far beyond the expected visual tease of cleavage. Nipples are the ground zero of a breast's meaning, the sign that animates the breast's contradictions. Both child and lover lay claim to the nipple as a site of pleasure. But Jackson's nipple introduced a third claim. What people ogled was not a nipple presenting itself simply as maternal or erotic, but rather one marked as autoerotic. In full view was the nipple accoutrement that, Jackson had explained earlier on the Oprah Winfrey Show, provided her many pleasures as she moved through her day. The explicitly self-pleasing nipple scandalized by announcing that the pleasures of Jackson's nipple were hers alone. The significance of Jackson's stareable nipple intensifies further when layered with the racist and sexist history of black women's bodies. African-American women have been exploited for their sexual, reproductive, and domestic labor and stigmatized as sexual predators or docile servants. The sign of a black woman owning her own sexual pleasure was an unexpected sight at the All-American Super Bowl.[8] Jackson's nipple became a cultural touchstone—so to speak—for contradictory meanings of breasts.

For women, the visual significance of breasts is their magnetism. The female breast is for the male eye. Breasts are women's erotic capital. Dolly Parton, Jayne Mansfield, Jane Russell, and Carol Doda found wealth and fame by inviting men to stare at their breasts. Throngs of nameless belly dancers, strip teasers, beauty queens, porn stars, and fashion models strut their breasts for a living. What propels this visual avalanche of breasts is an assumed gendered division of looking, as we saw in chapter 6.[9] In short, the social role of men is to be starers, and the social role of women is to be starees. The breast acts as the cultural icon for this visual relation. The social ritual of breast staring reiterates two fundamental lessons for man. First, looking at breasts reminds man of what he is not. Second, looking at breasts reminds man that he can and must get what he desires. Starers see the iconic breast as abundant and available, but always only for others, not the woman herself. The erotic breast provides sexual pleasure for male starers. The maternal breast provides nourishment for the child. Breasts almost never belong to the woman to whom they are attached, but are either ornaments or implements for male viewing comfort, excitement, or mastery.

As a result, women often dissociate from their breasts or worse yet are alienated from them. They are not-me but for-another. And yet, the breast is a source of profound sensual pleasure for everyone. Nipples are made for mouths, and all of nature urges their coupling. For women, however, the pleasure of the breast is in the touching, the feeling—whether that touch comes from the body of the lover, the mouth of the baby, her own hand, or Janet Jackson's self-pleasing sex toy. For women to take pleasure in their own breasts, they must move breasts from sight to touch.[10] The public sighting of a celebrity breast hinting at its own tactile pleasures is not what American viewers expected to see on Super Bowl Sunday. Whether startled, stimulated, or outraged, Americans stared.

UNEXPECTED BREASTS

If we are indeed a nation of gawkers, as Neil Postman (1985) and others have argued, unexpected breasts are stareable sights that rouse satisfactions, discomforts, and ambivalences.[11] The endlessly presented image of breasts is at once titillating—so to speak—and monotonous. Even though breasts can invoke visual boredom or excitement, almost all public breasts look remarkably uniform. One day at the beach or a short visit to the women's locker room, however, will reveal the truth that women's breasts are as distinct as the features on their faces. This difference between public breasts and real women's breasts is where commercialism does its most profitable work. Women labor to create and maintain media breasts, using normalization aids that range from shaping garments such as brassieres, to exercise machines, implants, and surgical modification. They learn early on that having proper breasts is the ticket to the good life, and in some way they are right.

Not only do we expect breasts to appear in certain places and shapes, we expect breasts to come in matched pairs. Symmetrical, bilateral conjoinment is the signature of proper feminine personhood and breastedness. A lone breast seldom appears outside of the maternal context. A third breast, which is not uncommon and which may have been part of Anne Boleyn's undoing, was called a "witch's teat" and thought to be a sign of having consorted with the devil. The twoness of breasts contributes to its visual fetish as well. Cleavage announces the breasts, promises their charms, and invites starers to nestle. Alluring necklines catch eyes; the luscious notch draws the tongue—and it all promises thrills. Cleavage depends upon the mates on either side for its definition. When that landscape is disrupted, when the elements of the scene do not match expectations, we are visually aghast.[12] An unpredictable, unrecognizable breasted landscape shocks the eye because it is something we do not know how to see.

The divergence between the breasts we see and the breasts we have provided the breast cancer advocacy movement with an effective visual tool beginning in the 1970s.[13] The national breast-cancer movement has developed widely to include a political advocacy agenda of aggressive lobbying, rallying public support, creating awareness and early detection campaigns, demanding action and funds, speaking out, and founding organizations such as the National Breast Cancer Coalition and events such as Race for the Cure. The first visual element was to put influential breast cancer survivors such as Shirley Temple Black, First Lady Betty Ford, and Happy Rockefeller, wife of the vice president, on view to speak out. Before these women went public, breast cancer was unmentionable and certainly unviewable in public. Later, however, protest and aggressive public engagement edged out the ladylike approach to presenting breasts in public.

Women who had cancer began to bare their breasts by the late 1970s when the women's movement was most strongly pushing against institutionalized sexism. Breastlessness on view sharply violated what people had learned to expect of breasts. These women mobilized American staring behavior to demand that people pay attention to breasts in new ways. Staring forces people to reorganize their understandings, which was exactly what the breast cancer movement sought to do. The shocking sight of amputated breasts pulled the public eye toward political awareness. This use of visual novelty to focus public attention on a political goal was a forerunner to the displays of Sierra Leonians' amputated hands we saw in the last chapter.

Figure 10.2. Hella Harnid, "The Warrior." Copyright Deena Metzger. Distributed by www.donnellycolt.com.

The first stareable sight was the now familiar photograph by Hella Harnid called "The Warrior" which shows writer Deena Metzger with outstretched arms, baring her naked chest toward the sky in a triumphant gesture of exuberance (figure 10.2). She intended the picture to accompany her 1978 publication of *Tree*, the book based on the journal she kept of her breast cancer experience, but the publishers were reluctant. The poster, however, slowly gained circulation and recognition in women's circles after she published it herself. "Warrior" is now a classic image of the women's positive identity politics initiative that honors differences among women. Metzger's triumphant pose celebrates survival, but more, it celebrates breastlessness. In the 1997 edition of her book, the picture is on the cover.

A grimmer look at breast cancer attends to the medical experience of breast cancer treatment rather than survival. The self-portraits of English photographer Jo Spence, for example, call up stares to reveal the realities of breast cancer treatment. Many of Spence's photographic series blend documentary and portraiture to put the middle-age breast at the center.[14] The most arresting of these pictures document her ten-year experience of breast cancer, starting in 1982. Spence's huge, saggy, scarred, and asymmetrical breasts are the central focus of "The Cancer Project," "The Picture of Health," and "The Final Project" (figure 10.3). Spence's pictures resemble bad family snapshots or even mug shots. So far are hers from the usual pert and sculpted breasts that they unsettle. There is not a hint of the cover girl or centerfold. Instead of the generic erotic breast we are used to seeing, Spence is all particularity in these pictures. One image shows Spence's surgically targeted breast with a huge X, scrawled with labels such as "property of Jo Spence?" while another mimics a mug shot, with Spence holding a sign with the date printed on it just under her stark breasts. One portrait juxtaposes a scarred and shrunken breast with a face concealed behind a motorcycle helmet. In another, called "Marked up for Amputation," a huge white X-ed breast emerges from her robe as a grim-faced Spence, with tinted granny glasses, coldly stares back at her gawkers. The last of these sensational and ironic self-portraits is set in a hospice just before she died in 1992. In the tradition of edgy, radical art, Spence's photographs have an enthusiastic but self-selected audience. People have to come to see Spence's pictures, rather than the pictures coming to them.

In 1993, breastlessness showed up where no one expected to see it. That year, a flamboyant, fabulous-looking artist and model who calls herself Matuschka changed the way we stare at breasts. Matuschka has made a career of showing her body; she was a go-go dancer, lingerie model, and photographer who began by making pictures of herself nude among abandoned buildings. She is obsessed with documenting her own figure, particularly her torso. One might say that Matuschka is a professional staree. In 1991, a

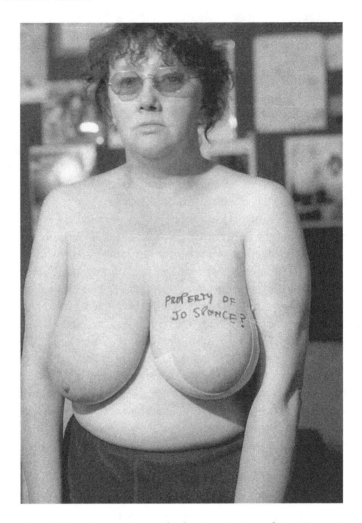

Figure 10.3. Jo Spence, Cancer Shock series. Courtesy of Terry Dennett.

cancer diagnosis and mastectomy forced her to reconsider her body, work, life, and mortality. With characteristic audacity, she continued making photo-biographic portraits, taking up the challenge of continuing to use her body to make beautiful pictures. Instead of luring eyes with a perfectly matched proper pair of breasts, however, these disquieting portraits compel astonished attention with a spectacular, jagged scar running half way across her chest where her right breast had been. In her post-mastectomy portraits, the stark center of interest gathers around a shocking scar that leaps out of the picture in loud contrast to the familiar stuff of the fashion shot or the smartly posed beautiful woman of art photography. Of the photographs, Matuschka says triumphantly, "now I can make art out of anything" (1993, 162).

Figure 10.4. Matuschka, "The New Deal" (1993), www.matuschka.net.

Matuschka did not simply now have a body that looked different from be-fore, but people looked at her differently from before. Her striking looks had always attracted stares, and her breasts had often been a destination for eager eyes. Her new body startled her spectators, and their responses startled her. She began to understand her photographs as "a new vocabulary of images" that gave breast cancer activism more than a face (Peterson 2003, 1). At that time, silence and invisibility shrouded breast cancer. There were no pink ribbons, walk-a-thons, talk shows, awareness campaigns, or Dr. Susan Love books—and almost no pictures of breastlessness. So she put together a se-ries of self- portraits called "Beauty Out of Damage" (figures 10.4 and 10.5). These photos flung into the public's face an image that had only appeared

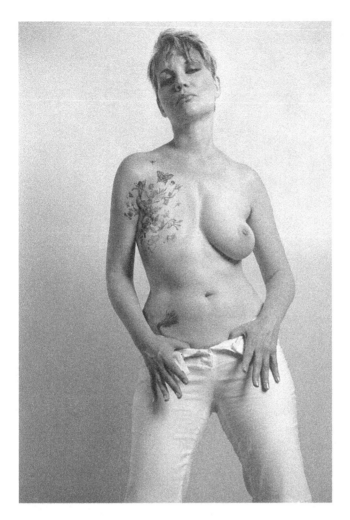

Figure 10.5. Matuschka, "Tattooectomy" (2003), www.matuschka.net.

in women's centers and activist offices. At first it seemed no one wanted to buy Matuschka's "honest photographs" (Matuschka 1993, 162). But then a writer for the *New York Times* saw the artist walking around a rally with her photographs hanging on her body like a sandwich sign and called her for an interview. In August 1993, one of the self-portraits from "Beauty Out of Damage" appeared on the cover of the Sunday *New York Times Magazine*, and Matuschka became what she calls "the first topless cover girl" in the emerging breast cancer movement (Matuschka 2005, 8; figure 10.6).[15] What distinguished Matuschka's single-breasted "Beauty" picture from Deena Metzger's earlier "Warrior" poster and Jo Spence's sensational photographs was simple: Matuschka was a fashion model on the cover of a slick, high-end

The New York Times Magazine

AUGUST 15, 1993

'You
Can't Look
Away
Anymore'

The Anguished Politics
Of Breast Cancer

By Susan Ferraro

MATUSCHKA,
ARTIST
AND ACTIVIST

Figure 10.6.   Matuschka, "Beauty Out of Damage" (1993), *The New York Times Magazine*.

news magazine. Whereas Jo Spence occupied the alternative realm of radical art photography, Matuschka beckoned stares from within a mainstream visual arena. With her high fashion portraits, Matuschka takes up the visual aesthetic tradition of the nude, whereas Spence captures nakedness with a hint of the tabloid. Matuschka made breastlessness a public spectacle that almost no one expected to see.

People stared. They had seen lots of lovely breasted women in the *New York Times*, but they had never seen breastlessness on such a woman. What we first see seems an unremarkable picture that follows the conventions of high fashion photography. A slender elegant model strikes a chic pose, face in a sophisticated profile, head stylishly turbaned, full front torso with a plunging, off-the-shoulder white gown. The image gains some drama from a not-so-subtle allusion to the goddess Diana. But there, at the literal heart of the picture, is a purplish scar snaking across the place where we expect to see the soft globe of a breast. The picture is stunning, in both senses of the word. It arrests by fusing expected with unexpected, familiar with strange. The unholy visual union of a very sightly figure and a very unsightly scar invites us to look.

Matuschka's at once gorgeous and shocking image drew more than stares; it also pulled in hundreds of letters to the editor at the *New York Times*, as well as a rush of television, radio, newspaper, and magazine interviews, personal phone calls, hate mail, and love letters to Matuschka herself. Some called it "embarrassing," "disgraceful," or thought it exploited suffering for "shock value" (Matuschka 1993, 162). Breast cancer survivors, whose response Matuschka most wanted, generally praised the photograph for making their reality visible, putting forward here to be seen the body that matched their own. Many women responded negatively, however, feeling that the picture violated their privacy, that "what they really looked like" was now exposed to the stares of everyone. Others worried that the shocking revelation of Matuschka's appearance would turn women away from mammograms and treatment. The photograph stirred a conversation about the scandal of ignoring breast cancer by insisting that breast cancer happened and that people should do something about that.

Matuschka's picture stokes anxieties about cancer—but also about staring. The headline printed over the photograph on the *New York Times Magazine* taunts: "You Can't Look Away Any More." That exposed wound and the unexpected difference of her body make people awkward starers in spite of their mothers' injunctions. She forces everyone to look hard, not so much at what we do not want to see, but that at which we are not supposed to stare. To see a wound where we expect a breast demands not just attention, but an explanation, a new reality. That we cannot look away anymore occasions a moment of political ripeness that breast cancer advocates have harvested particularly effectively. Unwavering stares at Matuschka's scar are a kind of upscale rubbernecking. The gut response may be horror, fascination, or stimulation, but the eye response is baroque staring. That stuck look is the raw material of political activism.

Matuschka's portrait on the cover of the *New York Times Magazine* was in a way a turning point for breast cancer advocacy, which has evolved an entire culture of visual symbolism, ranging from ubiquitous pink ribbons to intricate tattoos adorning mastectomy scars. In 2000, for instance, The Breast Cancer Fund, a San Francisco-based nonprofit organization dedicated to research and education, mounted a public awareness campaign called "Obsessed with Breasts" (figure 10.7).[16] The campaign put up three

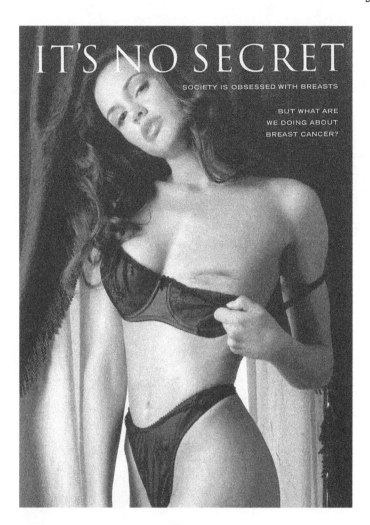

Figure 10.7. Obsessed with Breasts, Breast Cancer Fund Campaign.

different posters in public bus shelters and on building walls. One poster looked like the cover of Cosmopolitan magazine; another simulated an ad for a Calvin Klein perfume line called Obsession; the other replicated a Victoria Secret catalog cover. Instead of the expected visual offering of usual breasts, however, these models boldly flaunted scars. This campaign pushed Matuschka's cover girl image toward politicized parody. Not unlike Janet Jackson's autoerotic breast, these images provoked controversy and roused political protests over what constitutes acceptable and unacceptable looking at women's breasts.[17]

Switching out the ceaselessly circulated erotic breast for startling scars snags eyes by fusing two opposing visual genres: the pinup girl and the medical photograph. The medical subject would have been posed with slumping and resigned posture and a black rectangle covering the eyes; the pinup would have been properly cleavaged. The cognitive confusion intensifies our impulse to resolve the contradiction between these divergent expected sights. By mocking the sensationalism of both kinds of images, these pictures protest against the refusal of contemporary America to literally and figuratively look at breast cancer.

A perhaps even more novel sight than breastlessness appeared in London's Trafalgar Square in September 2005. A statue called "Alison Lapper Pregnant" was unveiled to the curious eyes of the public gathered for the momentous occasion (figure 10.8). This much-anticipated and controversial statue by the British sensationalist artist Marc Quinn was selected to occupy the Fourth Plinth, a public spot of honor that had been vacant for 150 years in a public space dominated by the towering memorial to Lord Nelson, Britain's one-armed famed war hero. Quinn's realistic portrayal of a nude, pregnant woman—which won over proposed statues of both Nelson Mandela and the Queen Mother—stirred up disagreements about what ought to be seen in public.

Figure 10.8. People watch as British artist Marc Quinn's white, thirteen-ton statue inspired by artist Alison Lapper, who was born with no arms and shortened legs, is unveiled in central London's Trafalgar Square, Thursday, September 15, 2005. Lapper posed naked for Quinn when she was eight months pregnant, in what the artist says was a tribute to motherhood and people with disabilities. The sculpture remained in place for eighteen months (AP Photo/Lefteris Pitarakis).

Viewers' responses to "Alison Lapper Pregnant" ranged widely, judging it as "indecent," "confrontational," "repellent," "ugly," and "beautiful" (Jury 2005; Leitch 2005). One observer wrote in a letter to a newspaper that there was "discomfort with the subject matter" (Olsen 2004). The statue's sculptor, Marc Quinn, offers an insight as to why people stare at his statue. Quinn asserts that most public sculpture is "invisible" to most people because it is such an unremarkable sight. "Alison Lapper Pregnant," however, is "vexingly visible." Quinn says that his statue makes people "see things that are there." In other words, it invites them to stare because it is something novel they do not expect to see. "That's why people are outraged by it," Quinn concludes (Darwent 2005).

A fifteen-foot high white marble nude woman on a pedestal is not uncommon among works of art. But to publicly memorialize a pregnant belly flanked with its heavy breasts presents a radical view of womanhood. Pregnancy, like mastectomy scars, is a usually hidden aspect of women's bodies. A look at "Alison Lapper Pregnant" jolts you with this visual juxtaposition between the familiar female nude and the rarely displayed pregnant woman. "Alison Lapper Pregnant" gets people staring, however, for more than just the unexpected trio of the heavily fecund belly and breasts naked in Trafalgar Square.[18] Surrounding the realistic representation of Alison Lapper's seldom-exposed but still ordinary torso is that of her actual, very unusual set of limbs. Lapper is armless and has shortened legs ending with singularly shaped feet.[19]

Lapper's marble portrait does similar cultural work to the picture of Matuschka on the cover of the *New York Times Magazine*. The venue, pose, medium, and context of both representations are familiar and legible to viewers: one is a white marble nude statue in a public square; the other a high fashion magazine cover shot. Embedded in these ordinary sights, however, are forbidden sights, the sort that would elicit a mother's "don't stare!" These hybrids of the to-be-looked-at and not to-be-looked-at create a stareable scene. They demand baroque staring, that intensely interrogative looking in response to startling visual novelty.

New sights ask new questions that can lead to new understandings. What Matuschka's picture asks is how what we have learned to think of as beauty—the ideal woman—might be crosshatched by what we think of as ugly—a scar replacing the breast. What "Alison Lapper Pregnant" asks is how a woman with significant disabilities merits being seen in Trafalgar Square with national heroes such as Nelson, how she might be sexual, and how she might be fit to parent a child. Viewers may come to these public sights with often unacknowledged ideas that the kinds of bodies such as Matuschka and Lapper have are somehow disqualified from womanhood. The cultural work of these images is to make us look at them long enough to change our minds. We may be discomforted, moved, outraged, enlightened, or offended. But we cannot look away any more.

RECOGNITION

If staring has done its work, the next time people see such bodies, they will be familiar, if only vaguely. When the visual novelty that sparks stares subsides, the bodies that life has given Matuschka and Lapper can be recognizable as belonging to the human spectrum. In other words, these representations put the distinctive details of these women's bodies in people's faces until they get used to them. The individual shapes and marks of these bodies bear witness to human variation, to the way our particular life etches itself onto our bodies. This work is the potentially mutually revivifying aspect of staring encounters.

Recognition, according to the political philosopher Nancy Fraser (2003), is essential not simply for individual self-realization but, more important, is the cornerstone of an ethical political society. Recognition is "an ideal reciprocal relation between subjects in which each sees the other as its equal and also as separate. . . . [O]ne becomes an individual subject only in virtue of recognizing, and being recognized by, another subject" (2003, 10). Implicit in Fraser's concept of political recognition is that persons be seen as they are, as particular individuals embedded in their own lives. To be recognizable a person must appear as distinct from a generic, generalized figure. To be recognized is to become familiar, no longer strange, to be seen and accorded the status of fellow human. Recognition, then, relies on a combination of identification and differentiation. The trajectory of recognition is this: I recognize you by seeing your similarity and your difference to me, and then I make your strangeness familiar. In other words, I see you as you are.

But all too often we see each other not as we are, but as we are expected to be. This misrecognition disparages or ignores a person's "distinctive characteristics," according to Fraser, which "prevent[s] one from participating as a peer in social life" (2003, 29). What's wrong about misrecognition is that it is unjust.[20] Misrecognition is a form of discrimination that Kenji Yoshino (2006) terms "covering." People of racial, ethnic, and sexual minorities, as well as people with disabilities, often try, according to Yoshino, to meet dominant group expectations by either minimizing or hiding the visible markers of their subordinated status. In other words, they mute their "distinctive characteristics," the ones Fraser calls to be recognized in an ethical society. This is why, according to Yoshino, blacks might straighten hair, the blind wear sunglasses to hide their eyes, or the unusually shaped get reconstructive surgery. This is also, to return to an earlier example, why Sergeant Doyne sometimes wears a "normal" hand. These appearance adjustments help quiet stigmatization and provide civil inattention, but they also invite misrecognition.[21]

Covering, in Yoshino's sense of the term, is an escape from stares. The problem with covering our distinctiveness is that it forfeits recognition. By literally refusing to cover themselves, Metzger, Matuschka, Spence, and Lapper provoke recognition by making themselves stareable sights. They initiate a feminist activist tradition that performance poets Cheryl Marie Wade and Lezlie Frye follow in baring their unusual hands. Moreover, these visual revelations rebuke the cover-ups of padded bras, falsies, implants, cosmetic prostheses, or baggy clothes. One particular cover-up they challenge are breast prostheses, which are an expected response to mastectomy. The self-proclaimed "warrior poet" Audre Lorde writes in *The Cancer Journals* of being urged toward a prosthetic breast so that "nobody'll ever know the difference" (1997, 42). Lorde rejects the prosthesis, not for its look, but for its feel. She elects sensation over appearance, concluding that the prosthesis is "awkwardly inert and lifeless, and having nothing to do with me . . ." (44). Facing herself in the mirror after her surgery, her new body makes her stare at herself: "I look strange and uneven and peculiar to myself, but somehow, ever so much more myself, and therefore so much more acceptable than I looked with that thing stuck inside my clothes. For not even the most skillful prosthesis in the world could undo that reality, or feel the way my breast had felt, and either I would love my body one breasted now, or remain forever alien to myself" (44). Lorde expresses in words here what Metzger and Matuschka convey in pictures.[22] These women exchange the visual anonymity that an artificial breast affords for the same opportunity Lorde seeks in refusing to cover: to "come to terms with their own pain and loss, and thereby, with their own strength" (49). The exposed bodies of the women who bare their breasts cover the reality of all our distinctive bodies. What breast cancer advocates and the larger disability rights movement wants is not simply stares but recognition, not separated but engaged stares. To look hard is potentially to recognize that devalued human variations do not diminish but testify to our humanness.

11

Bodies

Here I am! Take a good look!
—Peter Dinklage, *The Station Agent* (2003)

SPECTACULAR BODIES

Perhaps the most spectacular form of visual novelty that can prompt stares are breaches of the common human scale and shape. Characters with unusual forms and sizes abound in our folktales, literature, art, and material culture. Diminutive creatures such as dwarfs, elves, fairies, gnomes, goblins, hobbits, imps, leprechauns, and Lilliputians, for instance, have large roles in our shared stories. These miniature versions of average sized people range from delightful to spiteful, from Santa's Elves, Munchkins, Brownies, Rumpelstiltskin, Thumbellina, Snow White's Seven Dwarfs, Dickens' Tiny Tim and Quilp, Shakespeare's Puck, to Poe's Hop-Frog. On the more threatening side of unfamiliar size are the enormous creatures such as giants, cyclopses, dragons, ogres, titans, and trolls which stretch through cultural myths from the classical to contemporary. Atlas, Prometheus, Goliath, Leviathan, Swift's Brobdingnagians, Rabelais' Gargantua, Paul Bunyan, Bigfoot, King Kong, The Jolly Green Giant, the Incredible Hulk, and Shrek overwhelm our attention with their impressive scale. The miniature delights and titillates, for the most part. We have a few gentle giants, but mostly the exaggerated scale of our imaginary giants thrills or terrorizes.

Mythical creatures often look stranger yet in their forms. Homer's giant Polyphemus, for example, was a man writ huge with a single eye in the center of his forehead. Similarly, the ferocious dog Cerberus who guarded the gates of the underworld had three heads. Frankenstein was a man made up of dead body parts. A profusion of hybrids that merge humans and beasts enliven narratives across cultures as well. The fusion of a human body with a bull, fish, horse, lion, snake, goat, wolf, bird, or elephant give us Minotaurs, Mermaids, Centaurs, Sphinxes, Medusas, Satyrs, Werewolves, Gargoyles, Angels, and Cherubs, as well as gods such as Bast and Ganesha. The extraordinary size and shape of these creatures dazzle eyes and fire imaginations.

EXTRAORDINARY SCALE

Simply changing the ordinary scale of any object makes it visually novel. Making familiar things unfamiliar opens them up to new meaning—and to stares. A good example of this comes from contemporary artists who use scale violation to distort realism. The effect of Roy Lichtenstein's comic book paintings depends in part upon their enormity. Claus Oldenburg and Coosje van Bruggen's monumental outdoor sculpture of a spoon and cherry as big as a bridge or their huge circular eraser expand familiar objects into something novel. Christo's enormous drapings and wrappings stretch our conception of modest domestic coverings. Diminutive scenes in public gardens and theme parks such as Disneyland attract even more visual attention when they are populated by adorable humanlike mice or chipmunks.

Anything that looks too big or small assaults our sense of what is proper. "Scale," Susan Stewart observes, "is established by means of a set of correspondences to the familiar" (1984, 46). The large and the small mutually define one another. Their ocular punch comes from contrast to the ordinary. David becomes a plucky little underdog, for instance, only in relation to Goliath's hulking enormity. The verb *dwarf* means to make smaller by comparison. With this scale relationship come all of the associations of the enormous and the miniature. The miniature represents order whereas the enormous represents disorder. The miniature invites stewardship and appropriation whereas the enormous inspires fear and awe. The miniature is charming where the enormous is sublime. The miniature feminizes while the enormous masculinizes. As principals, the enormous acts as container and the miniature acts as contained. The effect of scale relies primarily on visual perception. Familiar things made diminutive or gigantic distort our sense of a stable reality. In the face of these juxtapositions, what counts as typical slips away. Moreover, viewers are themselves in scale relation to what they see. Seeing scale violation distorts our sense of our own proportions. The gigantic dwarfs us and the diminutive makes us gigantic. We can experience ourselves in new ways in the presence of these unfamiliar sights. Whether these scale violations delight or frighten, our eyes respond to these novel sights (figures 11.1).

Figure 11.1. "The Tom Thumb Wedding Group" (1865), Ronald G. Becker Collection of Charles Eisenmann Photographs/Special Collections Research Center, Syracuse University Library.

EXTRAORDINARY SHAPES

Whereas violations in scale give us figures such as giants and dwarfs, violations in shape give us monsters. Monsters are unusually formed beings whose bodies are simultaneously ordinary and extraordinary. The visual strangeness of monsters increases when atypical scale augments unusual form. Gigantic monsters, for example, become more threatening and diminutive ones more charming. Cultural representation tends to exaggerate even more the differentness of monsters. The use of caricature furthers distances these already unreal figures from actuality. Disney movies, for example, render the skin and hair tones of their hybrid creatures in vivid colors. Illustrations of these figures in books are usually elaborately rendered. So too, endless collectible figures such as trolls and winged ponies attract consumers with appealing pastels, bright colors, or bold patterns. Features distorted in shape and size attract further attention. Exaggerated eyes and lashes suggest cuteness, or huge hands suggest simple minds.[1]

The long history of monster and freak shows offers the most florid example of how and why people look at dissonant shapes and scales. These shows are publicly staged staring encounters that use extraordinary bodies to challenge the human need for order and certainty.[2] Unusual and inexplicable bodies have been on display in royal courts, street fairs, dime museums, sideshows, and sensational media. Monstrous bodies were a particular type of prodigy—similar to comets and earthquakes—which drew great attention and inspired awe. Early travel writers such as Marco Polo and Mandeville and early men of science such as Ambrose Paré scrutinized unfamiliar bodies as marvels.[3] Monarchs kept *Wunderkammern*, or cabinets of wonder. From its first usages in English in 1300, the word *monster* meant a rarity, an unusual occurrence in the natural world that invited interpretation and challenged common understandings of what was predictable and ordinary. The word *monster* is related to the word *demonstrate*, meaning to show or reveal through looking. The whole vocabulary of *marvel, prodigy,* and *wonder* describing extraordinary bodies faded into vagueness when staring at disabled people came to be considered bad taste.[4]

Whereas monsters were prodigious wonders in the ancient world, freaks were profitable performers in the developing commercial economy of the last several centuries.[5] The term *freak* has also been unmoored in contemporary times from its original meaning. *Freak* meant whimsical or capricious rather than today's concept of abnormal. Freaks were public displays of novelty that drew viewers who gladly paid to stare. A freak merited staring because it bore evidence of "nature's sport," God's infinite capacity for mysterious surprise, or simply inspired delight. The shows exaggerated unusual bodies through costuming, staging, props, and hyperbolic narrative. For example, what we now consider the medical skin condition vitiligo, gave promoters the act of Spotted Boys. People with giantism and those with dwarfism or other forms of restricted growth appeared posed together to highlight their differences. One promotional photograph for a female giant, for a example, juxtaposes an otherwise average looking woman suited up in a gown next to an ordinary woman over whom she towers and amply outsizes (figure 11.2). A fat man and a human skeleton, both dressed in tight fitting outfits to accentuate their form, pose in another example as a boxing couple.

We must now get our most spectacular visual novelty mostly from images rather than actual unusual bodies. In the last two centuries, medical science moved many startling bodies from the public eye into laboratories, operating rooms, and medical clinics.[6] The study of monsters became the science of teratology, discussed further later in this chapter, which established the borders of normal and abnormal, transforming wonders into pathological specimens.[7] Medical treatment, surgical normalization, prenatal testing, and selective abortion now actually eliminate many would-be marvels or freaks. Nevertheless, some of the intractably unusual or inexplicably passed over slip still into contemporary tabloids, talk shows, or films.

Figure 11.2. "Amalie-Giantess," Ronald G. Becker
Collection of Charles Eisenmann Photographs/Special
Collections Research Center, Syracuse University Library.

Techniques that produce, reproduce, and disseminate images now sup-
plant most of the live staring encounters the shows previously provided.[8]
The advent of photography in 1839 moved much public staring to the private realm of Victorian photo albums, ephemeral advertisements, or later
the work of photographers such as Diane Arbus or Joel Peter Witkin, who
place unusual bodies in art galleries rather than on stages.[9] The entertainment industry now gives us bionic action figures such as Terminator and
Star Wars creatures instead of live freaks and monsters. Contemporary
charitable institutions, which have always displayed people with disabilities,

now use television telethons and advertising campaigns to put unusual bodies in the spotlight.[10] As the history of monster and freak shows suggests, staring encounters between extraordinary and ordinary people are always in some sense staged, even theatrical; moreover, the visual etiquette that squelches stares in our contemporary day-to-day life has eviscerated the extravagant dramas of staring that these shows mounted. Nonetheless, dramatic staring exchanges ignited by novel scale and shape still lurk persistently in the mundane world.

SHAPE AND STORY

Spectacularly shaped and sized creatures such as giants, dwarfs, and monsters offer up theatrical staring encounters where ordinary humans can escape the mundane. The folk tales, myth, fantasy, and science fiction they inhabit take common-seeming folk to a phantasmal world where the rules do not apply. As novelty embodied, they staunch ennui and vivify blunted perceptions. We seem ordinary to ourselves, almost regardless of our own shape and size. Yet by staring at figures with extraordinary scales and forms, we become strange to ourselves. In stories, these creatures seem wholly imaginary, exaggerated to the point of being impossible. All are a breed apart from the familiarly human, like us enough to engage us yet different enough to unsettle us.

What is less recognized is that these mythical creatures are elaborations on infrequent, yet regularly occurring, actual human beings. People that we now diagnose with a range of medical conditions have throughout history served as models for fantastic giants, dwarfs, and monsters. Medical diagnoses reconceptualize spectacular characters such as Giants, Lion Faced Women, Lobster Boys, and Armless Wonders into cases of acromegalia, hypertrichosis languinosa, ectrodactyly, and limb deficiency. When people who are the living referents of imaginary giants, dwarfs, or monsters enter into our visual field, they interrupt what Susan Stewart calls the "conservatism of everyday life" (1984, 18). This tendency toward convention, repetition, and predictability that characterizes the familiar world provides the unremarkable landscape we inhabit most of the time. The sight of a radically unusual body provokes cognitive dissonance, perhaps not so much because of what the bodies themselves look like but because they disrupt the placid visual relation that we expect between foreground and background. Psychologist Len Sawisch explains that people need to manage an enormous amount of available sensory stimulation. They do this by filtering out visual sameness and directing their attention to "dissonance," "incongruity," and "differentness" (Sawisch quoted in Kennedy 2003, 61). Something seems either too big, too small, too much, or not enough as people try to make sense of the seeming incongruity presented by unusually embodied people. The jolt of pleasurable dopamine this "differentness" provides arrests their eyes to stay the task with determination.

Here staring takes on its storied quality. As we saw in the case of Kevin Connolly in chapter 7, only an explanation of the extraordinary sight will end our baroque stares, allowing us to sink back into an unruffled routine visual landscape. Caroline Walker Bynum (1999) elegantly formulates this relation between vision and narrative by observing that "shape structures story" ("Shape and Story"). Bynum says, "[S]hape or body is crucial, not incidental, to story. It carries story; it makes story visible; in a sense it is story. Shape (or visible body) is in space what story is in time. . . . Identity is finally shape carrying story." Bynum's understanding suggests that different shapes require different stories. Conservative shapes make conservative stories. Extraordinary shapes require extraordinary stories. The quotidian world has embroidered certain minority forms of embodiment into bestiaries and grotesqueries through which it marvels, scares, or ponders itself.

These stranger- or larger- or smaller-than-life tales can overwhelm the realities of the actual people whose bodies have given rise to these stories. Thus, our unusually shaped fellow humans can often blur into these creatures for whom they are the human referents. We see people with restricted growth, for example, through folk legends of curmudgeonly dwarfs under bridges or Disney versions of Snow White and her diminutive singing entourage. Tales of Goliaths bested by regular fellows and of plucky boys climbing beanstocks to conquer giants mold conceptions of very large people. Our notions of monsters come from horror stories designed to frighten.

In this way, story structures staring. The sight of living people with unusual bodies invites us to remap fantastic stories of giants, dwarfs, and monsters onto those people. People who look like dwarfs, giants, and monsters draw stares because they are unfamiliar as flesh and too familiar as narrative. Often lost in this exchange is a sense of the particular lives and looks of the people whose shapes have across history given rise to these stories. The people who inhabit such bodies are misfits in the literal sense of the word. Their unexpected bodies do not fit into a world built for others. Somehow their lives got set on the wrong stage, so that often their stories are as compelling as their sight. The cultural imagination thus ever threatens to thrust those who are too large, too small, or too irregular outside of the circle of common humanity.

GIANTS

Giants in our world exist within such staring stories. Take the example of Robert Wadlow, the tallest man in recorded history. Born into seeming ordinariness to a farm family in Alton, Illinois in 1918, Wadlow's growth soon exceeded all expectations, as did the attention his size garnered. First, the neighbors began to notice. "And still they gazed and still the wonder grew," one florid biography notes (Fadner 1944, 18). Wadlow eventually grew close to nine feet tall and weighed four hundred pounds. No one thought to track his growth until his scale began to be considered extraordinary, but by the time he was nine years old he was taller than his father; at twelve he was twice as large as other children. As he became enormous, accounts of his amazing size—such as his size thirty-seven shoe and his weight at age fifteen of 355 pounds—abounded (figure 11.3). All of the many images of him show him with people or objects of typical scale.

A medical condition made Wadlow grow large, but staring made him into a Giant. In his youth, he was big but led an ordinary life. He was a Boy Scout, worked on the high school yearbook, joined the YMCA, and aspired to be a lawyer. By the time of his death at age twenty-two, however, he had given himself over to his starers. He toured eight hundred towns in forty-one states promoting the company that provided him with free shoes. A perpetual target of photographs, he showed himself in theaters and town squares, commanded huge crowds, and appeared at least once in a circus. Eventually, his only role in life was to be seen. The preface to his 1944 biography, *The Gentleman Giant*, claims that "thousands of people who saw Robert Wadlow for the first time looked with wild eyes upon him and could hardly believe their senses when they actually saw a perfectly harmless giant smiling kindly down upon them . . ." (Fadner 1944, 5). He became a startling sight to even his familiars, so that by 1936 even his own father "looked up and saw the most astonishing sight of his life" as he walked down the street of Alton, Illinois (Brannan 2003, iv). People eagerly offered up accounts of having seen him. His appearance dominated his livelihood and most all of his relationships. Wadlow patiently endured endless photo stunts such as ordinary men trying to reach a five dollar bill placed on the top of his head or poses of his starers next to a real Giant. After his death, the town of Alton erected a life-size bronze statue as a memorial to Wadlow. The statue continues to offer his fellow citizens an invitation to stare so as to thrill at his enormity and contemplate their newly miniature size.

Perhaps the most stareable giant in America is Eddie Carmel, who enters the public eye by way of Diane Arbus's famous photograph called "Jewish Giant at Home with His Parents in the Bronx, N.Y., 1970." As with Robert

Figure 11.3. Robert Wadlow. Courtesy of Alton Museum of
History and Art.

Wadlow, being stared at became Eddie Carmel's life. Carmel tried to earn a
living as a staree by making horror movies, recording silly songs, and ex-
hibiting himself in carnival sideshows. Ill health compromised his career,
however, and he died at age thirty-six in 1972. According to a radio documentary narrated by Carmel's cousin, Eddie's life had two difficulties. First
was that his body would eventually grow so large that his organs could no
longer maintain it. Second was that his body had outsized its world. His size
literally diminished everything around him, from furniture, implements,
clothes, to coffins. Not only could his body not support itself, but the world
around him could not support his body.

Arbus's renowned photograph of Carmel captures this visual dissonance between body and world. In doing so, the scene that Arbus's photograph stages makes Carmel into a Giant. Next to his diminutive and perplexed parents, squeezed into the cramped living room whose ceiling menaces his head, Carmel overwhelms the space. The picture induces visual vertigo with its hyperbolic scale violation. This family portrait throws into chaos the familiar domestic scene of mother, father, and their child. The surprising reversal of the huge child next to his tiny parents violates our expectations. Novelty here comes from the juxtaposition of elements rather than the elements themselves. If considered separately, father, mother, sofa, curtains, lamps, chairs—even Eddie by himself—are the unremarkable stuff of a domestic scene. This jarring family portrait holds our eyes by showing us what is both recognizable and at the same time unrecognizable. Evidently Carmel himself understood the contextual nature of his giantness. His aunt reports that Eddie used to laugh and say, "Isn't it awful to have midget parents? Why did you have to happen to me? My luck, I have to have midget parents" (Abramson 1999). The permission to stare that the Carmel family portrait grants is in part what makes Diane Arbus's photographs discomforting and controversial. Perhaps it is less the Jewish Giant himself that unsettles viewers, but rather more their own urge to stare at this startling disruption of the ordinary world. Yuben Yee, photo librarian at the MOMA during an exhibition of some of Arbus's early prints in 1965, called this invitation to stare the "direct and primitive" gaze of Arbus's photographic style. "She stripped away all artiness, which the public wasn't used to," Yee explained. In doing so, Arbus creates an opportunity to see the strange as mundane and the mundane as strange, which both attracts and repels viewers (Bosworth 2005, 234–235). As a memorial to Eddie Carmel, Arbus's famous photograph accomplishes somewhat different cultural work from the memorial statue of Robert Wadlow in Alton, Illinois. The statue of Wadlow makes him a giant and invites viewers to be miniature in his presence. The photograph of the Jewish Giant makes Carmel a giant and his parents midgets. The difference in effect between the two images, then, is that Wadlow's statue makes us small, whereas Arbus's photograph makes us starers.

The relics of giants, like those of saints, are sought after as stareable remnants that call up the wonder of the vanished extraordinary body. Like postage stamps with errors, rarity makes valuable any material traces giants and other very unusually embodied people leave behind. Carmel's family was able to sell many of his possessions, especially clothes, to a sideshow collector after his death. In contrast, Wadlow and his family refused to circulate his relics. After his death, his mother destroyed most of his possessions and blocked exhibitions about him at the Alton Museum until after her death in 1980. Wadlow himself, along with his family, worried about possible desecration of his body and skeleton by collectors, both medical and commercial. Unusual bodies and their visible vestiges attract stares whether their bearers are alive or dead. Medical museums around the world have and still do display bodily relics of celebrated and often exploited people with unusual bodies. Some of the most notorious are Eng and Chang Bunker, the original Siamese twins, whose autopsy was performed at the Mutter Museum in Philadelphia, and Sara Baartman, the famous Hottentot Venus, whose 1815 caricature image we saw in chapter 3, and whose remains were once displayed at the Museum de l'Homme in Paris and have now been repatriated to her native land.[11] To ensure that Robert Wadlow would not be caught up in this tradition, his family arranged for him to be buried in a concrete bunker (Brannan 2003).

These men's shapes structured their stories. And their stories took shape through staring. They lived within stares because they had no other place to live. They were never visually anonymous except perhaps to a few very familiar people. The unsought and often uncivil attention that their size aroused apparently incapacitated both Carmel and Wadlow, not necessarily because it made them feel bad but rather because it made moving through the world of human action and relations almost impossible. Both men were described as exceedingly sensitive and gentle, which could be a reasonable response to constant stares or perhaps a counter to the truculent giant role. Carmel's aunt noted that he "did stand out in a crowd, you couldn't help but take another look and he was aware of it and it bothered him, terribly" (Abramson 1999). The attention their bodies drew was so intense that they existed primarily in the frozen moment and isolated space of a stare. The staring even shaped family relations. Self-pity evidently plagued Carmel's father, and Wadlow's mother dedicated her life to defending him from stares. Stares called them from the mundane world into a hypervisible space where actual people cannot live out ordinary lives. Apparently, the stares that made Wadlow and Carmel such giants did not yield a validating recognition but rather the spectacle of their giantness overran their stories.

DWARFS

Actual human giants are fragile and, therefore, few. Dwarfs, on the other hand, are a sturdier lot. Because people considered too small and too large are routinely normalized through medical treatment nowadays in the developed world, most of the gigantic or the very tiny people who in the past made their living as starees are no more (Rothman and Rothman 2003). Nevertheless, people with restricted growth diagnosed in such categories as chondrodystrophy, achondroplasia, or many other unalterable conditions comprise a significant physical minority in the world today. Yet even this particular minority is under significant threat from prenatal selection and eugenic abortion, making those who remain perhaps an even more novel sight.

As with giants, mythical narratives precede people of short stature and structure how most ordinary people see them. The sight of a real-life dwarf can call up predetermined reactions. Recognizing people with small stature takes place for most of us through a filter of shared stories inhabited by dwarves caricatured from sentimental and cute to grotesque and vengeful

Figure 11.4. "Drinking in Style," January 1, 1943. Shorty, the "Bowery Cherub," celebrates New Year's Eve at Sammy's Bar, in the Bowery district of New York. (Photo by Weegee [Arthur Fellig]/International Centre of Photography/Getty Images.)

(figure 11.4). The sight of a person with restricted growth can also trigger curiosity over the mechanics of how such short people manage ordinary tasks such as reaching their beer at the bar or getting something down from the top shelf.[12] The default understanding, however, is to think of small people as children and treat them accordingly (Ablon 1984). One father who has dwarfism, for example, finds that children, especially friends of his young daughter, stare in an effort to think through what seems to them the paradox of a gray-bearded father figure who is also their size. Their stares hold the question, he feels, of how he can be both child and adult at the same time (anonymous, 2006 interview). Shared cultural assumptions regarding proper scale and shape turn short-statured people into figures of contradiction to the eye of an ordinary starer. As this father experienced, stares mark him as socially illegible.

The critically acclaimed 2003 independent hit film, *The Station Agent,* presents a powerful dramatization of how one short-statured staree manages the tedious indignity of stares and the narratives they put upon him. The film tells the story of an otherwise ordinary man named Finbar McBride, played to great acclaim by actor Peter Dinklage. With this virtuoso performance, Dinklage upends the conventional use of short-statured actors as what he calls "sight gags" (Banks 2003). In the story, McBride is a quiet trainspotter who inherits a small train station from his boss. This film's main plot involves a friendship among three outsiders, through which each flourishes.[13] Many shots of McBride also include the perpetual starers around him, whom he generally ignores. He actively refuses the role of staree by simply declining to acknowledge stares. The film suggests that while such a strategy protects McBride's dignity by short-circuiting all staring encounters, this stare management guards against spontaneous engagement and helps make him reclusive and lonely. *The Station Agent* provides one scene in which McBride does confront his starers, however. In a testosterone-charged barroom full of bold gawkers to whom this small man is a conundrum, the sensitive Fin, animated with drink, reverses his earlier approach and dramatically demands stares. The scene recalls the famous moment in *The Best Years of Our Lives,* discussed in chapter 9, when war veteran Homer Parrish emphatically taunts the tormenting children with his prosthetic hands. In *The Station Agent,* McBride leaps up on the bar, spreads his arms wide and shouts, "Here I am! Take a good look!" He then climbs down and walks disgustedly out the door. In other words, McBride shifts his strategy from refusing stares to engaging them as a way to publicly shame his starers for their intrusive curiosity and their cowardly furtive stares. His ringing self-assertion, "Here I am!," at once exposes them as starers and commands that they recognize him as he is, as distinguished from them by his stature but bonded to them by shared manhood (figure 11.5).

Figure 11.5. Peter Dinklage in *The Station Agent.* Photograph courtesy of Miramax Film Corp.

In contrast to Fin McBride's hostile evocation or rejection of stares, the short-statured performer Tekki Lomnicki creates a very different invitation to stare. Lomnicki is a little woman who has made a career of her paradoxical appearance. A successful actor and director, she is cofounder and artistic director of Tellin' Tales Theater. Lomnicki earns her living by offering entertaining performances and her own unusual body up for contemplation, much like several of the other stareable disabled performers we considered in earlier chapters. "On stage . . . ," she says, "my disability works for me . . . being so different looking, people really take notice . . . people really get it. On the flip side, my disability works *against* me as a performer in that I'm most likely not going to be cast in the female romantic lead," but rather in "the circus performer stereotype." Although she does both comic and dramatic roles that refer to her size, she seeks and supports nontraditional casting as well as. Of small-statured actors, she says, "We need to keep going out there for conventional roles until people start to see us for who we are: everyday people who go to work, drive cars and have kids—not just someone in a Mickey Mouse costume" (Lomnicki and Benz 2000–04).[14] Lomnicki explains that she appears to be a visual conundrum. She considers herself very attractive and dresses well; at the same time, she is three-and-one-half feet tall and uses crutches. She presents her starers with a contradictory figure that fuses scripts of the pretty, fashionable woman and the stereotypical crippled dwarf. Lomnicki plays up her role as a staree with stories. She likes to tell about being stared at as if she were "some sort of goddess" by an African dignitary in a Chicago department store. When she goes round the corner and is out of sight, the African asks Tekki's companion, "What tribe is she from?" Lomnicki does indeed perform her unusual size and shape as if it were a form of ethnic identity. She displays herself in unusual costume and in character to her curious audiences. Her charismatic flamboyance, however, seems intended to delight rather than to estrange. Lomnicki's method is to evoke engaged stares from her audiences, to seduce from them a charmed stare that is open to interaction and recognition. Although her strategy differs from Fin McBride, her performances every bit as strongly assert "Here I am! Take a good look!"

Figure 11.6. Riva Lehrer, *Circle Story #2: Tekki Lomnicki,* 1999, acrylic on panel, 48 in. × 36 in.

A portrait of Tekki Lomnicki painted by Riva Lehrer sums up Lomnicki's particular invitation to stare (figure 11.6). The painting portrays the persona she crafts for her starers, every detail of which highlights her distinctiveness. Lehrer depicts Lomnicki in bold planes and colors that put forward a solid, sturdy woman with a strong personality. She hunkers solidly amid a scattering of brightly patterned, discarded clothes she has strewn about herself during a charmingly careless toilette. Interrupted in media res, she smiles out engagingly as if to the paparazzi. Comfortable with such exposure, she greets her starers dressed in a sexy and sweet white slip, shiny black Mary Janes, and one arm crutch, its partner tossed amongst the pile of outfits. Buxom, lipsticked, coiffed, feminine, and substantial, Tekki Lomnicki is mistress not victim of the stares she draws and the world in which she lives.

The story of the Ovitz Family offers a grimmer instance of the complicated relations between starers and starees. A troupe of Jewish musicians and entertainers from Transylvania, the Ovitzes were a sophisticated and successful group of second-generation performers by the time they were deported to Auschwitz in May 1944. At the center of this large and extended family entertainment business was the Lilliput Troupe, composed of the seven short-statured Ovitz siblings. All ten Ovitz children were born of a short-statured father and two different average-sized mothers. Perla Ovitz, the last survivor of the Lilliput Troupe, gives an account of the family's time at Auschwitz (Koren 2004; Rozen 1999). On the infamous train platform at Auschwitz, Josef Mengele, the Nazi doctor who scrutinized arriving prisoners to evaluate their fitness, saw the seven short-statured Ovitzes and selected them for special treatment in his camp laboratory where he conducted experiments on inmates. Mengele was particularly interested in collecting twins and people with dwarfism for his pseudoscientific experiments in eugenics and heredity. It was the appearance of the seven siblings, then, that saved them from the usual immediate gassing that awaited the majority of new arrivals and almost all people with disabilities who came to Auschwitz.

Mengele was obsessed with staring at the Ovitzes, according to Perla. During their time at Auschwitz, the Ovitzes evidently performed several roles as starees for Mengele. Perla tells that he called them to entertain him with their musical performances, photographed them naked as scientific specimens, looked at them as droll pets, and paid visits to their rooms. They wore lavish clothes and stayed in special quarters with miniature furniture. The Ovitzes functioned as Mengele's court jesters, accorded a perverse celebrity because they amused him. They were exempt from beatings, roll calls, and forced labor. Their special torture, however, was the knowledge that they would all be killed at Mengele's will when he was finished with his experiments. Almost all of his human specimens were in fact killed as part of Mengele's experiments, to make them into forensic specimens, or because they were no longer valuable. As with most unusually embodied prodigies who went before them, the seven Ovitz siblings were just as valuable dead as alive to their starers. Remarkably however, all ten siblings survived until liberation, including at least thirteen others who the Ovitzes claimed as relatives. They returned to entertaining after the War and immigrated to Israel in 1949, where they performed successfully until their retirement.

In the documentary film *Liebe Perla*, the aged Perla Ovitz expresses her ambivalence about this chilling relationship with Mengele. He alone, she acknowledges, was responsible for their survival, a fact about which she is guardedly grateful and deeply distrustful. They were protected as novelties, not as human beings. Their bodies were of great interest and value to him, but not their lives. She realizes the impersonality and narcissism of that gesture. Being stareable, marked by the visible differences of disability, was at once their redemption and their damnation.

Tekki Lomnicki and Perla Ovitz, along with her siblings, follow in a long tradition of unusually small entertainers who went before them. Egyptian court dwarfs were indulged and exchanged. Diego Velázques' painted portraits of renowned European court dwarfs. Probably the most famous small statured celebrity was P.T. Barnum's General Tom Thumb, perhaps the most photographed American of the nineteenth century. Public figures ranging from Alexander Pope to Henri de Toulouse-Lautrec either reluctantly or explicitly traded in their own diminutive stature (Adelson 2005). As recently as 2000, a fifty-five-year-old Haitian woman known as "Tiny Tasha" displayed herself on the midway at the Maryland and Virginia State Fairs (Frey 2000, C1). The actress Linda Hunt won the Academy Award for best supporting actress in 1982 for her role as the Chinese male dwarf photographer in the film *The Year of Living Dangerously*. Hunt's artful performance firmly established her as a serious, first-rate actress who is cast widely both with and against her small stature.[15]

Perla's Auschwitz story of staring certainly complicates any easy celebratory interpretation of the dwarf performances short-statured people have put forward. The Nazi doctor was clearly more than a simple audience for the Ovitz family. They were his prisoners, and he had the power of life and death over them. Yet apparently their visual novelty drew him to them. His fascination played out through two different yet oddly complementary ways of looking at the Ovitzes. One was a scientific stare, Foucault's clinical gaze that sought pathological evidence of their supposed degeneracy. Perhaps equally intense may have been a baroque engaged stare that responds to the novel performance of novel bodies. That Mengele had the power and probably the intention to eliminate the Ovitzes turns both of the ways he looked at them into dominating, hostile stares. Medical science looks at the particular shape and size of people like the Ovitz siblings as a form of pathology. Staring through such a lens at people of short stature can produce a particular kind of hostile stare that might be called a eugenic stare. The eugenic stare is a perverse form of recognizing human particularity in order to extirpate it. The received narrative that shapes the eugenic stare is the recent story that tells us that the human variations we think of as dwarfism should be eradicated from our human community.

Although we of course cannot know most of these people's motivation or the degree of co-optation involved in their self-display, it seems clear that Tekki Lomnicki and Perla Ovitz—like David Roche, the Schappell sisters, Mary Duffy, or Matuschka—intentionally cultivate the inevitable stares their bodies draw as an opportunity for self-determination, expression, art, and a good livelihood. By embellishing their stage personae, often with flamboyance and always with dignity, they turn common starers into appreciative audiences. Both of these women embrace the conventions of feminine performance with relish, adapting these scripts to the particularities of their bodies. In *Liebe Perla*, Perla is a vibrant, aged beauty of eighty whose wheelchair, small stature, and frailty are oddly congruent elements of her resplendent personae. Theatrical and elegant, Perla costumes herself in red satin and rhinestones for the camera lens. A consummate entertainer, she sings, smiles, and charms as she tells her tale of Auschwitz.

MONSTERS

Authentic monsters are born, never made. Today's high-tech, pop-culture monsters such as King Kong, Yeti, and Mummies may thrill or frighten, but they cannot match the visual novelty of a living monster. Historically, a monster was an animal or human born with a deviation from type, or a so-called "congenital malformation." In the nineteenth century, the science of teratology studied born monsters and worked toward producing animal monsters. In the twentieth century, teratology has shifted toward genetics, a science dedicated to preventing monsters. Modern medical science shifted the understanding of monsters from wonder to error, from message to mistake (Garland Thomson 1996). With this change, looking at human monsters moved from street to laboratory, from stage to asylum. This inclination to sequester rather than display born monsters changed who and how ordinary people saw monsters.

To the typically bodied, perhaps the most unsettling monstrous beings are conjoined twins. This very rare form of embodiment challenges what we take as a fundamental aspect of humanness: our separateness. A mid-eighteenth-century book on midwifery lays out this distinction between single and conjoined, "When two children are distinct they are called twins," but they are "monsters, when they are joined together" (*Oxford English Dictionary*, s.v. "Monster"). Monstrous as it may seem, conjoinment is a recognizable albeit rare form of human embodiment that occurs regularly throughout history. Everyone knows about conjoined twins, but few have seen them. Nonetheless, all humans share an experience of conjoinment: even though people live most of their lives as singletons, the universal experience of human gestation is one of conjoinment. Continued conjoinment, however, seems so intolerable that when possible, conjoined twins are surgically separated, despite a risk of significant mutilation or death for one or both twins.[16]

The most startling forms of conjoinment are probably those that most violate singleton form. Twinning that commingles, redistributes, or reshapes standard bodily configuration upsets our sense of proper personhood. The shared faces of Lori and Reba Schappell that we saw in chapter 8, for example, drew stares of amazement. One of the most spectacular forms of conjoinment to the singleton eye is what medicine terms *dicephalic* twinning. In this form of conjoinment, monozygotic twins share a single lower body and legs, often including a trunk and arms. They have separate upper bodies and distinct heads. The number of arms varies from couple to couple. Most of these twins have two sets of internal upper body organs such as hearts and one set of internal lower body organs. Because these conjoined twins are so rare, most people's understanding of them comes from stories or images. Figures such as the sideshow's "two-headed monster" haunt the way the ordinary world sees dicephalic twins. While families of conjoined twins often must contend with their children's health problems, another challenge is managing how to present their children to the world outside their family.[17]

The way one family managed the increasing stares focused on their conjoined twin girls offers an opportunity to more fully understand staring dynamics. Abigail and Brittany Hensel are healthy dicephalic twins born in 1990 into a previously undistinguished Midwestern family. The family vigilantly protected the girls from the eyes of world outside a close circle of family and community for the first several years of the girls' lives. When Abigail and Brittany were six years old, the family brought the girls out before the public view on the pages of *Life Magazine*. The choice to introduce the girls in this magazine structured the way people would see and understand them. *Life Magazine* was as far from a sideshow as the family could get. Known for decades as a venue for the best journalistic and art photography, *Life* was a popular, general interest magazine that told the story of America through photographs from the Great Depression through the Vietnam War. *Life* featured the Hensel twins in its revived monthly incarnation during the 1980s and 90s that emphasized nostalgia for the wholesome bygone era in which its photographs defined the character of American life and identity. The romance of national commonality, decency, and simplicity which animated the images in *Life* made it the perfect venue to work against the sensational entertainment narratives of monsters and freaks that defined the lives of most of the people in history who looked like Abigail and Brittany.

The Hensel twins' emergence from their domestic haven into the wider world was a carefully crafted invitation to stare. The 1996 *Life* article is a photo essay accompanied by a text that is no more than a set of expanded captions.[18] Readers get to know Abigail and Brittany by seeing them rather than reading about them. All of the ten photographs of the girls going about their six-year-old lives convey the central message of the article's title, "Two Sisters Together Forever: the Ordinary Life of Extraordinary Twins." The black-and-white photographs capture typical family scenes of the girls learning to ride a bike with Dad, playing with their siblings in the unfinished basement, collaborating in tying their sneakers, saluting the flag in their school room, reading stories together, and going to swim lessons with Mom. There is a snapshot from the family photo album of the girls having their first bath. The cover photo is a tender cameo portrait done in soft pastels of Brittany gently kissing Abby on the cheek. Every image reaches toward the sentimental and avoids the sensational.

The pictures of the Hensel twins are unremarkable but at the same time unnerving. They fuse unexceptional sights with extraordinary ones. The sweet scene of Brittany kissing Abby's cheek, for example, also reveals the merging of their two distinct necks into a single pair of shoulders and one chest. One of the less posed shots shows cute girlish outfits that have two turtlenecks and two sleeves. The familiar bike riding lesson becomes unfamiliar as the two little-girl legs support the top-heavy twins. Family, schoolmates, and teachers in the photographs seem for the most part not to notice what to readers is an astonishing sight. Indeed, the pages of *Life* magazine invite stares more than they show stares. In the community of more than twenty-five potential starers featured in the magazine's ten pictures, there is only a single starer. This compositional choice certainly makes the girls seem more ordinary. Perhaps more important however, not having to see other starers can serve to soothe readers' anxiety over the guilty pleasure of staring.

The sole scene of staring in the *Life Magazine* feature sprawls across two pages and is the visual heart of the article (figure 11.7). The story of staring it tells reveals some of the logic of how we look. The photograph is theatrical in the sense that it is filled with characters, action, and drama. The scene is a community pool during lesson time, where everyone watches someone else in the

Figure 11.7. Steve Wewerka, Brittany and Abby Hensel, *Life Magazine,* 1996.

absorbing business of learning and teaching swimming. On the pool's edge, the children wait their turn to leap into the water toward the expectant instructors. Parents idly look on. The boy who is up next concentrates on getting it right as the teachers inspect his form. The real drama, however, takes place at the end of the line of kids where you would not expect anything special. The shivering kids dawdle, waiting their turn. The little boy nearest the pool's edge glances over his shoulder to the fellow swimmer behind him. There, a few feet back, he sees Abby and Brittany, their two arms folded over their shared chest, comforting and warming each other, standing in the comportment of the cold and wet, their two feet planted solid and drippy on the wet tile floor. The six eyes of these three children are locked together in a mutual stare of recognition. The boy sees the girls. The girls see the boy seeing them. The boy sees the girls seeing him see them. The mouths are solemn and expressionless. Their eyes express the dynamics of the encounter. For him it is new; for them it is old. His surprised stare says that he has never noticed them before. Their placid looks suggest that they are used to notice. There is a sense of the momentary in this exchange of looks, a suggestion that the staring encounter cannot hold. His stare is intent yet ephemeral. But more important is the look that the girls return: Abigail and Brittany are staring back, but without rebuke or hostility. In their six-year-old eyes is a calm, constant insistence on their own humanity. The scene suggests that the boy's sharp interest must soon give way to the tasks of the swim lesson.

Yet in this moment of engagement caught by the camera, the girls have stood their visual ground, inviting their new friend to look away and return his concentration to swimming, unnerved less by their confusing bodies and perhaps dimly or even explicitly aware that they are all peers.

The swimming lesson is a transitional staring space, one of neither complete visual anonymity nor total visual familiarity. Because the lesson gathers its community regularly, many of the actors have moved through staring toward knowledge while others have not. For people who come often to the lessons, the unexpected bodies of the dicephalic twins have become the expected and accepted Hensel girls. The teachers have clearly moved from arrested stares to engaged stares. They seem to see the girls not as an assault to the order of things, but rather as a teacherly opportunity to foster human adaptability. Their job, their look implies, is to help the Hensel twins learn to swim. This scene of staring also hints that perhaps more than just swimming, everyone has learned a fuller range of ways to look at each other.

This snapshot of staring suggests that by six years old, the Hensel twins have become accomplished starees. They have already acquired the sophisticated skills they need to manage their starers. Becoming a staree is like learning another language: the earlier you do it the better you are at it. The foreign language of staring management is at once visual, gestural, and interpersonal. Staring, like language, is an interchange, for while staring is often an unintentional physiological impulse, responding to a stare is usually the staree's deliberate decision. The look starees return can range from a mind-your-own-business command to a generous lesson in tolerance and empathy. The structuring cues a staree directs to a starer can range from the feigned obliviousness Fin McBride initially uses in *The Station Agent* to the hostile command McBride issues to his barmates toward the end of the film to the explicit invitation to stare that people such as Tekki Lomnicki offer in their performances. The swimming lesson photograph presents a more subtle staring encounter, one in which starees do not simply endure or encourage stares but instead adeptly preside over the startled eyes of the world into which they were born.

PART VI

A Last Look

BEHOLDING

> It's not that I'm ugly. It's more that most people don't know
> how to look at me.
> —Harriet McBryde Johnson in *New York Times Magazine*,
> February 16, 2003

AN ETHICS OF LOOKING

We all stare. Sights that stimulate our eyes—the magic show extravaganza, the burning Towers, the twisted cars on the freeway—lead to wonder, horror, or just thrills. When we stare at one another, as we have seen, things get more complicated. We are all potential starees as well as starers, and between people, staring is a communicative gesture. Between strangers, staring is uncomfortable, especially the intense, prohibited, baroque staring that does not disguise itself. That discomfort can be positive, however, rather than oppressive. A stare is a response to someone's distinctiveness, and a staring exchange can thus beget mutual recognition, however fleeting. In this way, how we look at one another can be a productive aspect of our interpersonal, even our political, lives. If all this is so, then the question for starers is not whether we *should* stare, but rather *how* we should stare. The question for starees is not whether we *will* be stared at, but rather *how* we will be stared at. As a productive, albeit volatile social relationship, staring necessarily brings with it these ethical dilemmas.

The cultural critic Susan Sontag (2003) takes up the question of whether and how we should stare in her last book, *Regarding the Pain of Others*.[1] The book considers the ethics of looking at photographs of suffering, hurt, or dead bodies. For Sontag, staring is a one-way dynamic, in part because she is considering photographs rather than lived interactions but also because she is concerned about the ethics of looking rather than the ethics of being looked at. She evaluates whether we ought to be looking at what she broadly takes to be other people's suffering and ponders how we should respond when we do look.

What Sontag considers these "repulsive attractions," of course, are exactly sights that most attract stares (96). The intense attraction to such scenes, the compelling human impulse to stare at them, is for Sontag an "unworthy desire," which she condemns (96). Her thinking is in line with the familiar American disapproval of staring as inappropriate looking—as visual intrusion, a surrender to the sensational, or unconstrained, voyeurism. Sontag sees "the attraction of mutilated bodies" both in lived experience and in photographic images as unseemly. Viewing human pain, she insists, particularly from the distance that images and anonymity involve, is "a prurient interest" that should be in all of us a "despised impulse" (95, 97). Staring is an ethical violation, Sontag concludes, because it is motivated by "curiosity," which is only worthy if tempered by "reason" that quashes any "voyeuristic lure" (96, 97, 99).

Even though Sontag maintains that the urge to stare at human pain, death, and disability is a "despised impulse," she nonetheless claims that staring can be redeemed by a proper response. Accordingly, she lays out a model of good and bad staring—in other words, of how and when we should stare. Bad staring satisfies supposedly salacious curiosity and leads to the ethical dead end of schaudenfreude, of taking satisfaction in someone else's misfortune. For Sontag, looking at photographs of human pain is bad if our interest in them affirms that "This is not happening to *me*" (99). This response kindles indifference and complacency born of feeling secure and produces an unethical "passivity." Bad staring, in short, is inadequate identification between starer and staree. Rather than responding with this-could-be-me, a bad starer concludes this-cannot-be-me. Bad staring fails to make the leap from a place of discomfort, shock, or fear toward empathic identification. This unethical stare, in other words, is looking without recognizing, a separated stare that refuses to move toward one's fellow human.[2] To use Martin Buber's (1958) language, bad staring is all I and no Thou.

Good staring, Sontag suggests, reaches out. So the "unworthy desire" to look hard at "repulsive attractions" can be transformed into an ethical relation if it is mobilized into political action. If starers can identify with starees enough to jumpstart a sympathetic response that is then "translated into action," staring turns the corner toward the ethical (101). It would be unethical, then, to gawk in the checkout line at shocking pictures of human mutilation and grotesqueness on the cover of the *National Inquirer*. Yet the same pictures in the *New York Times*, at a thoughtful art exhibition, or in a documentary film—contexts that ask for political engagement— could produce good staring. The shocking pictures from Sierra Leone of amputated hands that appear in the *Washington Post*, the stark photos in a medical textbook, or the amputee beggar on the street corner may rivet eyes equally. But only one that has the capacity to move us to volunteer our time or to petition Congress rather than recoiling and forgetting is ethical. The stareable sight is the same; the response, however, is different. Ethical action is the provenance of starers in Sontag's account of separated and engaged staring encounters.

But what of living and breathing starees? In *On Beauty and Being Just*, Elaine Scarry (1999) augments Sontag's ethics of looking by realizing the object of stares have an active role in an encounter. Intense looking, Scarry claims, initiates an interactional "compact" between a perceiver and a perceived object of beauty (90). Whereas Sontag contemplates what horrifying images do to starers, Scarry ponders how beautiful objects affect them. For Scarry, beauty, like the "repulsive attractions" Sontag contemplates, is a stareable sight that attracts attention and demands engagement. It is not that beauty attracts us per se but rather that by attracting us something becomes beauty.

Scarry's compact between starer and staree is not static but collaborative. Beauty is what beauty does. Staring at beauty, according to Scarry, generates social justice.[3] Beauty is a perceptual process and a transitive action: it catches interest, prompts judgment, encourages scrutiny, creates knowledge. Being seized by beauty conveys "a sense of the newness of the entire world" (22). Even though a thing of beauty might be mundane in another context, its reception renders it extraordinary. In other words, beauty is novelty at work. Scarry's theory of beauty's work also inadvertently helps us understand how baroque engaged staring might work. Beauty, she says, catches you unprepared and provokes unexpected wonder, a reverential awe lost from our modern, disenchanted world.[4] An encounter with beauty is epiphanic, drenched in knowledge-producing narrative drama. Openness to beauty, she concludes, "is the basic impulse underlying education" (7). Looking at beauty generates social justice, Scarry argues, through moving its perceivers toward active "stewardship" of everyone's opportunity for access to beauty. Staring at beauty animates people to extend equity to fellow humans. This is exactly the "action" Sontag expects from good staring at bad pictures. One might say that such staring works to preserve the distinctiveness, the novelty, that animates the staring encounter.

Although Sontag discusses looking at "repulsive attractions" and Scarry at "beauty," together they offer a model with which to consider staring encounters. Scarry's concept of beauty is capacious; a sight becomes beautiful by doing the work of beauty. This understanding suggests that the unbeautiful is the unremarkable, the unnoticeable. We can conclude, then, that the capacity of both "beautiful" and "repulsive" attractions to make us look is similar and has comparable ethical potential. We become ethical starers by being conscious in the presence of something that compels our intense attention. What gives such attractions power in these formulations is their capacity to vivify human empathy through bearing visual witness. In other words, Sontag's and Scarry's accounts suggest that the impulse to stare at novel sights, whether we understand them as conventionally beautiful or repulsive, can move us toward recognizing a "newness" that can be transformative. These stareable sights disturb not just the visual status quo but the ethical status quo as well. Crucial to these interactions, this book asserts, is the role of the staree in the encounter.

SEEING RARE BEAUTY

Many starees we have considered find themselves in the uncomfortable position in a staring encounter of being someone's idea of what Sontag calls a "repulsive attraction." As we have seen, they have developed in response a range of strategies for directing staring interactions. The late disability rights lawyer, activist, and storyteller Harriet McBryde Johnson used media and public appearances to coach the public eye to see her distinctiveness according to her own story rather than the one they may have learned about people who look like her.

"It's not that I'm ugly," Johnson begins in the February 16, 2003, cover story of the *New York Times Magazine*, "It's more that most people don't know how to look at me" (52). With this edgy, yet understated flourish, Johnson begins a story of looking that illustrates how an ethics of staring might work. The photograph of Johnson on the cover shows her seated in her wheelchair, a surprising pose for a cover girl. Boldly beneath her picture sits the unsettling question that Johnson herself poses for many readers: "Should I Have Been Killed at Birth?" The inexplicable combination of this picture, this venue, and this question is startling. With the *New York Times* as her stage, Johnson gathers up starers and proceeds to show them "how to look."

> The sight of me is routinely discombobulating. The power wheelchair is enough to inspire gawking, but that's the least of it. Much more impressive is the impact on my body of more than four decades of a muscle-wasting disease. At this

stage of my life, I'm Karen Carpenter thin, flesh mostly vanished, a jumble of bones in a floppy bag of skin. At 15, I threw away the back brace and let my spine reshape itself into a deep twisty S-curve. Now my right side is two deep canyons. To keep myself upright, I lean forward, rest my rib cage on my lap, plant my elbows beside my knees. Since my backbone found its own natural shape, I've been entirely comfortable in my skin. (52)

In this description, Johnson takes charge of the staring encounter that began with her cover photo. She accounts for her unusual body, casually, even chirpily, letting us know what "happened" to her. The seeming contradiction between "four decades of a muscle-wasting disease" and the fact that she is "entirely comfortable in [her own] skin" (52) already disturbs our shared understandings of what it means to inhabit a body. Her compelling what-happened-to-you story makes what most of us would consider harrowing into an ordinary experience:

> I am in the first generation to survive to such decrepitude. Because antibiotics were available, we didn't die from the childhood pneumonias that often come with weakened respiratory systems. I guess it is natural enough that most people don't know what to make of us . . . Two or three times in my life . . . I have been looked at as a rare kind of beauty . . . some people call me Good Luck Lady. (52)

In this passage, Johnson continues to undermine complacent understandings by advancing yet another set of contradictions. Following the unlikely partnership of "disease" and "comfortable," comes "decrepitude" and "beauty." This "beauty," however, is not ordinary but "rare" in several ways. First, it is a beauty seldom recognized, only "two or three times in [her] life." Second, it is fragile and infrequent; she is one of the few survivors, not only of "childhood pneumonia" but potentially from the threat of being "killed at birth." Finally, this "rare beauty," this not-ugly, is distinct from typical beauty; it has a form and logic of its own, much like the unconventional beauty Doug Auld's portraits of burn survivors presents.

In showing us how to look at her, Johnson retells our shared story about beauty (figure 12.1). This is a novel beauty made of an elegant "twisty S-curve," of "deep canyons" in unexpected places. Hers is baroque beauty: irregular, exaggerated, and peculiar. Such "rare beauty" is hard to see, both difficult to look at and to appreciate. Like Sontag's pictures of pain, it is hard not to read Johnson's looks as an image of suffering or an occasion for pity or horror. Johnson's picture is hard to see as well because most of us lack the skills to properly appreciate the way she looks without her guidance. If we learn from her how to look, we may come away knowing how to recognize "rare beauty" when we see it again. If Johnson's story succeeds, the wide audience of *The New York Times* may be moved toward a kind of conservation campaign to

Figure 12.1. John Madere, portrait of Harriet McBryde Johnson (2005).

value and save from extinction the "rare beauty" Johnson has showed them how to appreciate.

The possibilities for misrecognition, of seeing "ugly" where there is "beauty," are perpetual. When strangers catch sight of her, "most often" she reports, "the reactions are decidedly negative" (52):

> Strangers on the street are moved to comment:
> *I admire you for being out; most people would give up.*
> *God bless you! I'll pray for you.*
> *You don't let the pain hold you back, do you?*
> *If I had to live like you, I think I'd kill myself.* (52)

What people usually see, Johnson suggests, is unbearable pain, insurmountable adversity, a diminished life, and a fervent desire for a cured body. Johnson's starers bring with them these usual kinds of stories when they encounter the unusual sight of someone like her. Similarly to the way she showed her starers how to look at her, she proceeds next to show them how to imagine her life:

> I used to try to explain that in fact I enjoy my life, that it's a great sensual pleasure to zoom by power chair on these delicious muggy streets, that I have no more reason to kill myself than most people. But it gets tedious. . . . they don't want to know. They think they know everything there is to know, just by looking at me. That's how stereotypes work. They don't know that they're confused, that they're really expressing the discombobulation that comes in my wake. (52)

What makes people who see Johnson "confused" and "discombobulated" is perhaps not so much how she looks but instead how she ended up on the cover of the *New York Times Magazine* rather than on a telethon, a medical textbook, or begging on the street corner. How could she say, "I enjoy my life"? This is not a life most people would claim to enjoy.[5] Johnson has the kind of body and the kind of life that people have learned is a sentence of suffering. She is the kind of person that genetic or prenatal tests screen out for elimination, whose feeding tube gets removed, or mostly who no one wants to become. And yet, with a closer look at her picture, you see fondly plaited long hair in a lovely, dark rope that winds across her slender shoulder. She wears those chic Chinese Mary Janes on feet that will never touch pavement. She is dressed in a flowing, gypsy outfit that hints at an artistic, sensual soul. She looks pretty hip, in her own way. This shot, upon closer look, feels much like the usual fashionable photos on the cover of magazines. In fact, with help from her story, a scene may begin to emerge of her enjoying "great sensual pleasure" zooming around "delicious muggy streets." The power wheelchair in which she seems so comfortably settled perhaps enables rather than confines. Maybe she does not have any reason to kill herself, after all.[6]

Johnson's tutorial on looking is no etiquette lesson about not staring at people with disabilities. Instead, she puts forward an invitation to stare and skillfully crafts its effect, much like other starees we have seen in this book who with great skill show their starers how to look at them. By confronting the readers of the *New York Times* with what they have learned to see as an unlivable life, she tells the story of a livable life—indeed, an enjoyable life of rare beauty.[7] She moves her audience from what they do not expect to see to perhaps expecting to see people like her again. In other words, she gets them accustomed to looking at her by making herself more familiar than strange, by bringing her life story closer to their own. By getting them to see her as unremarkable in her distinctiveness, she makes it possible to identify with her own aliveness, which as she tells it, seems pretty much like theirs. By both showing and telling her experience as if it were ordinary, Johnson reaches toward the work of Scarry's beauty and Sontag's good staring. If Johnson's approach succeeds, the staring encounter she stages will shift her audience from curiosity to knowledge. She will turn them away from arrested stares and set them on a path toward empathetic identification. To use Sontag's and Scarry's terms, she will rescue them from the "repulsive attraction" of bad staring and offer them an opportunity to enact social justice.

By staging strategic staring encounters that teach her audience a new way to look at her, she enables them to recognize her full humanity, to stare without stigmatizing. Understanding that people with stareable bodies can have livable lives contributes to a larger ethical goal of accepting and accommodating devalued human differences. Intolerance for human variation, Michael Ignatieff argues, is an unintended consequence of the "liberal experiment," which fostered sameness as a measure of equality (1997, 66). To counter this intolerance Ignatieff calls for "a polity based on equal rights with the full incorporation of all available human differences" (69). By putting forward what in political terms might be termed her minority embodiment, Johnson asks for recognition of her "differences," her rareness, as distinctive beauty rather than damning deviation. By looking at her closely, they can know her life as she knows it, not as they have learned to imagine it. In showing her audiences that she is not really "ugly," she undertakes the social justice work of "beauty," so that they might recognize "the newness of the entire world" (Scarry 1999, 22). This is her modest offering, then, to making ours a more equitable and inclusive world.

Johnson forges her particular contribution to social justice by using the expertise she has gained as a lifetime staree. One story she tells suggests how she, together with her family, developed staring management techniques. Here for example she describes learning to turn away unwanted stares and to meet them with wry humor:

In public places, I am stared at so routinely that I typically don't notice it. . . . I do notice when it goes from staring to gawking or more active interaction. A gawking experience I remember as being particularly egregious was when I was 18, going through a crowded museum with my mother. In front of me was a girl, maybe 9 years old, who was actually walking backwards to gawk at me. My mother spoke to the parents: "Your daughter thinks my daughter is the most interesting thing in the museum." The parents grabbed her by the arm, "Come on Gayle, don't stare!" She turned, but 3 seconds later she was gawking again. The parents hollered "Come on Gayle," a couple more times, but then gave up. The aisles were too narrow for us to put space between us (my mother was behind me, pushing my chair), so we had to go through the whole exhibit with this backwards-walking child. It became a family saying for a while, whenever a child was staring: "Gayle's here." (2006 interview)

The skill set Johnson developed learning to manage the many "Gayles" in her life gives her a deep understanding of the way staring works and what it might accomplish. Johnson brings that expertise to her staring project in the *New York Times*. Like a fading language with only a few native speakers remaining, this knowledge is endangered. The picture Johnson presents of herself recommends that we conserve such rare beauty. Deeply settled in her wheelchair, charismatic rather than cute, ironic rather than pathetic, self-assured rather than suffering, Johnson answers the cover's provocative question: "Should I Have Been Killed at Birth?" This is what a life worth living looks like.

VISUAL ACTIVISM

By putting themselves in the public eye, saying "look at me" instead of "don't stare," people such as Matuschka and Johnson practice what might be called visual activism. In 1993 Matuschka exposed her scars and commanded "You Can't Look Away Anymore" to make the public accountable for knowing the reality of her body. Ten years later Johnson presented herself on the same *New York Times Magazine* cover to make the public accountable for knowing that people like her can flourish in their own distinctive way. In doing so, these twin cover girls put to work a three step process of visual activism: look, think, act. First, they use the human urge to look at new things to make people look at them. Second, they use the way they look, the way we look at them, and what they say about it to ask the public to think differently about people like them. The last step depends on their starers' receptiveness. If their visual politics of deliberatively structured self-disclosure succeeds, it can create a sense of obligation that primes people to act in new ways: to vote differently, to spend money differently, to build the world differently, to treat people differently, and to look at people differently.

The risk of all activism is that it will not make this last leap from intent to effect. The intense attentiveness of staring, however, might be particularly supple and effective raw material stareable people can invoke to influence others. To do their work, Matuschka and Johnson appropriate the model of lived face-to-face visual interactions between starers and starees. In other words, the women take what they know from life about how people look at them and go public with it on the pages of *The New York Times Magazine*. They draw on the can't-take-your-eyes-off-it quality of visual engagement, or what we have called baroque staring, that drives starers to keep looking and stay interested. Using a picture and story, they freeze the spontaneous face-to-face relation, expand it to a wide audience, and deliberately direct their starers' responses.

In contrast, lived staring encounters are pliable interventions that respond to the immediate needs and aims of both starers and starees. Stares can be broken off, turned away, continued, softened, or hardened as the participants move through the encounter. An experienced staree, as we have seen, often can take the lead, but a starer must be willing to follow, to stay with the staree if the interaction is to generate any mutual recognition. Because staring strives toward knowing by reducing unfamiliarity, if it is not short-circuited, it can be coaxed toward transformative interaction through the kind of deft management Johnson demonstrates so clearly in her staged staring encounter and starees often practice in their day-to-day lives. The cultural critic bell hooks describes the potential of intense visual interpersonal interaction as a conduit to relations of mutual equality. According to hooks, "eye-to-eye contact, the direct unmediated gaze of recognition . . . affirms subjectivity" (1992, 129–30).[8] To use the language of political philosophy put forward in chapter 10, "the look of recognition" hooks calls for constitutes us as equal citizens and equally legitimate reciprocal participants in the public sphere. To be shut away through segregation or to cover up devalued human differences thwarts opportunities for this recognition. To be recognized, one needs literally to be seen.

In other words, what begins as simple staring, a visual groping toward a new and stimulating sight, has the potential to enact something akin to what psychologist D.W. Winnicott (1965) calls the holding function.[9] To be held in the visual regard of another enables humans to flourish and forge a sturdy sense of self. Being seen by another person is key to our psychological well-being, then, as well as our civil recognition. Staring's pattern of interest, attention, and engagement, the mobilization of its essential curiosity, might be understood as a potential act of be-holding, of holding the being of another particular individual in the eye of the beholder. Staring as beholding is a way to bring visual presence to another person, to recognize fully their "distinctive characteristics" (Fraser 2003, 29). The affirmative recognition visual activists stage is the ethical looking Sontag (2003) calls for and what Martin Buber (1958) describes in theological terms as the face of God in the face of the other. The work of a beholding encounter would be to create a sense of beholdenness, of human obligation that inheres in the productive discomfort mutual visual presence can generate. The radical besiegement of both starer and staree in such an intense visual interaction holds an unexpected opportunity for generating mutual new knowledge and potential social justice. This is an act of generosity, of political and interpersonal leadership, that starees offer starers.

This kind of visual engagement that stays steady when the sight gets uncomfortable is an often deliberate and sometimes inadvertent activist strategy

Johnson and many other stareable people invoke every day in order simply to go about their lives with dignity.[10] Starees such as David Roche, Lori and Reba Schappell, Theresia Degener, Lezlie Frye, Mary Duffy, Cheryl Marie Wade, Brittany and Abigail Hensel, Tekki Lomnicki and many others teach starers how to look at them. Often without intention, stareable people, whether performing or just out on the street, reduce the unfamiliarity that the segregation of people with visually significant disabilities like theirs has created in the general public. Now that civil rights legislation has removed many barriers to equal access, people with disabilities are entering and being seen everywhere, from transportation, commercial spaces, employment to the political arena. The public venues for the very stareable have expanded from sideshows to all parts of public life. In contrast to the early decades in the twentieth century when the sight of President Franklin Delano Roosevelt in the wheelchair he used every day was hidden from stares, the sight of public figures who are openly disabled has changed the visual landscape of the public sphere. We now see and recognize as people with disabilities, for example, political figures such as Senator Max Cleland, the late Congresswoman Barbara Jordan, Congressman Jim Langevin, past EEO Commissioner Paul Steven Miller, and New York governor David A. Paterson. Celebrities such as the late actor Christopher Reeve; actors Michael J. Fox, Chris Burke, Peter Dinklage, Marlee Matlin, and Emmanuelle Laborit; journalist John Hockenberry; artist Chuck Close; violinist Itzak Perlman; supermodel Aimee Mullins; and landmine activist Heather Mills claim disability as part of their public persona. The public presence of people with disabilities stretches our shared understanding of the human variations we value and appreciate and invites us to accommodate them.

Positioning oneself in the public eye can be a strategy to "claim disability," explains visual activist and arts consultant Simi Linton. In her memoir *My Body Politic* (2005) Linton, who uses a wheelchair, writes about negotiating a new body and a new visibility after becoming disabled.[11] Linton's is not the expected story about tragedy, loss, or suffering but instead about a "robust and excitable" young woman's transition from "the walking world" into the unfamiliar world of disability and her sudden forfiture of civil inattention. Linton re-enters the world via her wheelchair with the support of peers from the disability community. With verve and wonder, she discovers her new body's new pleasures, hungers, surprises, hurts, strengths, limits, and uses. In "absorb[ing] disability," she also learns that her young body draws attention in a completely new way. Newly stareable, she is seen differently by people. Other disabled people teach her how to be stareable out in the world, how not to hide or cover, and what access routes she can take—from accessible buses, disability rights protests, to college degrees. The circle of collaborators who ease the way as she learns to be "a substantial person" also show her how to flaunt the visible marks of her disability and engage stares.

"This new cadre of disabled people," she writes, "has come out of those special rooms set aside just for us. Casting off our drab institutional garb, we now don garments tailored for work and play, love and sport. Indeed, as an indicator of our new social standing, the high-toned among us even appear in television commercials wearing such finery. . . . [W]e wield that white cane or ride that wheelchair or limp that limp" (Linton 1998, 108). Here Linton captures the *relish* with which many practiced starees present themselves to the startled eyes of a public made insensate to the spectacular range of human variation by the social pressure toward visual conformity. The starees we have looked at together in this book show us how to look by showing us how they look. It is all a fine spectacle to behold (figure 12.2).

Figure 12.2. Ruth Morgan, portrait of Simi Linton (2005).

NOTES

1. Cognitive psychologists tell us that staring is a universal neural reflex. Even blind people get involved in staring. For more on this idea consider the Berkeley Art Museum's "Blind at the Museum" exhibition which, in its own words, examines how "art objects can address all of the senses—sight, touch, hearing, scent, taste—and thus offer an opportunity to reconsider the process of 'viewing' or responding to art. Visual artists often think about the very nature of vision: What does it mean to 'see'? How does an artwork address the viewer? What are the behaviors of looking? And what are the limits, or the liabilities, of the gaze?" For a synopsis of the full exhibition, see http://blindatthemuseum.com/index.html.

2. See Berns (2005).

3. For more on this topic, see the *MIT Encyclopedia of Cognitive Sciences,* s.v. "Language and Thought."

4. Here I quote Ervin in a personal interview from November 22, 2005.

5. Here I quote Meile in an e-mail interview from November 14, 2005.

6. For studies on staring behavior and preferences, see both Langer (1976) and Rutter (1984).

7. Sociologist Fred Davis (1961) described this process as "deviance disavowal."

8. For more on the disability rights movement, see the following documents about disability civil rights legislation: Section 504 of the Rehabilitation Act of 1973, which advocates that no qualified individual with a disability in the United States can be excluded from, denied the benefits of, or be subjected to discrimination under any program or activity that either receives federal financial assistance or is conducted by any executive agency or the U.S. Postal Service; the Individuals with Disabilities Education Act (IDEA), which requires public schools to make available to all eligible children with disabilities a free appropriate public education in

the least restrictive environment appropriate to their individual needs; the Americans with Disabilities Act (ADA), which prohibits discrimination on the basis of disability in employment, state and local government, public accommodations, commercial facilities, transportation, and telecommunications. Find descriptions of this legislation at the U.S. Department of Justice's "A Guide to Disability Rights Laws" Web page, http://www.usdoj.gov/crt/ada/cguide.htm. For more information, see also the National Organization on Disability Web site, http://www.nod. org, and the Center for Universal Design at N.C. State University, http://www. design.ncsu.edu/cud.

9. I considered casting the book into the genre of *meditation* as well, but have been reluctant to call it a *cultural history* or the more fashionable *micro history* because it does not follow the methods or conventions of an historical study. Of course, *anatomy* has the charming benefit of the double meaning that this reading suggests. In this sense, it follows in the tradition of *The Anatomy of Disgust* by William Ian Miller (1997).

10. There is much analysis and research on visual perception in general, but not on staring per se, which is surprising considering the voluminous recent scholarship on visual culture and what is sometimes called the visual turn. Social psychologists have conducted studies on staring. In researching this book, I longed for a subject that more readily conformed to the keyword system. I envied the scholar Jonathan Crary, for example, whose new work on "attention," *Suspensions of Perception: Attention, Spectacle, and Modern Culture* (1999), is buttressed by a surfeit of commentaries from the ancients to the defenders of medicating inattentive children with Ritalin in schools. I, conversely, could only infer about staring.

11. As I describe in chapter 4, the gaze has been defined by critical theorists as a type of look implicated in gendered objectification and the colonizing aspects of sight.

12. Miller, *Anatomy of Disgust* (1997, xiii).

CHAPTER 2

1. See Nancy Burson and J. McDermott's *Faces* (2003, npn.)

2. See "Language and Thought."

3. Gervase of Tillbury, *Otia imperialia*, circa 1210. Tillbury is quoted in Daston and Park (1998, 73).

4. Berns understands our desire for novelty as an evolutionary adaptation, as the need to be alert to unpredictability as dangerous and predictability as safe. Langer understands the desire for novelty more as a psychological impulse with social consequences.

5. Recently, for example, the press brought forward the fact that the playwright Arthur Miller, whose work and life were committed to social justice, not only

institutionalized his son who has Down syndrome but did not for the most part ever acknowledge his son's existence.

6. An enormous literature exists to document social prejudice against disability and disabled people. See Eiseland and Johnson (1996). Social scientists agree that disability creates social discomfort on the part of those who identify as nondisabled. The widely known work of Erving Goffman (1986) on stigma and asylums, which is discussed later, as well as Beatrice Wright (1960) and many other social scientists confirm disability prejudice and the refusal to accept and recognize disability. Social scientists keenly measure the variegations of bias or discomfort the nondisabled feel in encounters with people with disabilities, thus providing a hierarchy of discrimination that begs for critical analysis. Repeated studies show that the majority "rejected intimacy" with the disabled minority (Eiseland and Johnson 1996, 68). Most studies agree that facial disfigurement provokes the greatest degree of what Harlan Hahn (1988) has called "aesthetic anxiety" among the nondisabled. Mental illness, cognitive impairment, seizure disorders, and senility make the nondisabled majority group very nervous as well, often more uncomfortable than the presence of the least accepted of ethnic minority groups. Persons with cerebral palsy, paraplegia, or those of small stature are considered unacceptable even as neighbors. Around half or more of the population is uncomfortable interacting with blind or deaf people or with wheelchair users. For examples of the historical denial of disability and discrimination against people with disabilities, see Trent (1994), Rothman (2005), Rothman (1990), Baynton (1996), and Turner (2006).

7. I take the term "social capital" from Pierre Bourdieu. In "Forms of Capital," Bourdieu explains that capital "presents itself in three fundamental guises": economic capital is directly convertible into money (i.e., property rights); cultural capital includes accumulated cultural knowledge that confers power and status (i.e., educational qualifications); social capital is made up of social obligations or connections (i.e., a title of nobility) (1986, 243). James Colman (1988) alternately defines social capital as "a resource for social action" and considers it as manifested in obligations and expectations, information channels, and social norms.

8. See James's *The Principles of Psychology,* Vol. 1.

9. See also Wolfe's essay "Visual Search" in Pashler (1998).

10. Pashler notes that, "An object that is unique and therefore stands out against its background definitely intrudes on a person who is trying to search for something that is unique in some other feature" (1998, 243–44).

11. Psychologists call "attention" searching for a target element; see Pashler (1998, 243).

12. In *Democracy and Education,* John Dewey says the stare occurs in "the abnormality of a situation in which the bodily activity is divorced from the perception of meaning" (quoted in Levin 1988, 492).

13. For an analysis of the social meaning of eye contact, see Kleege, *Sight Unseen,* especially chapter 5.

14. See Goffman (1959).

CHAPTER 3

1. For overviews of ocularcentricity, see Jay, *Downcast Eyes* (1993), Levin (1993), and Crary (1990).

2. By modernity, I mean the gradual, uneven, and unintended historical shift in social organization, material circumstances, communal values, behavioral patterns, and individual character that began in Renaissance Europe, intensified in Enlightenment Europe, and was most intensely realized in late in nineteenth- and twentieth-century European and North American culture. Modernity is characterized by secularization, mobility, nationalism, urbanization, industrialization, technological and scientific development, capitalism, literacy, egalitarianism, democracy, individualism, and the imperative for social change rather than stability. In modernity, literacy and the proliferation of technologically reproduced and disseminated images makes visuality the dominant means of perception.

3. See Martin Jay (1993), Harris (1973), and Ricky Jay (2005).

4. For various historical accounts of the cultural significance of vision, see DeBord (1994), Freedberg (1989), Blumenberg (1983), Kaplan (1997), Jameson (1990), Mulvey (1989), Doane (1987), Cartwright (1995), Foucault (1979), and Berger (1972).

5. In contrast, in ancient militaristic Sparta blindness was a neutral condition since what mattered was being able to march shoulder-to-shoulder in a military phalanx with spear extended. See Rose (2003, 43–45).

6. See Gould (1981), Tavris (1992), and Ehrenreich and English (1978).

7. See Jameson (1991), Featherstone (1991), Bowlby (1985), and Friedberg (1993).

8. For discussions of the flaneur figure, see Tester (1994).

9. Again, see Crary (1999) on the distinction between the spectator and attentiveness.

10. For more on malls as sites of consumption, spectacle, and social interaction, see Kowinski (1985), Shields (1992), Goss (1993), and Cohen (2000),

11. See Kracauer (1995).

12. See Weber (1968) as well as Beniger (1986).

13. For discussions of normality, also see Baynton's (1996) work.

14. See Canguilhem (1989).

CHAPTER 4

1. Lofland (1973) estimates that the limit of how many people we can live with and in some way know personally is about three to four thousand, which means that most everyone in contemporary U.S. culture must confront anonymity quite often.

2. For an example of how visual cues are used to signal identities, see Chauncey (1994). On how visual and other cues influence stereotyping, see Dunning and Sherman (1997).

3. See also Sennett (1978).

4. Gilman (1998) has argued that the purpose of what he calls "aesthetic surgery" is to make us visually anonymous rather than outstanding. For an account of self-presentation in consumer capitalism, see Featherstone (1991, 170–96) and Bordo (1993).

5. See Sacks's essay "On Doing 'Being Ordinary'" (1984).

6. See Leder (1990).

7. In his methodological discussion of thick description, for example, anthropologist Clifford Geertz uses an example taken from Gilbert Ryle to explain the difference between a blink and a wink. The blink is an involuntary, physical twitch of the eye, while the wink is an intentional, symbolic gesture, which is communicative (often of private information between two individuals). While the physical movement of the eye is the same in each case, a blink has a different meaning from a wink, "as anyone unfortunate enough to have had the first taken for the second knows" (1973, 6). George Lakoff and Mark Johnson (1980) show how the body is a source of metaphor we use to understand and value the world. For example, up is more and down is less. By extension, an upstanding citizen is a metaphor for a good citizen, which perhaps inadvertently implies that a citizen who uses a wheelchair cannot be upstanding.

8. I take the phrase "waist-high in the world" from Nancy Mairs (1996).

9. According to Rutter (1984), Ellsworth was a primary investigator of staring. Staring was used in many definitive experiments in the 1970s as a way to set off normative looking behaviors. Most of the experiments involved three kinds of looking: staring, normal looking, and the averted gaze.

10. See Mitchell and Maple (1985).

11. A study of visual dominance behavior in relations between male ROTC cadets and their superiors revealed that cadets looked less when speaking to partners than when listening. Officers looked equally when speaking and listening. See Ellyson and Dovido (1985, 130–31).

12. For readings of the gaze, see Mulvey (1989), Kaplan (1997), Bobo (1995), Silverman (1992), Mayne (2000), and Straayer (1996).

13. For more on this idea see Althusser (2001).

14. For accounts of the colonizing gaze, see Kaplan (1997) and Fanon (1991).

15. See, for example, Dennett (1997), Reiss (2001), Garland Thomson (1996), Rydell (2000), Lutz (1993), and Halberstam (1998).

16. For more on this idea, see Baynton (2001).

17. See Goodheart (1984) and Melville (1996).

18. See Foucault's *Discipline and Punish* (1979).

19. "Normate" is a deliberately clunky neologism that calls attention to itself by mocking the clinical. Normate is "the constructed identity of those who, by way of the bodily configurations and cultural capital they assume, can step into a position of authority and wield the power it grants them" (Garland Thomson 1997, 8). The

word fills the critical need to name a heretofore under if not un-theorized position. The work of this deliberately awkward term is to defamilarize the privileged designation of "ablebodied," shifting it out of the body and into the realm of social and political relations.

20. For all his insistence that the narcissism of minor differences abrogates the potential for empathy and makes us dehumanize one another, it is ironic that Ignatieff (1997) cites and apparently endorses Enzensberger's "useful word"—autism—to capture the pathological character of nationalist identity. In Ignatieff's plea for tolerance and his liberal argument for individual rather than group identities, the use of "autism" replicates precisely the process that he critiques by metaphorically enlisting the stigmatized, pathologized group identity of autistic to stand as a negative descriptor of the ethnic nationalism he excoriates. Thus he inadvertently supports his own argument that variation imbued with negative significance is the ground of violent exclusion—in this case the eugenic ideology, medicalization, and segregation to which "the autistic" have been subjected. Ignatieff employs the fantasy of "us" and "them" made from the differences that autism pathologizes to describe the same system of identity creation he so vehemently decries. For more on this critique, see Enzensberger (1994).

21. Much recent work on ethics recognizes human vulnerability, need for care, and dependency as fundamental to our humanity and a source of commonality. See, for example, Butler (2004), Fineman (2004), Kittay (1999), Nussbaum (2006), and Turner (2006).

CHAPTER 5

1. See Gilmore (2003).
2. See Greenblatt (1991) and Paulson (1996).
3. For more on Johnson's notion of curiosity, see Thomas's essay in Elsner and Cardinal (1994).
4. See Elsner and Cardinal (1994), especially chapters by Kaufmann and Shelton.
5. See Foucault (1975, 1965) as well as Canguilhem (1989).
6. See works by Cartwright (2001), Gould (1981), Tavris (1992), and Rothman (1998).
7. I am borrowing the notion of baroque looking from French philosopher Buci-Glucksmann who takes the term "madness of vision" from Merleau-Ponty (1968, 75).
8. In "Scopic Regimes of Modernity" in Force Fields (1993), Jay suggests that the baroque vision celebrated by Buci-Glucksmann (1994) may not be so attractive to the postmodern age because it thwarts the legibility so highly valued in modernity (125). Neither Jay nor Buci-Glucksmann considers that the object of baroque vision might be a subject, a person; both tacitly assume that it is always an inanimate object.

9. Jonathan Sawday's *Body Emblazoned* (1995; paperback ed., 1996) has an excellent discussion of the anatomic gaze and philosophical/religious self-scrutiny (110ff.)

10. This is Daston and Park's 1998 argument. It contradicts the usual historical progress narrative—and even their own earlier one (as well as the ideas of Weber and Canguilhem)—that attributes the rise of science to discrediting wonder.

11. This gap between visual and experienced perception of the self has been postulated by psychoanalytic theorist Jacques Lacan as the mirror stage, in which the illusion of wholeness that looking in the mirror offers consolidates the developing child's subjectivity out of its fragmented interior perception of self. Thus the mirror stage produces the illusion of wholeness that constitutes subjectivity.

12. See also Serge Roche et al. (1985).

13. For more on the history of portrait photography, see Kozloff (2007) and Lewinski and Magnus (1982).

14. This notion comes from Robert Burns's poem, "To A Louse."

15. See also Banner (2002).

16. What Jonathan Sawday (1995) calls a "culture of dissection" in medical theaters arose in the early modern period and aimed the exploratory eye at the body's interior, enabling early scientists to see the inside of our bodies, a sight like the face that was denied ordinary people. For a discussion of public dissections, see also Richardson (2000) and Reiss (2001).

17. See Blanchot's *The Gaze of Orpheus* (1981), especially pages 63–77, as well as Leder's *The Absent Body* (1980).

18. See Winnicott (1965).

CHAPTER 6

1. On the history of curiosity in America, see American Antiquarian Society, "A Cabinet of Curiosities" (2004); also Benedict (2001).

2. These ideas come from a history of the term "curiosity" in *The Oxford English Dictionary*.

3. See Brown (1976), Blumin (1989), and also Weber on rationalization in Gane (2002).

4. See Harris (1973), Halttunen (1982), and Henry James (1893).

5. See also Sennett (1978).

6. Veblen (1919) has pointed out that even though middle-class men were not objects of display, middle-class women were assigned the role of ornaments that provided visual evidence of their men's status.

7. See Halttunen (1995) on sentimentality and benevolence.

8. This fact is an important example of the way an analysis of staring can complicate the current theoretical conversation about the gaze. From John Berger to

Laura Mulvey, the male gaze is conceived as a gendered privilege. These conduct manuals on the one hand support that reading of the male gaze as a disciplinary practice but they also suggest that the very possession of such a powerful social privilege might itself need to be regulated.

9. The very idea of being civilized in the modernizing West is synonymous with developing self-restraint. See Elias (1978).

10. This poem comes from the Web site: http://www.picturingwomen.org/home.php.

11. See Lerner (1986) for discussions about women's vulnerability to being de-classed.

12. See Schweik's *The Ugly Laws* (2009). The phrase "ugly law" was coined in the source for all citations of the ordinance: a single paragraph in a landmark work of legal scholarship, Marcia Pearce Burgdorf and Robert Burgdorf, Jr.'s "A History of Unequal Treatment: The Qualifications of Handicapped Persons as a 'Suspect Class' Under the Equal Protection Clause" (1975). The authors cited a version of the wording in the Chicago Municipal Code that they said was in force "until recently," and they offered footnotes to codes in three cities: Chicago (listed as "Mun. Code 36–34 [1966], repealed 1974"), Columbus (listed as "Gen. Offense Code 2387.04 [1972]"), and Omaha (listed as "Unsightly Beggar Ordinance," Omaha, Neb. Mun. Code of 1941, 25"). Offering these three examples, they named them ugly laws, probably directly inspired by reports of the Omaha case.

13. See Whitman's poem in *American Literature: A Prentice Hall Anthology* (1991).

14. The term "society of the spectacle" comes from the title of Guy Debord's 1960 foundational critique of rising modern consumer capitalism in the West.

15. See Leach (1993) and Bowlby (1985).

CHAPTER 7

1. Press Release, "Permission to Stare." *Jack the Pelican Presents*. http://www.jackthe pelicanpresents.com/rushpr.html (accessed 18 August 2006). See also the artist's Web site at http://chrisrushartist.com/.

2. Almost all the research on staring involves gathering information about starers. For this book, I collected thirty-five responses from people with stareable disabilities about their experiences with staring. Their mostly anonymous responses are included throughout the book as the major source of information about starees. Several people who completed the questionnaire about staring requested that their names be included along with their quotes, and I have done so in deference to those requests.

3. The philosopher Butler discusses lives imagined as livable and not livable in *Precarious Life* (2004).

4. See Karen Halttunen (1995) on sentimentality and Garland-Thomson essay from *Beyond the Binary* (1999).

5. This kind of interpersonal dynamic is also required in the case of racism. The importunate postures required of people who are targets of racism as well as the accompanying indignities and outrages are explored in Franz Fanon, *Black Skin, White Masks* (1991).

CHAPTER 8

1. For more on this idea, see Gilman's work in both *Creating Beauty to Cure the Soul* (1998) and *Making the Body Beautiful* (1999).

2. History has of course shown Levinas to be wrong when it comes to human action. We are able to kill one another face-to-face with grim regularity.

3. What Chancer (1998) calls "looksism" and what Synnott (1993) terms "aesthetic discrimination" haunt our face-to-face encounters.

4. For discussion of encounters between what Goffman calls "normals" and people stigmatized by socially subordinated differences such as disability, racialization, and other discredited categories, see Goffman's book, *Stigma: Notes on the Management of Spoiled Identity* (1986).

5. All quotes in this and the above paragraph reference Roche's essay "Finding My Voice." For more on Roche, see also his award-winning documentary, *The Perfect Flaw: Triumphing over Facial Disfigurement* (2003), and his book, *The Church of 80% Sincerity* (2008).

6. The Schappell twins were institutionalized in a hospital for the developmentally and intellectually disabled for the first twenty-four years of their lives. Reba, with the support of the hospital staff and the First Lady of Pennsylvania, Ginny Thornburgh, pushed for their independence much more assiduously than Lori. Although they were institutionalized from birth, they apparently were not abandoned by their family, who visited regularly and most probably made the decision to institutionalize them based on medical advice and the lack of an accessible environment for them. Part of the rationale for their institutionalization was that it was repeatedly predicted that their condition was not compatible with life, and that they were expected to die soon, as is not an unusual diagnosis for people with significant and rare disabilities. (Harriet McBryde Johnson writes about this constant prediction of death in her 2005 memoir.) Upon deinstitutionalization, both women immediately experienced extreme employment discrimination but have eventually come to make a living as celebrities. See Dreger (2004).

7. The exception to this may be fetus and mother, whose conjoinment is generally mutually agreeable if not always mutually beneficial. The term "singleton" is used by the medical historian Alice Dreger to name the kind of human being who is not conjoined. The critical work of this term is extremely important because it names

a term which is imagined to be so normal as to not need to be named, In other words the term *singleton* calls attention to the minority embodiment of conjoinment by naming the previously unnamed majority term. See again Dreger (2004) as well as Couser, "Double Exposure: Performing Conjoined Twinship in *Signifying Bodies*" (2009).

8. Reba, who has appeared with Lori on several television programs, has cut a single song called "Fear of Being Alone" and has changed her name from Dori to Reba, in honor of the country singer Reba McIntyre.

CHAPTER 9

1. Distinct from rather than derived from spoken language, sign language forms the basis for the claim to a distinctive Deaf culture that grows out of minority language practice. As a result, an important difference exists between the use of *Deaf* and *deaf*: *Deaf* refers to the cultural groups or communities who use sign as their primary language or to shared cultural practices of people who use sign language, whereas *deaf* refers to the larger group of individuals with hearing loss. Deaf culture consists of not just sign languages, but such cultural products as Deaf poetry, theater, films, and publications as well as the interactions and institutions developed within the spaces of Deaf community such as schools, clubs, neighborhoods, and other social venues (Padden and Humphries 2005).

2. Geographic and national groups develop and employ culturally specific sign languages, of which American Sign Language, or ASL, is only one form. Not unlike vocal languages, sign languages are complex systems made up of arbitrary signs, natural language, and, specifically, finger spelling. As digital representations of the alphabet letters used in written language, finger spelling links sign language to written language, for which there is no signed form, rather than to spoken language, to which sign language is not related. Sign language is much more than word chains or mimetic gestures; it is a concise, complex, combinatorial code shared by its practitioners. Sign language users, just like spoken language users, develop aphasia as result of specifically located brain injuries. Deaf children acquire sign language in the same graduated, age-appropriate process that hearing children acquire speech. See Stokoe (2005) and Lane (1992)

3. For more on this notion, see "Morphology" and "Laterality" in *Encyclopedia Britannica Online*.

4. See Theodore Edel's *Piano Music for One Hand* (1994). Single-handed piano performances are an uncommon but significant musical repertoire. Single-handed pianists must play from a small body of compositions and arrangements for performers intending to strengthen their left hand and players who have use of only their left hand. A surge of one-handed piano works appeared in the 1870s and 1880s in the United States for the enormous amputee population created by the Civil War.

5. One-handed piano playing might be appreciated on its own terms. Instead of perpetual compensation, the one-handed pianist can forge unique relationships between bodies and instruments. As Michael Davidson has argued, "disability, far from limiting possibilities of design or performance, liberates and changes the terms for composition" (2005, 619). Ravel recognized this potential, saying, "the [single-handed] concerto must not be a stunt. The listener must never feel that more could have been accomplished with two hands. The part must be complete, beautiful and transparent" (Flindell 1971, 122). Understanding the one-handed pianist as "complete" requires imagining the distinctiveness rather than the deficiency of single handedness and the concerto as an occasion for realizing its beauty.

6. A subgenre of horror films features severed hands that haunt and terrorize in hysterical plots of disability revenge, according to Neil Lerner. Such plots are featured in *The Beast with Five Fingers* (1946), *The Crawling Hand* (1963), *Dr. Terror's House of Horrors* (1965), *And Now the Screaming Starts* (1973), and Oliver Stone's 1981 film *The Hand*. The theme music for *The Beast with Five Fingers*, perhaps ironically, is Brahms's adaptation of Bach. The roaming amputated hand is also a feature of *Un Chien Andalou*, the 1928 surrealist film by Salvador Dali and Luis Buñuel and *The Exterminating Angel* made in 1962 by Buñuel. The discomforting trope of the disembodied hand also engaged the stare of terror-seeking audiences in television series episodes from *The Addams Family* to *Buffy the Vampire Slayer*.

7. Only establishing independence in 1962, Sierra Leone has been in constant dispute since the first democratically held elections occurred in 1996. The conflict over control of the diamond-producing areas of this West African nation officially ended in January 2002. This intra-ethnic form of violence was unique to Sierra Leone and to this war. The rebels first used amputations to talk back to the newly elected president, whose campaign slogan was, "The future is in your hands." They told their victims to go ask the new president for new hands. The rebels also sometimes told victims to ask the United Nations for new limbs. Most fundamentally, the severed hands communicated that the rebels could seize control by disrupting the daily life of the communities from which they came. For example, a handless 47-year-old man named Tommy Foday, who had been a driver, was told by the rebels that cutting off his hands would keep him from ever driving again (Fisher-Thompson 2006, n.p.). More generally, however, the handless could no longer farm, feed themselves or others, or find marriage partners.

8. See Gerber (2000). Media technology has advanced to the point where nondisabled actors can now convincingly play the kinds of roles only Harold Russell could act in earlier films. The nondisabled actor Gary Sinese plays a double amputee in *Forrest Gump* and has become a spokesperson for the disabled veterans' memorial in Washington, D.C.

9. For more on freak performances, see Garland Thomson (1996), Adams (2001) and Mitchell and Eisenmann (1979).

10. Mary Duffy and Cheryl Marie Wade's performances are available on video in *Vital Signs, Crip Culture Talks Back*, directed and produced by David T. Mitchell and Sharon Snyder (1996). I have seen Duffy's and Wade's performances live; my readings of all these performances are influenced by the editing and thematic framing of Mitchell and Snyder's important film. The quotes here are from *Vital Signs*.

11. Unpublished poem from author, performed at the Society for Disability Studies Annual Conference, June 2005, San Francisco State University.

CHAPTER 10

1. In this chapter, I am indebted to Iris Marion Young's seminal essay on breastedness, "Breasted Experience," in *On Female Body Experience* (2005).

2. See Susan Bordo (1994).

3. The floral paintings of American artist Georgia O'Keeffe suggest vaginas, even though the artist has insisted they are simply pictures of flowers; American artist Judy Chicago's 1979 feminist celebration of women's culture, "The Dinner Party," explicitly uses stylized vaginal imagery in its series of dining plates; and Eve Ensler's 1996 blockbuster play, "The Vagina Monologues," which is a meditation on the significance and semantics of vaginas, is filled with narrative accounts of looking at vaginas.

4. See Annette Kolodny (1975).

5. See Urla and Swedlund (1995).

6. See Yalom (1997) as well as Latteier (1998).

7. For a provocative, subjective account of testosterone's effects, see Sullivan (2000).

8. Kimberly Wallace-Sanders (2008) discusses this question in her essay "Nipplegate: Black Feminism, Corporeal Fragmentation and the Politics of Public Consumption."

9. This gender dynamic of seeing describes normative cultural scripts, not necessarily the behavior or motivations of actual individuals. How people place themselves along the continuum of sexual identity structures the way actual people look at men and women, of course (Berger 1972).

10. See Young (2005).

11. See Postman (1985) and Debord (1994).

12. About one out of two hundred women have a supernumerary nipple (Yalom 1997, 61).

13. The breast cancer movement was a political recognition initiative that was part of not only the women's movement but the larger cluster of civil rights movements that characterized and transformed the political and social landscape of mid-twentieth-century America.

14. See works by Jo Spence (1988, 1995, 2006).

15. See Ferraro (1993).

16. In 1998, the Breast Cancer Fund published a book called *Art. Rage. Us: The Art and Outrage of Breast Cancer.* Composed of writing and art by women with breast cancer, this beautiful coffee-table book with an epilogue by breast cancer survivor and environmentalist novelist Terry Tempest Williams is representative of the activist art produced by a breast cancer advocacy movement.

17. At present, the user-populated Internet image archive Flickr hosts a number of self-portraits of breast cancer survivors presented in the mode of these public displays of breastlessness.

18. See, for example, Annie Liebovitz's controversial *Vanity Fair* magazine cover photo of pregnant Demi Moore published in August 1991.

19. Alison Lapper is herself an artist and a single mother. Abandoned to a foundling home for disabled children at birth, she eventually earned a First in Fine Art at Brighton University and became a successful artist. In her youth, she discovered increased freedom and flexibility by discarding the prosthetic limbs she was encouraged to wear. She works for the Mouth and Foot Painting Artists Association designing greeting cards that are sold in seventy-three countries. She also has made a series of photographic self-portraits and in 2006 published an autobiography with Guy Feldman called *My Life in My Hands.*

20. The philosopher Charles Taylor also explored political recognition, using the example of how Canadian Francophone culture gets recognition through legislated bilingualism; see Taylor (1994).

21. See Goffman (1986).

22. For a dissenting argument on breast prostheses, see Herndl (2002).

CHAPTER 11

1. See Cohen (1999; 1999). See also Davidson and Foucault (2003), Shildrik (2002), and Haraway (1995) on monsters and monstrosity.

2. The prodigy plot informs many of the foundational narratives of Western culture. Genesis's account of Eve being born from Adam's side may refer to the astonishing prodigy known as a teratoma or *fetus in fetu,* a tumor, often containing hair and teeth, that is the residual presence of an absorbed twin hidden in the body of the surviving sibling, waiting patiently to reveal itself to some medical intruder. The story of the Christ child's birth, for example, can be understood as a convergence of prodigious events. The star of Bethlehem is the comet—a common prodigy foretelling the future—that signals the wise men that a prodigious birth has taken place and that they should travel to witness the extraordinary body as a conduit to truth. Prodigious births came in the form of unusual bodies that could be distinguished from run-of-the-mill births so as to provide a discernable

text. While Jesus is not represented as monstrous per se, his body at both birth and death functions as a prodigy: its distinction offers it up as a preternatural gesture to be read. Like monsters, Jesus was imagined as a sign from the gods. The Christian pageantry of the Crucifixion, as well, takes its narrative structure from the practice of public executions that were rituals of staring intended to provide lessons to a rapt audience. In the Crucifixion story, the faithful heedfully attend the suffering body of Jesus as a sign of God's order and plan for humanity.

3. See works by Friedman (1981), Campbell, and Greenblatt (1991).

4. For more on premodern freaks and monsters, see Daston and Park (1998) and Altick (1978).

5. See works on freaks by Bogdan (1988), Dennett (1997), Garland Thomson (1996), and Adams (2001).

6. Bogdan claims that medicalization eliminated the freak show, Garland Thomson adds that sentimentality attenuated the freak show, while Adams, Weinstock, and Dennett point out it only shifted its form.

7. See works by Canguilhem (1989), Garland-Thomson, Rothman, and Hubbard (1990).

8. I am borrowing Anne Friedberg's useful term "virtual gaze" here to describe the kind of modern mediated looking that removes the actual object of looking from the act of looking through the use of visual technologies such as photography, television, film, and so forth.

9. What can be called freak scholarship has several important conversations: first is the cause of the freak show's demise; second is whether the shows provided dignity with employment that medicalization robs people of; third is whether the shows ended or just shifted into other venues; see, for example, Chemers (2008).

10. Telethons allow Americans to reassure themselves that the excesses of individualism have not corroded their moral and communal commitments by establishing themselves as generous "givers." These collective rituals of staring display bodies marked as "disabled" as objects of the supposed compassion of their viewers. Entangled in that compassion, however, is contempt for the ostensible "takers," who function as recipients of this largess by being stripped of the morality, agency, and productivity so valued in the concept of "giving." Telethons thus enable citizens who are implicitly positioned as nondisabled to counter the accusation of "conspicuous consumption," Veblen's indictment of consumer capitalism, with what Longmore calls "conspicuous contribution," which endows them with considerable social capital (Longmore 1997, 134). See also Johnson (2006).

11. For accounts of the Bunkers, see Dreger (2004); for Baartman, see Crais and Scully (2008).

12. Lisa Abelow Hedley's documentary film *Dwarfs: Not a Fairytale* presents several people of short stature explaining ordinary-sized people's responses to them.

13. Dinklage won the Emerging Actor Award at the Aspen Film Festival as well as several festival awards. He was nominated for Best Actor by the Screen Actors

Guild and the IFP Independent Spirit Award. The movie itself won many awards at Sundance and other prestigious festivals. He also played the part of Shakespeare's Richard III in a production at New York's Public Theater.

14. Lomnicki says that her work is becoming more minimalist and that she is using her own body to become a character. For more on this idea, see Mauro (2003) on the actress's career.

15. Hunt has played a wide range of roles in stage dramas such as Brecht's *Mother Courage and Her Children* and Chekhov's *The Cherry Orchard*, as well as the role of Alice B. Toklas in an American Playhouse film (Adelson 2005, 261–67).

16. Conjoined twins are rare, occurring approximately once every fifty thousand to one hundred thousand births, and approximately seventy-five percent of conjoined twins are stillborn or die within twenty-four hours. The overall survival rate is estimated at between five and twenty-five percent. Although more male twins are conjoined in utero, females are three times more likely to be born alive, resulting in approximately seventy percent of conjoined twins being girls. Thus, there are usually only a dozen or so sets of living conjoined twins in the world at one time. Most people never see conjoined twins face-to-face in their lifetimes (Piccolo 2004).

17. Parents that elect not to initiate the family health care crisis of surgically separating their twins may face more stares. However, according to medical historian Alice Dreger (2004), conjoined twins who are not subjected to surgical separation generally have fewer significant health problems in childhood than separated ones.

18. The article contains one obligatory chart about the configuration of the Hensel twins' internal organs. Almost all media articles about the girls feature either an explanation or illustration that follows the conventions of medical language, drawn to satisfy the reader's curiosity about the physiology of the girls' conjoinment. These pieces of medical information seem designed to protect the reader from feeling intrusive or voyeuristic.

CHAPTER 12

1. Sontag's 1977 book *On Photography* might have been titled *Against Photography*, according to W. J. T. Mitchell in *What Do Pictures Want?* (2005). Sontag's later work *Regarding the Pain of Others* (2003) reconsiders her arguments about the power of photography.

2. This kind of bad staring is particular to modernity, Sontag (2003) suggests. The kind of premodern staring at images of human suffering codified in Christian icons such as Saint Sebastian pierced by arrows from head to toe depicts suffering as "a kind of transfiguration," which "links pain to sacrifice," Sontag approves (99). I would continue her analysis by adding that the rhetorical

purpose of such premodern sights of suffering and mutilation as the Crucifixion—the central image of Western religious culture (which Sontag surprisingly does not mention)—is to inspire the kind of identification good staring
requires. But the intent of this identification is quite distinct from the modern
dynamic of good staring at suffering Sontag calls for. The ubiquitous representation of the mutilated, dead, suffering body of the crucified Jesus in western
iconography does not command us to work toward the social justice that will
eliminate such suffering. In fact, this scene of suffering asks us to accept and
transcend human pain, to endure rather than fix it, even to celebrate it. Sontag
rightly observes that such depictions "could not be more alien to a modern
sensibility, which regards suffering as something that is a mistake or an accident or a crime. Something to be fixed. Something to be refused. Something
that makes one feel powerless" (99). Thomas Haskell (1985) has elaborated
this same point more fully if less eloquently in his historical analysis of the
relationship between the tandem rise of capitalism and benevolence in the
nineteenth-century West.

3. Scarry (1999) does not use the word *staring* specifically as the perceptual means
of apprehending beauty. However, beauty is available primarily through the visible register. The intensity and unexpectedness of the perception is what characterizes an encounter with beauty for Scarry. In this sense, apprehending beauty is
a similar process to staring as I have elaborated it here.

4. See Horkheimer and Adorno (1987) and Campbell (1999).

5. The longer part of Johnson's story recounts her debate with Princeton philosopher and ethicist Peter Singer, who advocates euthanizing significantly
disabled newborns. For Singer's argument, see his book, co-authored with
Helga Kuhse (1985). Also see Harriet McBryde Johnson, "Not Dead At All"
(2005).

6. Social psychologists Ellen Langer, et al. (1976) find that people with disabilities
are avoided, but discovers that such a response is not aversion, fear, disgust, or
perhaps even prejudice but rather this avoidance is about staring. Avoiding or
being uncomfortable around people with disabilities is a response caused by conflict between the desire to stare and the social injunction against staring at people.
The evidence suggests that when the "stimuli" of difference becomes routine,
avoidance and discomfort diminish.

7. For discussion of discrediting supposedly unlivable lives, see Butler (2004); for
an examination of what might constitute a livable life, see Nussbaum and Sen
(1993).

8. See especially chapter 7, "The Oppositional Gaze: Black Female Spectators."

9. See especially Winnicott (1965, 37–55). For Winnicott, the holding function is
performed both by the mother's mirroring gaze and her literal holding of the
infant close to her body.

10. Sociologist Fred Davis (1961) described this process as "deviance disavowal." While the stigma management techniques Davis describes are parallel to the performances of the visual activists discussed here and also to the strategies used by many of the informants here, the language of deviance disavowal does not address the full scope in the sociopolitical world of these social interactions.

11. See both of Linton's books: *My Body Politic* (2005) and *Claiming Disability* (1998).

REFERENCES

Abell, L. G. *Woman in Her Various Relations: Containing Practical Rules for American Females, the Best Methods for Dinners and Social Parties, a Chapter for Young Ladies, Mothers, and Invalids, Hints O the Body, Mind, and Character.* New York: Holdredge, 1851.

Ablon, Joan. *Little People in America: The Social Dimension of Dwarfism.* New York: Praeger, 1984.

Abramson, Stacy, prod. "The Jewish Giant: A Sound Portrait." Narrated by Jenny Carchman. *All Things Considered.* National Public Radio, 6 October 1999.

Ackerman, Diane. *A Natural History of the Senses.* New York: Random House, 1990.

Adams, Rachel. *Sideshow U.S.A: Freaks and the American Cultural Imagination.* Chicago: University of Chicago Press, 2001.

Adelson, Betty M. *The Lives of Dwarfs: The Journey from Public Curiosity Toward Social Liberation.* New Brunswick, N.J.: Rutgers University Press, 2005.

Alcoff, Linda Martín. *Visible Identities: Race, Gender, and the Self.* New York: Oxford University Press, 2006.

Allen, James. *Without Sanctuary: Lynching Photography in America.* Santa Fe, N.M.: Twin Palms, 2000.

Althusser, Louis. *Lenin and Philosophy, and Other Essays.* New York: Monthly Review Press, 2001.

Altick, Richard Daniel. *The Shows of London.* Cambridge, Mass.: Belknap Press, 1978.

American Antiquarian Society and Florida State University Department of History. "A Cabinet of Curiosities." *Common-Place: A Common Place, An Uncommon Voice* 4, no. 2 (January 2004), www.common-place.org (accessed 31 August 2006).

Argyle, Michael, and Mark Cook. *Gaze and Mutual Gaze.* Cambridge: Cambridge University Press, 1976.

Arieli, Yehoshua. *Individualism and Nationalism in American Ideology.* Cambridge: Center for Study of History of Liberty in America, 1964.

Aristotle. *Historia Animalium*, translated by A. L. Peck. London: Heinemann; Cambridge: Harvard University Press, 1965.

Art, Rage, Us: Art and Writing by Women with Breast Cancer. San Francisco: Chronicle Books, 1998.

Auld, Doug. "Mission." 2005–08. http://dougauld.com (accessed 3 November 2008).

Baldrige, Letitia. *The Amy Vanderbilt Complete Book of Etiquette.* New York: Doubleday & Co., 1978.

Banks, Wendy. "Peter Dinklage: Sundance Fave's Powerful Performance Makes the Station Agent This Season's Big Indie Hit." *NOW*, 9–15 October 2003, n.p.

Banner, Stuart. *The Death Penalty: An American History.* Cambridge: Harvard University Press, 2002.

Baron-Cohen, Simon. *Mindblindness: An Essay on Autism and "Theory of Mind."* Learning, Development, and Conceptual Change. Cambridge: MIT Press, 1995.

Barnum, P. T. *Struggles and Triumphs; Or, Forty Years' Recollections of P. T. Barnum.* Hartford: J. B. Burr, 1869.

Barsley, Michael. *The Left-Handed Book: An Investigation into the Sinister History of Left-Handedness.* London: Souvenir Press, 1966.

Baynton, Douglas C. "Disability and the Justification of Inequality in American History." In *The New Disability History: American Perspectives,* edited by Paul Longmore and Lauri Imansky. New York: New York University Press, 2001.

———. *Forbidden Signs: American Culture and the Campaign Against Sign Language.* Chicago: University of Chicago Press, 1996.

Bell, Charles. *The Hand, Its Mechanism and Vital Endowments as Evincing Design.* Philadelphia: Carey, Lea & Blanchard, 1833.

Benedict, Barbara M. *Curiosity: A Cultural History of Early Modern Inquiry.* Chicago: University of Chicago Press, 2001.

Beniger, James R. *The Control Revolution: Technological and Economic Origins of the Information Society.* Cambridge: Harvard University Press, 1986.

Berger, John. *Ways of Seeing.* London: BBC and Penguin, 1972.

Berns, Gregory. *Satisfaction: The Science of Finding True Fulfillment.* New York: Henry Holt, 2005.

The Best Years of Our Lives, directed by William Wyler. Samuel Goldwyn Productions, Inc., 1946.

Beuf, Ann H. *Beauty Is the Beast: Appearance-Impaired Children in America.* Philadelphia: University of Pennsylvania Press, 1990.

Blanchot, Maurice, and P. Adams Sitney. *The Gaze of Orpheus, and Other Literary Essays.* Barrytown: Station Hill Press, 1981.

Blumenberg, Hans. *The Legitimacy of the Modern Age.* Studies in Contemporary German Social Thought. Cambridge, Mass.: MIT Press, 1983.

Blumin, Stuart M. *The Emergence of the Middle Class: Social Experience in the American City, 1760–1900.* Interdisciplinary Perspectives on Modern History. Cambridge: Cambridge University Press, 1989.

Bobo, Jacqueline. *Black Women as Cultural Readers*. New York: Columbia University Press, 1995.

Bogdan, Robert. *Freak Show: Presenting Human Oddities for Amusement and Profit*. Chicago: University of Chicago Press, 1988.

Bordo, Susan. "Reading the Male Body." In *The Male Body*, edited by Laurence Goldstein, 265–306. Ann Arbor: University of Michigan Press, 1994.

———. *Unbearable Weight: Feminism, Western Culture, and the Body*. Berkeley and Los Angeles: University of California Press, 1993.

Bosworth, Patricia. *Diane Arbus*. New York: W. W. Norton & Company, 2005.

Bourdieu, Pierre. "The Forms of Capital." In *Handbook of Theory: Research for the Sociology of Education*, edited by John G. Richardson, 241–58. New York: Greenwood Press, 1986.

Bowker, Geoffrey C., and Leigh Star. *Sorting Things Out: Classification and Its Consequences*. Cambridge: MIT Press, 1999.

Bowlby, Rachel. *Just Looking: Consumer Culture in Dreiser, Gissing, and Zola*. New York: Methuen, 1985.

Brannan, Dan. *Boy Giant: The Story of Robert Wadlow, the World's Tallest Man*. Alton: Alton Museum of History and Art, 2003.

Brant, Ethel Cushing. *Standard Etiquette for All Occasions: What to Do, What to Say, What to Wear*. New York: J. H. Sears & Co, 1925.

Braun, V., and S. Wilkinson. "Socio-cultural Representations of the Vagina." *Journal of Reproductive and Infant Psychology*. 19:1 (February 2001): 17–32.

Bremmer, Jan N., and Herman Roodenburg. *A Cultural History of Gesture*. Ithaca, N.Y.: Cornell University Press, 1992.

Brown, Bob. "Man without Legs Harnesses Public Gaze." 1 January 2007. *ABC News*. http://abcnews.go.com/2020 (accessed 8 January 2008).

Brown, Richard D. *Modernization: The Transformation of American Life, 1600–1865*. New York: Hill and Wang, 1976.

Bruce, Vicki. *Recognizing Faces*. Essays in Cognitive Psychology. Hove: Lawrence Erlbaum Associates, 1988.

Brundage, W. Fitzhugh. *Under Sentence of Death: Lynching in the South*. Chapel Hill: University of North Carolina Press, 1997.

Buber, Martin. *I and Thou*. 2nd ed. New York: Scribner, 1958.

Buci-Glucksmann, Christine. *Baroque Reason: The Aesthetics of Modernity*. London and Thousand Oaks: Sage Publications, 1994.

Bulwer, John, et al. *Chirologia; or, the Natvrall Langvage of the Hand. Composed of the Speaking Motions, and Discoursing Gestures Thereof*. London: printed by T. Harper and sold by R. Whitaker, 1644.

Burgdorf, Marcia Pearce, and Robert Burgdorf, Jr. "A History of Unequal Treatment: The Qualifications of Handicapped Persons as a 'Suspect Class' Under the Equal Protection Clause." *Santa Clara Law Review* 15 (1975): 861–91.

Burns, Stanley. *Sleeping Beauty: Memorial Photography in America*. Altadena, Calif.: Twelvetrees Press, 1990.

Burson, Nancy, and Jeanne McDermott. *Faces*. 1st ed. Santa Fe, N.M.: Twin Palms, 1993.

Butler, Judith. *Gender Trouble: Feminism and the Subversion of Identity*. New York: Routledge, 1990.

———. *Precarious Life*. New York: Verso, 2004.

Bynum, Caroline Walker. "Shape and Story: Metamorphosis in Western Tradition." National Endowment for the Humanities Jefferson Lecture in the Humanities. Concert Hall of the Kennedy Center for the Performing Arts, Washington, D.C., 22 March 1999.

Campbell, Mary B. *Wonder & Science: Imagining Worlds in Early Modern Europe*. Ithaca, N.Y.: Cornell University Press, 1999.

Canguilhem, Georges. *The Normal and the Pathological*. New York: Zone Books, 1989.

Cartwright, Lisa. *Screening the Body: Tracing Medicine's Visual Culture*. Minneapolis: University of Minnesota Press, 1995.

Carey, Martha. "Survival Is Political: History, Violence and the Contemporary Power Struggle in Sierra Leone." In *States of Violence: Politics, Youth and Memory in Contemporary Africa*, edited by E. G. Bay and D. L. Donham. Charlottesville: University of Virginia Press, 2006.

Chancer, Lynn S. *Reconcilable Differences: Confronting Beauty, Pornography, and the Future of Feminism*. Berkeley: University of California Press, 1998.

Chauncey, George. *Gay New York: Gender, Urban Culture, and the Making of the Gay Male World, 1890–1940*. New York: Basic Books, 1994.

Chemers, Michael M. *Staging Stigma: A Critical Examination of the American Freak Show*. New York: Palgrave Macmillan, 2008.

Cohen, Jeffery, ed. *Monster Theory: Reading Culture*. Minneapolis: University of Minnesota Press, 1999.

———. *Of Giants: Sex, Monsters and the Middle Ages*. Minneapolis: University of Minnesota Press, 1999.

Cohen, Lizabeth. *A Consumer's Republic: The Politics of Mass Consumption in Postwar America*. New York: Knopf, 2003.

Cohen, Richard A. *Face to Face with Levinas*. SUNY Series in Philosophy. Albany: State University of New York Press, 1986.

Coleman, James S. "Social Capital in the Creation of Human Capital." *American Journal of Sociology* 94, Supplement: Organizations and Institutions: Sociological and Economic Approaches to the Analysis of Social Structure (1988): S95–S120.

Colwell, John, Sadi Schroder, and David Sladen. "The Ability to Detect Unseen Staring: A Literature Review and Empirical Tests." *British Journal of Psychology* 91, no. 1 (February 2000): 71–85.

Connolly, Kevin. "The Rolling Exhibition," 2007. www.therollingexhibition.com (accessed 8 January 2008).

Couser, G. Thomas. *Signifying Bodies: Disability in Contemporary Life Writing*. Ann Arbor: University of Michigan Press, 2009.

Crais, Clifton, and Pamela Scully. *Sara Baartman and the Hottentot Venus: A Ghost Story and a Biography*. Princeton, N.J.: Princeton University Press, 2008.

Crary, Jonathan. *Suspensions of Perception: Attention, Spectacle, and Modern Culture.* Cambridge, Mass.: MIT Press, 1999.

———. *Techniques of the Observer: On Vision and Modernity in the Nineteenth Century.* Cambridge, Mass.: MIT Press, 1990.

Darwent, Charles. "A Marble Sculpture of a Pregnant Woman with Shortened Legs and Arms." *The Daily Telegraph* (London), 16 September 2005: 6.

Daston, Lorraine, and Katharine Park. *Wonders and the Order of Nature, 1150–1750.* New York: Zone Books, 1998.

Davidson, Michael. "Concerto for the Left-Hand: Disability (in the) Arts." *PMLA* 120, no. 2 (2005): 615–19.

Davis, Fred. "Deviance Disavowal: The Management of Strained Interaction by the Visibly Handicapped." *Social Problems* 9 (1961): 120–32.

Davis, Lennard J. *Enforcing Normalcy: Disability, Deafness, and the Body.* New York: Verso, 1995.

de Beauvior, Simone. *The Second Sex,* edited and translated by H. M. Parshley. New York: Vintage Press, 1974; first published, 1952.

Debord, Guy. *The Society of the Spectacle.* New York: Zone Books, 1994.

Dennett, Andrea Stulman. *Weird and Wonderful: The Dime Museum in America.* New York: New York University Press, 1997.

Doane, Mary Ann. *The Desire to Desire: The Woman's Film of the 1940s.* Theories of Representation and Difference. Bloomington: Indiana University Press, 1987.

Dreger, Alice Domurat. *One of Us: Conjoined Twins and the Future of Normal.* Cambridge: Harvard University Press, 2004.

Dunning, D., and Sherman, D. A. "Stereotypes and Tacit Inference." *Journal of Personality and Social Psychology* 73 (1997): 459–71.

Edel, Theodore. *Piano Music for One Hand.* Bloomington: Indiana University Press, 1994.

Ederly, Sheryl. *365 Manners Kids Should Know: Games, Activities, and Other Fun Ways to Help Children Learn Etiquette.* New York: Three Rivers Press, 2001.

Ehrenreich, Barbara, and Deirdre English. *For Her Own Good: 150 Years of the Experts' Advice to Women.* 1st ed. Garden City: Anchor Press, 1978.

Eiseland, Nancy L., and Cathryn Johnson. "Physical Ability as a Diffuse Status Characteristic: Implications for Small Group Interaction." *Advances in Group Processes* 13 (1996): 67–90.

Elias, Norbert. *The Civilizing Process: The History of Manners.* New York: Urizen Books, 1978.

Ellsworth, P., J. Carlsmith, and A. Henson. "The Stare as Stimulus to Flight in Human Subjects." *Journal of Personality and Social Psychology* 21 (1972): 302–11.

Ellsworth, Phoebe C., and Ellen Langer. "Staring as a Call for Help." *Victimology* 1, no. 2 (1976): 342.

Ellyson, Steve L., and John F. Dovidio. *Power, Dominance, and Nonverbal Behavior.* Springer Series in Social Psychology. New York: Springer-Verlag, 1985.

Elsner, John, and Roger Cardinal. *The Cultures of Collecting*. Cambridge, Mass.: Harvard University Press, 1994.

Encyclopædia Britannica Online. 2005, s.v. "Laterality" and "Morphology." http://search. eb.com (accessed 28 October 2005).

Enzensberger, Hans Magnus. *Civil Wars: From L.A. to Bosnia*. New York: New Press, 1994.

Ervin, Michael. Phone interview with author. 22 November 2005.

Fadner, Frederic. *The Gentleman Giant: The Biography of Robert Pershing Wadlow*. Boston: Bruce Humphries, 1944.

Fanon, Frantz. *Black Skin, White Masks*. New York: Grove Weidenfeld, 1991.

Featherstone, Mike. "The Body in Consumer Culture." In *The Body: Social Process and Cultural Theory*, edited by Mike Featherstone et al., 170–96. London: Sage, 1991.

Ferraro, Susan. "The Anguished Politics of Breast Cancer." *New York Times Magazine*. 15 August 1993: 24–27.

Fineman, Martha. *The Autonomy Myth: A Theory of Dependency*. New York: W. W. Norton, 2004.

Fisher-Thompson, Jim. "Amputees Bring Conflict in Sierra Leone Home to Congressmen." *Washington File*. 27 April 2005. Office of International Information Programs, U.S. Department of State. http://usinfo.state.gov (accessed 1 July 2006).

Flindell, Fred. "Paul Wittgenstein, 1887–1961: Patron and Pianist." *Music Review* 32 (1971): 107–27.

Foucault, Michel. *Abnormal: Lectures at the Collège de France, 1974–1975*, with Valerio Marchetti et al. 1st Picador USA ed. New York: Picador, 2003.

———. *Discipline and Punish: The Birth of the Prison*. New York: Vintage Books, 1979.

———. *The Birth of the Clinic: An Archaeology of Medical Perception*. New York: Vintage Books, 1975.

———. *Madness and Civilization: A History of Insanity in the Age of Reason*. New York: Pantheon Books, 1965.

Frank, Geyla. *Venus on Wheels: Two Decades of Dialogue on Disability, Biography, and Being Female*. Berkeley: University of California Press, 2000.

Fraser, Nancy, and Axel Honneth. *Redistribution or Recognition? A Political Philosophical Exchange*. London: Verso, 2003.

Frazier Lisa. "A Precious Gift for Victims of the Sierra Leone Civil War." *Washington Post*, 28 September 2000, M02.

Freedberg, David. *The Power of Images: Studies in the History and Theory of Response*. Chicago: University of Chicago Press, 1989.

Frey, Jennifer. "29 Inches Tall but Looming Large; Fairgoers Beat a Path to Tiny Tasha." *Washington Post*, 4 September 2000, C1.

Friedberg, Anne. *Window Shopping: Cinema and the Postmodern*. Berkeley and Los Angeles: University of California Press, 1993.

Friedman, John Block. *The Monstrous Races in Medieval Art and Thought*. Cambridge: Harvard University Press, 1981.

Frye, Leslie. Performance at the Society for Disability Studies Annual Meeting. San Francisco, Calif., June 2005.

Gane, Nicholas. *Max Weber and Postmodern Theory: Rationalization Versus Re-Enchantment.* New York: Palgrave, 2002.

Garland-Thomson, Rosemarie. "Seeing the Disabled: Visual Rhetorics of Popular Disability Photography." In *The New Disability History: American Perspectives,* edited by P. Longmore and L. Umansky, 335–74. New York: New York University Press, 2000.

———. "Narratives of Deviance and Delight: Staring at Julia Pastrana, 'The Extraordinary Lady.'" In *Beyond the Binary,* edited by Timothy Powell, 81–106. New Brunswick, N.J.: Rutgers University Press, 1999.

———. *Extraordinary Bodies: Figuring Physical Disability in American Culture and Literature.* New York: Columbia University Press, 1997.

———, ed. *Freakery: Cultural Spectacles of the Extraordinary Body.* New York: New York University Press, 1996.

Geertz, Clifford. *The Interpretation of Cultures: Selected Essays.* New York: Basic Books, 1973.

Gerber, D. A. *Disabled Veterans in History.* Ann Arbor: University of Michigan Press, 2000.

Gifford, Edward S. *The Evil Eye: Studies in the Folklore of Vision.* New York: Macmillan, 1958.

Gilbert, Mark. "Saving Faces." 2004. *The Facial Surgery Research Foundation.* http://www.savingfaces.co.uk/gallery/index.htm (accessed 10 June 2006).

Gilman, Sander L. *Making the Body Beautiful: A Cultural History of Aesthetic Surgery.* Princeton, N.J.: Princeton University Press, 1999.

———. *Creating Beauty to Cure the Soul: Race and Psychology in the Shaping of Aesthetic Surgery.* Durham N.C.: Duke University Press, 1998.

Gilmore, Michael T. *Surface and Depth: The Quest for Legibility in American Culture.* Oxford: Oxford University Press, 2003.

Goffman, Erving. *Stigma: Notes on the Management of Spoiled Identity.* New York: Simon & Schuster, 1986.

———. *Interaction Ritual: Essays on Face-to-Face Behavior.* 1st Pantheon Books ed. New York: Pantheon Books, 1982.

———. *Behavior in Public Places: Notes on the Social Organization of Gatherings.* Westport: Greenwood Press, 1980.

———. *The Presentation of Self in Everyday Life.* Garden City: Doubleday, 1959.

———. "The Nature of Deference and Demeanor." *American Anthropologist* 58 (1956): 472–502.

Goffman, Erving, P. Drew, and A. J. Wooton. *Erving Goffman: Exploring the Interaction Order.* Boston: Northeastern University Press, 1988.

Goodheart, Eugene. *The Skeptic Disposition in Contemporary Criticism.* Princeton Essays in Literature. Princeton, N.J.: Princeton University Press, 1984.

Goss, Jon. "The 'Magic of the Mall': An Analysis of Form, Function, and Meaning in the Contemporary Retail Built Environment." *Annals of the Association of American Geographers* 83 (1993): 18–47.

Gould, Stephen Jay. *The Mismeasure of Man.* 1st ed. New York: Norton, 1981.

Graf, Fritz. "The Gestures of Roman Actors and Oratories." In *A Cultural History of Gesture,* edited by Jan N. Bremmer and Herman Roodenburg, 36–58. Ithaca, N.Y.: Cornell University Press, 1992.

Grealy, Lucy. *Autobiography of a Face.* Boston: Houghton Mifflin, 1994.

Greenblatt, Stephen. *Marvelous Possessions: The Wonder of the New World.* Chicago: University of Chicago Press, 1991.

Grundman, Mike, dir. *The Perfect Flaw: Triumphing over Facial Disfigurement.* Princeton, N.J.: Films for the Humanities & Sciences, 2002.

Habermas, Jurgen. "Public Space and Political Public Sphere: The Biographical Roots of Two Motifs in My Thought." Commemorative Lecture, Kyoto, 11 November 2004.

Hacking, Ian. *The Taming of Chance.* Ideas in Context. Cambridge and New York: Cambridge University Press, 1990.

Hahn, Harlan. "The Politics of Physical Difference." *Journal of Social Issues* 44, no. 1 (1988): 39–47.

Halberstam, Judith. *Female Masculinity.* Durham: Duke University Press, 1998.

Halttunen, Karen. "Humanitarianism and the Pornography of Pain in Anglo-American Culture." *American Historical Review* 100 (April 1995): 303–34.

———. *Confidence Men and Painted Women: A Study of Middle-Class Culture in America, 1830–1870.* New Haven: Yale University Press, 1982.

Haraway, Donna Jeanne. *Monströse Versprechen: Coyote-Geschichten zu Feminismus und Technowissenschaft.* Coyote-Texte. 1. Aufl. ed. Hamburg: Argument Verlag, 1995.

———. *Simians, Cyborgs, and Women: The Reinvention of Nature.* London: Free Association, 1991.

Harris, Neil. *Humbug: The Art of P. T. Barnum.* 1st ed. Boston: Little Brown, 1973.

Hartley, Lucy. *Physiognomy and the Meaning of Expression in Nineteenth-Century Culture.* Cambridge Studies in Nineteenth-Century Literature and Culture 29. New York: Cambridge University Press, 2001.

Haskell, Thomas L. "Capitalism and the Origins of the Humanitarian Sensibility, Part 2." *American History Review* 90, no. 3 (1985): 547–66.

———. "Capitalism and the Origins of the Humanitarian Sensibility, Part I." *American History Review* 90, no. 2 (1985): 339–61.

Heijden, A. H. C. van der. *Selective Attention in Vision.* International Library of Psychology. London and New York: Routledge, 1992.

Herndl, Diane Price. "Reconstructing the Posthuman Feminist Body: Twenty Years after Audre Lorde's *Cancer Journals.*" In *Disability Studies: Enabling the Humanities,* edited by Sharon L. Snyder, et al., 144–55. New York: Modern Language Association of America, 2002.

hooks, bell. *Black Looks: Race and Representation.* Boston: South End Press, 1992.

Horkheimer, Max, and Theodor W. Adorno. *Dialectic of Enlightenment.* New York: Continuum, 1987.

Howard, Timothy Edward, and Rebecca V. Roberts. *Excelsior; or, Essays on Politeness, Education, and the Means of Attaining Success in Life*. Baltimore: Kelly Piet & Co., 1868.

Hubbard, Ruth. *The Politics of Women's Biology*. New Brunswick, N.J.: Rutgers University Press, 1990.

Hurston, Zora Neale. "How It Feels to Be Colored Me." In *I Love Myself When I'm Laughing . . . and Then Again When I'm Looking Mean and Impressive: A Zora Neale Hurston Reader*, edited by Alice Walker, 152–55. Old Westbury, N.Y.: Feminist Press, 1979; first published, 1928.

Ignatieff, Michael. *The Warrior's Honor: Ethnic War and the Modern Conscience*. New York: Metropolitan Books, 1997.

James, Henry, and Henry James Collection (Library of Congress). *The Real Thing, and Other Tales*. New York: Macmillan, 1893.

James, William. *The Principles of Psychology*. New York: H. Holt, 1890.

Jameson, Fredric. *Postmodernism; or, the Cultural Logic of Late Capitalism*. Post-Contemporary Interventions. Durham, N.C.: Duke University Press, 1991.

———. *Signatures of the Visible*. New York: Routledge, 1990.

Jay, Martin. *Downcast Eyes: The Denigration of Vision in Twentieth-Century French Thought*. Berkeley and Los Angeles: University of California Press, 1993.

———. *Force Fields: Between Intellectual History and Cultural Critique*. New York: Routledge, 1993.

Jay, Ricky. *Extraordinary Exhibitions*. New York: Quantuck Lane Press, 2005.

Johnson, Harriet McBryde. *Too Late to Die Young: Nearly True Tales from a Life*. New York: Henry Holt, 2006.

———. "Not Dead at All: Why Congress Was Right to Stick up for Terri Schiavo." *Slate Magazine*, 23 March 2005. http://slate.msn.com/id/2115208/ (accessed 30 August 2006).

———. E-mail interview with author. 17 September 2005.

———. "Unspeakable Conversations." *New York Times Magazine*, 16 February 2003: 50–59.

Johnson, Mark. *The Body in the Mind: The Bodily Basis of Meaning, Imagination, and Reason*. Chicago: University of Chicago Press, 1987.

Johnson, M. H., and J. Morton. *Biology and Cognitive Development: The Case of Face Recognition*. Oxford: Blackwell, 1991.

Jonas, Hans. *The Phenomenon of Life: Toward a Philosophical Biology*. Westport: Greenwood Press, 1979.

Kaplan, E. Ann. *Looking for the Other: Feminism, Film, and the Imperial Gaze*. New York: Routledge, 1997.

Kasson, John F. *Rudeness & Civility: Manners in Nineteenth-Century Urban America*. New York: Hill and Wang, 1990.

Keil, F., ed. *MIT Encyclopedia of Cognitive Sciences*, s.v. "Language and Thought." Cambridge, Mass.: MIT Press, 2001.

Kennedy, Dan. *Little People: Learning to See the World through My Daughter's Eyes*. Emmaus: Rodale, 2003.

Kittay, Eva Feder. *Love's Labor: Essays on Women, Equality, and Dependency*. New York: Routledge, 1999.

Kleege, Georgina. *Sight Unseen*. New Haven: Yale University Press, 1999.

Kolodny, Annette. *The Lay of the Land: Metaphor as Experience and History in American Life and Letters*. Chapel Hill: University of North Carolina Press, 1975.

Koren, Yehuda. *In Our Hearts We Were Giants: The Remarkable Story of the Lilliput Troupe: A Dwarf Family's Survival of the Holocaust*. New York: Carroll & Graf, 2004.

Kowinski, William Severini. *The Malling of America: An Inside Look at the Great Consumer Paradise*. New York: William Morrow, 1985.

Kozloff, Max. *The Theatre of the Face: Portrait Photography Since 1900*. London and New York: Phaidon, 2007.

Kracauer, Siegfried, and Thomas Y. Levin. *The Mass Ornament: Weimar Essays*. Cambridge: Harvard University Press, 1995.

Lacan, Jacques. "The Mirror Stage." In *Écrits: A Selection*, translated by Alan Sheridan, 1–8. New York: Norton, 1977.

Lakoff, George, and Mark Johnson. *Metaphors We Live By*. Chicago: University of Chicago Press, 1980.

Laderman, Gary. *Rest in Peace: A Cultural History of Death and the Funeral Home in Twentieth-Century America*. New York: Oxford University Press, 2003.

Lamott, Anne. "Foreword." In *The Church of 80% Sincerity*, by David Roche, ix–xii. New York: Perigee Books, 2008.

Lane, Harlan L. *The Mask of Benevolence: Disabling the Deaf Community*. 1st ed. New York: Knopf, 1992.

Langer, Ellen J., et al. "Stigma, Staring, and Discomfort: A Novel-Stimulus Hypothesis." *Journal of Experimental Social Psychology* 12 (1976): 451–63.

Lapper, Alison, and Guy Feldman. *My Life in My Hands*. London: Simon & Schuster, 2006.

Lasch, Christopher. *The Culture of Narcissism: American Life in an Age of Diminishing Expectations*. Warner Books ed. New York: Warner Books, 1980.

Latour, Bruno. *Science in Action: How to Follow Scientists and Engineers through Society*. Cambridge, Mass.: Harvard University Press, 1987.

Latteier, Carolyn. *Breasts: The Women's Perspective on an American Obsession*. Haworth Innovations in Feminist Studies. New York: Haworth Press, 1998.

Leach, William. *Land of Desire: Merchants, Power, and the Rise of a New American Culture*. 1st ed. New York: Pantheon Books, 1993.

Leder, Drew. *The Absent Body*. Chicago: University of Chicago Press, 1990.

Lee, Alan, and Morton Goldman. "Effect of Staring on Normal and Overweight Students." *Journal of Social Psychology* 108, no. 2 (1979): 165.

Leitch, Luke. "Repellent Lapper Statue Looks Like Soap, Says Critic." *The Independent* (London), 16 September 2005, 11.

Lerner, Gerda. *The Creation of Patriarchy*. New York: Oxford University Press, 1986.

Lerner, Neil. "The Horrors of the Left Hand: Music and Disability in the Beast with Five Fingers." Unpublished paper. Society for Disability Studies Conference, San Francisco State University, 11 June 2005.

Levin, David Michael. *Modernity and the Hegemony of Vision*. Berkeley and Los Angeles: University of California Press, 1993.

———. *The Opening of Vision: Nihilism and the Postmodern Situation*. New York: Routledge, 1988.

Levinas, Emmanuel. *Emmanuel Levinas: Basic Philosophical Writings*, edited by Adriaan T. Peperzak, Simon Critchley, and Robert Bernasconi. Studies in Continental Thought. Bloomington: Indiana University Press, 1996.

Lewinski, Jorge, and Mayotte Magnus. *The Book of Portrait Photography*. New York: Random House, 1982.

Linton, Simi. *My Body Politic: A Memoir*. Ann Arbor: University of Michigan Press, 2005.

———. *Claiming Disability: Knowledge and Identity*. New York: New York University Press, 1998.

Lofland, Lyn H. *A World of Strangers: Order and Action in Urban Public Space*. New York: Basic Books, 1973.

Lombroso-Ferrero, Gina, and Cesare Lombroso. *Criminal Man, According to the Classification of Cesare Lombroso*. Montclair, N.J.: Patterson Smith, 1972.

Lomnicki, Tekki, and Laurie Benz. "Little Amazons in the Arts," 2000–04. http://www.geocities.com/ltl_renaissance_feminist/Artful-Amazons1.html (accessed 5 March 2006).

Longmore, Paul K. Personal interview with author. 10 June 2005.

———. "Conspicuous Contribution and American Cultural Dilemmas: Telethon Rituals of Cleansing and Renewal." In *Discourses of Disability: The Body and Physical Difference in the Humanities*, edited by D. Mitchell and S. Snyder, 134–60. Ann Arbor: University of Michigan Press, 1997.

Lorde, Audre. *The Cancer Journals: Special Edition*. San Francisco: Aunt Lute Books, 1997.

———. *Sister Outsider: Essays and Speeches*. Trumansburg, N.Y.: Crossing Press, 1984.

Lukatsky, Efrem. "Tiny Village Possibly Holds the World's Tallest Man." *USA Today*, 17 April 2004. http://www.usatoday.com/news/world/2004-04-17-tallest-man_x.htm (accessed 1 June 2004).

Lunettes, Henry. *The American Gentleman's Guide to Politeness and Fashion*. New York: Derby and Jackson, 1857.

Lutz, Catherine. *Reading National Geographic*. Chicago: University of Chicago Press, 1993.

Macgregor, Frances M. Cooke. *Transformation and Identity; the Face and Plastic Surgery*. New York: Quadrangle, 1974.

Mairs, Nancy. *Waist-High in the World: A Life among the Nondisabled*. Boston: Beacon Press, 1996.

The Manners That Win. Atlanta: L. A. Clarkson, 1883.

Mannix, Daniel Pratt. *Freaks: We Who Are Not as Others.* Rev. ed. San Francisco: Re/ Search Publications, 1990.

Masur, Louis P. *Rites of Execution: Capital Punishment and the Transformation of American Culture, 1776–1865.* New York: Oxford University Press, 1989.

Matuschka. "Balancing a Lopsided Act" (By Crinkle Tit). Unpublished essay, 2005.

———. "Why I Did It." *Glamour Magazine* 91 (November 1993): 162.

Mauro, Lucia. "Tekki Lomnicki in Stage Persona," 20 June 2003. http://www.performink. com/archives/stagepersonae/2003/LomnickiTekki.html (accessed 5 March 2006).

Mayne, Judith. *Framed: Lesbians, Feminists, and Media Culture.* Minneapolis: University of Minnesota Press, 2000.

McNeill, Dan. *The Face.* 1st ed. Boston: Little, Brown, 1998.

Meile, Joshua. E-mail interview with author. 11 November 2005.

Melchior-Bonnet, Sabine. *The Mirror: A History.* New York: Routledge, 2001.

Melville, Stephen. "Division of the Gaze, or, Remarks on the Color and Tenure of Contemporary 'Theory.'" In *Vision in Context: Historical and Contemporary Perspectives on Sight,* edited by Teresa Brennan and Martin Jay, 101–16. New York: Routledge, 1996.

Merish, Lori. *Sentimental Materialism: Gender, Commodity Culture, and Nineteenth-Century American Literature.* New Americanists. Durham, N.C.: Duke University Press, 2000.

Merleau-Ponty, Maurice. *Phenomenology of Perception.* London and New York: Routledge, 1962.

Merleau-Ponty, Maurice, and Claude Lefort. *The Visible and the Invisible; Followed by Working Notes.* Northwestern University Studies in Phenomenology & Existential Philosophy. Evanston: Northwestern University Press, 1968.

Miller, William Ian. *The Anatomy of Disgust.* Cambridge, Mass.: Harvard University Press, 1997.

Mitchell, David T., and Sharon Snyder, dir. and prod. *Vital Signs: Crip Culture Talks Back.* Marquette: Brace Yourself Productions, 1996.

Mitchell, G., and Terry L. Maple. "Dominance in Nonhuman Primates." In *Power, Dominance, and Nonverbal Behavior,* edited by Steve L. Ellyson and John F. Dovido, 49–66. Springer Series in Social Psychology. New York: Springer-Verlag, 1985.

Mitchell, Michael, and Charles Eisenmann. *Monsters of the Gilded Age: Photographs by Charles Eisenmann.* Agincourt, Ont.: Gage Publications, 1979.

Mitchell, W. J. T. *What Do Pictures Want? The Lives and Loves of Images.* Chicago: University of Chicago Press, 2005.

Mulvey, Laura. *Visual and Other Pleasures.* Theories of Representation and Difference. Bloomington: Indiana University Press, 1989.

Murphy, Robert. *The Body Silent.* New York: W. W. Norton, 1987.

Myser, Catherine, and David L. Clark. "'Fixing' Katie and Eilish: Medical Documentaries and the Subjection of Conjoined Twins." *Literature and Medicine* 17, no. 1 (1988): 45–67.

Napier, John Russell. *Hands*. 1st American ed. New York: Pantheon Books, 1980.

Newman, Andy. "Facing Their Scars, and Finding Beauty." *New York Times*, 18 June 2006, 1.25.

Newton, Adam Zachary. "'Nothing but Face'—'to Hell with Philosophy': Witold Gombrowicz, Bruno Schulz, and the Scandal of Human Countenance." *Style* (Summer 1998): 243–60.

Nussbaum, Martha. *Frontiers of Justice: Disability, Nationality, Species Membership*. Cambridge, Mass.: Belknap Press, 2006.

Nussbaum, Martha, and Amartya Sen, eds. *The Quality of Life*. New York: Oxford University Press, 1993.

Packer, George. "The Children of Freetown." *New Yorker*, 13 January 2003, 50–61.

Packer, George, and Sylvia Moreno. "For African War Victims, Visit for Care Becomes Lasting Stay." *Washington Post*, 26 May 2002, A01.

Padden, Carol and Tom Humphries. *Inside Deaf Culture*. Cambridge, Mass.: Harvard University Press, 2005.

Partridge, James. *Changing Faces: The Challenge of Facial Disfigurement*. London: Penguin Books, 1990.

Pashler, Harold E., ed. *The Psychology of Attention*. Cambridge: MIT Press, 1998.

Patchett, Ann. *Truth & Beauty: A Friendship*. 1st ed. New York: HarperCollins, 2004.

Patzer, Gordon L. *The Physical Attractiveness Phenomena*. New York: Plenum Press, 1985.

Paulson, Ronald. *The Beautiful, Novel, and Strange: Aesthetics and Heterodoxy*. Baltimore: Johns Hopkins University Press, 1996.

"Permission to Stare." July 2006. http://www.jackthepelicanpresents.com/rushpr.html (accessed 18 August 2006).

Pernick, Martin S. *A Calculus of Suffering: Pain, Professionalism, and Anesthesia in Nineteenth-Century America*. New York: Columbia University Press, 1985.

Peterson, Jennifer. "Case Re-Examined," 2003. http://www.matuschka.net/interviews/interview2003a.html (accessed 24 August 2006).

Peterson, Mary A., and Gillian Rhodes. *Perception of Faces, Objects, and Scenes: Analytic and Holistic Processes*. Advances in Visual Cognition. Oxford: Oxford University Press, 2003.

Phillips, Adam. *On Kissing, Tickling, and Being Bored: Psychoanalytic Essays on the Unexamined Life*. Cambridge: Harvard University Press, 1993.

Piccolo, Cynthia M. "Shared Lives: From the Types of Joining to Separation Surgeries, the Issues around Conjoined Twins Are Varied and Complex," 22 August 2004. http://www.medhunters.com/articles/sharedLives.html (accessed 16 March 2006).

"Picturing Women," 2004. http://www.picturingwomen.org/home.php (accessed 6 January 2004).

Postman, Neil. *Amusing Ourselves to Death: Public Discourse in the Age of Show Business*. New York: Viking, 1985.

Quetelet, Lambert Adolphe Jacques. *A Treatise on Man and the Development of His Faculties*. Edinburgh: W. & R. Chambers, 1842.

Quigley, Christine. *Conjoined Twins: Historical, Biological and Ethical Issues Encyclopedia.* Jefferson, N.C.: McFarland, 2003.

Rathbone, Belinda, and Walker Evans. *Walker Evans: A Biography.* Boston: Houghton Mifflin, 1995.

Reiss, Benjamin. *The Showman and the Slave: Race, Death, and Memory in Barnum's America.* Cambridge: Harvard University Press, 2001.

Reynolds, Nigel. "Whatever Would Nelson Think? Statue of Naked Disabled Artist Causes Controversy as It Is Unveiled in Trafalgar Square." *The Independent* (London), 20 May 2004, 3.

Rhodes, Gillian, and Leslie A. Zebrowitz. *Facial Attractiveness: Evolutionary, Cognitive, and Social Perspectives.* Advances in Visual Cognition V.1. Westport, Conn.: Ablex, 2002.

Rhodes, Gillian, and Tanya Tremewan. "Understanding Face Recognition: Caricature Effects, Inversion, and the Homogeneity Problem." *Visual Cognition* 2, no. 3 (1994): 275–311.

Richardson, Ruth. *Death, Dissection, and the Destitute.* 2nd ed. Chicago: University of Chicago Press, 2000.

Roberts, Roxanne. "Do Me a Favor, Keep a Lid on Your Double Latte." *Washington Post,* 15 August 2004, C01.

Roche, David. *The Church of 80% Sincerity.* New York: Perigee Books, 2008.

———. "About David," 1999–2006. http://www.davidroche.com/about.htm (accessed 3 March 2006).

———. E-mail interview with author. 22 September 2005.

———. "Finding My Voice," 1999–2006. http://www.davidroche.com/findingmyvoice.htm (accessed 3 March 2006).

———. "My Face Does Not Belong to Me," 1999–2006, http://www.davidroche.com/myface.htm (accessed 3 March 2006).

Roche, Serge, Germain Courage, and Pierre Devinoy. *Mirrors.* New York: Rizzoli, 1985.

Roodenburg, Herman. "The 'Hand of Friendship': Shaking Hands and Other Gestures in the Dutch Republic." In *A Cultural History of Gesture,* edited by Jan N. Bremmer and Herman Roodenburg, 152–89. Ithaca, N.Y.: Cornell University Press, 1992.

Rose, Martha L. *The Staff of Oedipus: Transforming Disability in Ancient Greece.* Corporealities. Ann Arbor: University of Michigan Press, 2003.

Rothman, Barbara Katz. *Genetic Maps and Human Imaginations: The Limits of Science in Understanding Who We Are.* 1st ed. New York: Norton, 1998.

Rothman, David J. *The Discovery of the Asylum: Social Order and Disorder in the New Republic.* Rev. 2nd ed. Boston: Little, Brown, 1990.

Rothman, David J., and Sheila M. Rothman. *The Willowbrook Wars: Bringing the Mentally Disabled into the Community.* New Brunswick, N.J.: Aldine Transaction, 2005.

Rothman, Sheila M., and David J. Rothman. *The Pursuit of Perfection: The Promise and Perils of Medical Enhancement.* 1st ed. New York: Pantheon Books, 2003.

Rozen, Shahar, dir. *Liebe Perla*. Hamburg: Keshet Broadcasting, New Israeli Foundation for Film and Television, Eden Productions Ltd. in partnership with Norddeutscher Rundfunk (NDR), 1999.

Rutter, D. R. *Looking and Seeing: The Role of Visual Communication in Social Interaction*. Chichester and New York: Wiley, 1984.

Rydell, Robert W. *Fair America: World's Fairs in the United States*. Washington, D.C.: Smithsonian Institution Press, 2000.

Sacks, Harvey. "On Doing 'Being Ordinary.'" In *Structures of Social Action: Studies in Conversation Analysis*, edited by J. Maxwell Atkinson and John Heritage, 413–40. Cambridge: Cambridge University Press, 1984.

Said, Edward W. *Orientalism*. 1st Vintage Books ed. New York: Vintage Books, 1979.

Sartre, Jean-Paul. *Being and Nothingness: An Essay on Phenomenological Ontology*. New York: Philosophical Library, 1956.

Sawday, Jonathan. *The Body Emblazoned: Dissection and the Human Body in Renaissance Culture*. London and New York: Routledge, 1995; paperback ed., 1996.

Sawsich, Len. E-mail interview with author. 13 March 2006.

Scarry, Elaine. *On Beauty and Being Just*. Princeton, N.J.: Princeton University Press, 1999.

———. *The Body in Pain: The Making and Unmaking of the World*. New York: Oxford University Press, 1985.

Schneider, Rebecca. *The Explicit Body in Performance*. New York: Routledge, 1997.

Schwartz, Vanessa R. *Spectacular Realities: Early Mass Culture in Fin-De-Siècle Paris*. Berkeley and Los Angeles: University of California Press, 1998.

Schweik, Susan. *The Ugly Laws*. New York: New York University Press, 2009.

Sennett, Richard. *The Fall of Public Man*. New York: Vintage Books, 1978.

Shields, Rob. *Lifestyle Shopping: The Subject of Consumption*. New York: Routledge, 1992.

Shildrick, Margrit. *Embodying the Monster: Encounters with the Vulnerable Self*. London: Sage, 2002.

Siebers, Tobin. *The Mirror of Medusa*. Berkeley and Los Angeles: University of California Press, 1983.

Silverman, Kaja. *Male Subjectivity at the Margins*. New York: Routledge, 1992.

Simmel, Georg. "The Aesthetic Significance of the Face." In *Essays on Sociology, Philosophy, and Aesthetics*, edited by K. H. Wolff, 276–81. New York: Harper & Row, 1965.

Simmel, Georg, and Kurt H. Wolff. *The Sociology of Georg Simmel*. New York and London: Free Press and Collier Macmillan, 1964.

Sims, Michael. *Adam's Navel: A Natural and Cultural History of the Human Body*. London: Allen Lane, 2003.

Singer, Peter, and Helga Kuhse. *Should the Baby Live? The Problems of Handicapped Infants*. New York: Oxford University Press, 1985.

Sontag, Susan. *Regarding the Pain of Others*. New York: Farrar, Straus and Giroux/Picador, 2003.

———. *On Photography*. New York: Farrar, Straus and Giroux, 1977.

Spence, Jo. *Beyond the Perfect Image: Photography, Subjectivity, and Antagonism*. Barcelona: Museu d'Art Contemporani de Barcelona, 2006.

———. *Cultural Sniping: The Art of Transgression*. London: Routledge, 1995.

———. *Putting Myself in the Picture: A Political, Personal and Photographic Autobiography*. Seattle: Real Comet Press, 1988.

The Station Agent, directed by Thomas McCarthy. Miramax, 2003.

Stewart, Susan. *On Longing: Narratives of the Miniature, the Gigantic, the Souvenir, the Collection*. Baltimore: Johns Hopkins University Press, 1984.

Stokoe, William C., Jr. "Sign Language Structure: An Outline of the Visual Communication Systems of the American Deaf." *Journal of Deaf Studies and Deaf Education* 10, no. 1 (2005): 3–37.

Straayer, Chris. *Deviant Eyes, Deviant Bodies: Sexual Re-Orientations in Film and Video*. Film and Culture. New York: Columbia University Press, 1996.

Strauss, Bonnie, and Lisa Abelow Hedley, dirs. *Dwarfs: Not a Fairy Tale*. New York: HBO Home Video, 2001.

Sturken, Marita, and Lisa Cartwright. *Practices of Looking: An Introduction to Visual Culture*. Oxford: Oxford University Press, 2001.

Sullivan, Andrew. "The He Hormone." *New York Times Magazine*, 2 April 2000, Health, SM 46–57.

Synnott, Anthony. *The Body Social: Symbolism, Self, and Society*. London: Routledge, 1993.

Tavris, Carol. *The Mismeasure of Woman*. New York: Simon & Schuster, 1992.

Taylor, Charles. "The Politics of Recognition." In *Multiculturalism: Examining the Politics of Recognition*, edited by Amy Gutmann, 25–74. Princeton, N.J.: Princeton University Press, 1994.

Terry, Jennifer and Jacqueline Urla. *Deviant Bodies: Critical Perspectives on Difference in Science and Popular Culture*. Bloomington: Indiana University Press, 1995.

Tester, Keith. *The Flâneur*. London: Routledge, 1994.

Titchkowsky, Tanya. *Reading and Writing Disability Differently: The Textured Life of Embodiment*. Toronto: University of Toronto Press, 2007.

Trent, James W., Jr. *Inventing the Feeble Mind: A History of Mental Retardation in the United States*. Berkeley and Los Angeles: University of California Press, 1994.

Turner, Bryan S. *Vulnerability and Human Rights*. University Park: Pennsylvania State University Press, 2006.

"Two Sisters Together Forever: The Ordinary Life of Extraordinary Twins." *Life Magazine*, April 1996, 46–56.

Urla, Jacqueline, and Alan Swedlund. "The Anthropometry of Barbie." In *Deviant Bodies: Cultural Perspectives in Science and Popular Culture*, edited by Jennifer Terry et al., 277–313. Bloomington: Indiana University Press, 1995.

U.S. Department of Justice. Civil Rights Division. "A Guide to Disability Rights Laws." 16 February 2006. http://www.usdoj.gov/crt/ada/cguide.htm (accessed 28 August 2006).

Veblen, Thorstein. *The Theory of the Leisure Class: An Economic Study of Institutions.* New York: B. W. Huebsch, 1919.

Wade, Cheryl Marie. "I'm Not One of The." *Sinister Wisdom* 35 (1988): 24. Reprinted in *Ms.* 12, no. 3 (2002): 77.

Wallace-Sanders, Kimberly. "Nipplegate: Black Feminism, Corporeal Fragmentation and the Politics of Public Consumption." In *Women in Popular Culture: Representation and Meaning,* edited by Marian Meyers. Cresskill, N.J.: Hampton Press, 2008.

Washington, George. *George Washington's Rules of Civility: Complete with the Original French Text and New French-to-English Translations,* edited by John T. Phillips. The Complete George Washington Series 1. 2nd, Collector's Classic ed. Leesburg, Va.: Goose Creek Productions, 2000; first published 1744–1748.

Weber, Max. *The Protestant Ethic and the Spirit of Capitalism.* London: Unwin University Books, 1968.

Weegee. *Naked City.* New York: Essential Books, 1945.

Weegee and John Coplans. *Weegee's New York: Photographs 1935–1960.* New York: Neues Publishing, 1996.

Weissbrod, Ellen, dir. *Face to Face: The Schappell Twins.* A & E Home Video, 1999.

Whitman, Walt. "Crossing Brooklyn Ferry." In *American Literature: A Prentice Hall Anthology,* edited by Emory B. Elliott, A. Walton Litz, Terence Martin, and Linda K. Kerber, 1072. Concise ed. Englewood: Simon & Schuster, 1991.

———. "Song of Myself." In *American Literature: A Prentice Hall Anthology,* edited by Emory B. Elliott, A. Walton Litz, Terence Martin, and Linda K. Kerber, 1024–69. Concise ed. Englewood: Simon & Schuster, 1991.

Williams, Clarence. "Life of Normalcy Rests in His Palm." *Washington Post,* 28 November 2005, B1.

Wilson, Frank R. *The Hand: How Its Use Shapes the Brain, Language, and Human Culture.* 1st ed. New York: Pantheon Books, 1998.

Winnicott, D. W. *The Maturational Processes and the Facilitating Environment: Studies in the Theory of Emotional Development.* New York: International Universities Press, 1965.

———. "The Theory of the Parent-Child Relationship." *International Journal of Psychoanalysis* 41 (1960): 585–95.

Wolfe, Jeremy. "Visual Search." In *The Psychology of Attention,* edited by H. Pashler. Cambridge: MIT Press, 1998.

Wolff, Kurt H. *Essays on Sociology, Philosophy, and Aesthetics.* New York: Harper & Row, 1965.

Wright, Beatrice. *Physical Disability: A Psychological Approach.* New York: Harper, 1960.

Yalom, Marilyn. *A History of the Breast.* New York: Alfred A. Knopf, 1997.

Yantis, Steven. "Control of Visual Attention." In *Attention,* edited by H. Pashler, 223–56. Psychology Press, 1998.

The Year of Living Dangerously, directed by Peter Weir. Jim McElroy, 1982.

Yoshino, Kenji. *Covering: The Hidden Assault on Our Civil Rights.* New York: Random House, 2006.

Young, Iris Marion. *On Female Body Experience: "Throwing Like a Girl" and Other Essays.* Studies in Feminist Philosophy. New York: Oxford University Press, 2005.

Yu, Ning. "What Does Our Face Mean to Us?" *Pragmatics and Cognition* 9, no. 1 (2001): 1–36.

Zacher, Christian K. *Curiosity and Pilgrimage: The Literature of Discovery in Fourteenth-Century England.* Baltimore: Johns Hopkins University Press, 1976.

Zandy, Janet. *Hands: Physical Labor, Class, and Cultural Work.* New Brunswick, N.J.: Rutgers University Press, 2004.

Zebrowitz, Leslie A. *Reading Faces: Window to the Soul?* New Directions in Social Psychology. Boulder, Colo.: Westview Press, 1997.

CPSIA information can be obtained
at www.ICGtesting.com
Printed in the USA
BVHW070252101019
560696BV00001B/5/P